T0357877

"This book is an investigation into ___ system that 'disproportionately' tar___ and that wreaks havoc on Black fam___ eye-opening tale."

—*The Philadelphia Tribune*

"This book will appeal to readers interested in social reform and the abolition of the carceral state, and it makes a strong pairing with Dorothy Roberts' *Torn Apart*."

—*Booklist*

"It's an invaluable insider account of a pressing social issue."

—*Publishers Weekly*

"Sharing real-life professional experience as well as key insight from caseworkers and Black women's experiences within the system."

—*Essence*

"Pryce opens readers' eyes to the systemic racism that is deeply rooted in the system and often creates a pipeline to incarceration."

—*The Root*

"Broken delivers an eye-opening, insider's perspective on the impact of 'standard practices' within the world and work of child and family services. This book should be required reading for every social worker. Using well-researched and documented case histories, Dr. Pryce shows that actions from within an outdated institutional framework, designed to protect itself as much as it safeguards a child, can often do more harm than good."

—Virginia Deberry, *New York Times* bestselling author of *Far from the Tree*

"*Broken* is a vital call to protect Black mothers. The stories of the women in this book will lodge themselves in the reader's heart. I couldn't put this book down, and I will be thinking about it for a long time to come."

—Andrea Dunlop, author of *Women Are the Fiercest Creatures*

"In this deeply moving and vulnerable work, Pryce examines the complexities of case work yet the complicity of the workforce in the systemic harm done to families. If you work within the system in any way, stop what you are doing and grab this book. By the end, the questions you ask yourself might just change your life and the lives of those you are trying to help."

—Vivek S. Sankaran, coauthor of
Representing Parents in Child Welfare Cases

"In this groundbreaking work Pryce shows us how a system designed to protect Black children and families often ends up harming them. Through powerful everyday stories, she shows the fault lines within child protective services and grounds us in new ways to think about and fix this beleaguered system."

—Michael Eric Dyson, *New York Times*
bestselling author of *Tears We Cannot Stop*

BROKEN

BROKEN

TRANSFORMING CHILD PROTECTIVE SERVICES
NOTES OF A FORMER CASEWORKER

Jessica Pryce

AMISTAD
An Imprint of HarperCollins*Publishers*

BROKEN. Copyright © 2024 by Jessica Pryce. All rights reserved. Printed in the United States of America. No part of this book may be used or reproduced in any manner whatsoever without written permission except in the case of brief quotations embodied in critical articles and reviews. For information, address HarperCollins Publishers, 195 Broadway, New York, NY 10007.

HarperCollins books may be purchased for educational, business, or sales promotional use. For information, please email the Special Markets Department at SPsales@harpercollins.com.

FIRST AMISTAD PAPERBACK PUBLISHED IN 2025

Library of Congress Cataloging-in-Publication Data is available upon request.

ISBN 978-0-06-303620-8

25 26 27 28 29 LBC 5 4 3 2 1

For my parents, Ramsay and Viola Pryce

CONTENTS

The true focus of revolutionary change is never merely the oppressive situations which we seek to escape, but that piece of the oppressor which is planted deep within each of us.

—Audre Lorde

AT THE BEGINNING OF THIS WRITING PROJECT, I HAD TEN BLACK women who I intended to include in the book. Most of them, I did not know. They found me online and reached out to share their tumultuous journeys with child protective services (CPS). I planned to weave all of their narratives throughout the book, emphasizing the systemic issues within child welfare. I wrote that iteration in the third person, as a researcher who was reporting on qualitative interviews. It was a solid manuscript, but my publisher and editor challenged me to dig deeper. They encouraged me to write a book that was *different*. A book of first-person accounts of my time working in CPS. That, for many reasons, frightened me. It required a level of vulnerability and culpability. But it also created an opportunity to get to the essence of how CPS plays out with families. As I made that pivot, I decided to only include cases on women I knew personally or worked with directly.

During this leg of the writing journey, I took a six-week online course on narrative nonfiction and read every book that I could find on it. This was the beginning of several months of narrative journaling, which allowed me to detail the CPS cases that had stuck with me over the years. This process also included a self-reflection period where I explored the impact of each of these cases on me personally and professionally. I spent considerable time with former colleagues and conducted interviews with some of the parents included in the book.

It is important to note that although there are firsthand accounts of events from my time in the field during 2008–10, this book is not asserting that the exact CPS context is the same today. Although it is clear that some CPS operations have persisted over the years, this book does not negate the improvements that child welfare agencies have made along the way.

Many of the events in this book I witnessed firsthand as an investigator, with the exception of case details that were provided to me through in-depth interviews. Each interview was recorded, and any additional follow-up communication with parents occurred via phone calls, email, and text messages. Direct quotes and dialogue in this book derived from my frontline casework, interview transcriptions, case notes, medical assessments, CPS reports, and court documents. To contextualize the interview content, I used public records, news media, research, data, and policy analysis. In certain instances, I have reconstructed the content of CPS reports, such as allegation narratives, based on my distinct recollections and interviews with my former colleagues. All names and identifying details have been changed in order to protect privacy, with the exception of a few individuals whose real names I have used at their request. No one interviewed for this book has a current case pending before or employment with CPS.

• • •

Please note that the terminology "child welfare professional" refers to an investigator, a family support social worker, or a caseworker/case manager who carries a caseload and works for or contracts through a child protective services agency. The terminology "child welfare community partner" refers to various family-serving professionals, such as (but not limited to) child welfare attorneys, judges, mental health providers, court-appointed advocates, educators, physicians, social workers, foster parents, and law enforcement.

IT STARTS WITH US

I HAD BEEN A CHILD PROTECTIVE INVESTIGATOR FOR ABOUT one year when I started having nightmares. In this particular one, I was getting ready for work, like any other day. I went into the bathroom to look at myself in the mirror. To my horror, my face was disfigured. I had thick webbed scarring, and my skin seemed waxy as if it were melting in place. It was the sort of disfigurement that frightened people and made them avert their gaze. I gasped and stared for a moment longer before I finished getting ready. I had to make a stop for a case on the way into the office. When I arrived at the house, I was shocked to find dozens of Black children lying across the lawn. All of them appeared dead, and their faces were disfigured in the same way as mine. Why did my face match all of these dead children?

I got out of my car and carefully stepped over their bodies, one by one, and I made my way to the house. It was as if their bodies were uneven bricks on a sidewalk. A woman opened the door before I knocked. But it wasn't just any woman; it was my best friend, Erica. I introduced myself as the child protective services (CPS) investigator and informed Erica that I had received a report regarding her children and needed to ask her some questions.

"There are dead children all over my yard and you want to ask me questions?!" She was livid. I noticed her face was unblemished, and I wondered if she could see my face the way I saw it that morning in the mirror.

"Yes," I said bluntly. "I need to get some questions answered, I need to walk through your home and see your children, complete a risk assessment, and—"

"And you need to go talk to the school and the neighbors and ask them if they have any concerns about the safety of these kids," my CPS supervisor said, as she appeared next to me, giving me additional directives. I nodded and quickly jotted down a single note: THE CHILDREN ARE ALREADY DEAD.

• • •

Psychophysiologists call dreams the *road to the unconscious*.[1] Science tells us that within five minutes of waking up, a person generally forgets 50 percent of their dreams. Within ten minutes, 90 percent has been forgotten. It has been fifteen years, and I still remember that dream. I will not claim to be a dream interpreter, but I do have a guess at what it meant.

In CPS, we often focus on the wrong things. We overlook the true essence of what is in front of us and engage in rudimentary queries about surface-level dynamics that do not get us to a genuine understanding of what is happening with families. When the approach is one-size-fits-all, then our priority is making it fit, no matter what is going on around us. Decisions are made that vilify parents, even when we know that families are stuck in a cycle of inequity, low access to support, intractable poverty, and the complexities of human relationships. With insufficient information, we wield elusive power,[2] and we require tasks that are focused on rehabilitation and surveillance.[3]

That dream disturbed me a lot. It made me realize that CPS work truly does change the professionals in the system. There is trauma in what professionals witness, what they endure, and also when they realize that their help is actually harm. When the realization of culpability surfaces, moral distress and shame often create a cycle that plagues your waking and sleeping hours. Although my dream showed external disfigurement, I believe that CPS disfigured me on the inside. That disfigurement was facilitated by the systemic harm I passed along to families and children. For me, the dream confirmed that not only are children and families being harmed by the system, so are the professionals.

Doing CPS work often felt as if the strings that were attached to investigators and caseworkers led back to a dehumanizing mandate or an outdated policy or procedure. Many families were so clearly in need, in crisis, but we had a process and an investigation to complete. Working with families is dynamic, and all questions shouldn't be the same, all inquiries shouldn't sound the same, and all investigations shouldn't produce the same result, which is often a family left powerless, fearful, angry, and dazed.

This book is largely about the strange odyssey of my child protective work. In 2007, the year before I started in the field, a group of authors posited that child welfare professionals should be given a warning: *beware, this may change you forever and can be dangerous.*[4] I came to realize that the dangers were far more than just physical. Moral injury and moral distress in child protective agencies have been explored by social scientists, and there is great need for mitigation tactics and support structures for child welfare professionals. If it is true that "hurt people hurt people," then the harm to families will continue and likely become more pronounced as the workforce continues to suffer.[5]

I am (and have been) a sort of satellite in the orbit of the CPS system. I don't think I ever belonged there, but I am certain that my purpose was to be there. And I have been there in many ways—as an intern, as a social worker, as an investigator, as a friend, as a relative, and as a subject matter expert. At the onset of my time working in CPS, I did not know how subjective the job could be. Our childhood and upbringing is a lens through which we, subjectively, see the world. I grew up in a tight-knit family in a small neighborhood. The insularity of my childhood didn't prepare me to fully understand the vulnerability of my community or the structural challenges that ensnare many families.

I hope this book will be helpful for a wide variety of readers, but I wrote this book for the professionals who are currently in the child welfare field, students who are interested in social work, and the CPS system's partners like therapists, educators, medical professionals, attorneys, judges, court-appointed advocates, guardians ad litem, and law enforcement. Child protective work is interconnected with other family-serving organizations, so if your work affects the well-being and safety of families and children, I hope you will read with an open mind and open heart. I invite the reader into my personal journey through deep moral conflict. This book brings together firsthand accounts from my child protective field work and additional stories of the experiences of Black women. It includes the difficult situations that professionals face daily, and also the desperate situations that many families are in.

Before this book, I had written academic articles, thought-pieces, court affidavits, and trial testimony. I have prepared countless speeches and presentations. But I have not shared my personal journey. In this book, I have highlighted how my personal values, education, and training all affected my frontline experience as a young CPS investigator. My mindset has certainly changed in and through my experience with CPS. Today it is hard to recognize myself back when I received my very first case.

The journey to this book was more than sifting through eighty-five hours of recorded interview content, reading and rereading transcriptions, synthesizing research and policies, and years of revisions. It was a journey of self-awareness, self-discovery, and finally, self-actualization. *Broken: Transforming Child Protective Services—Notes of a Former*

Caseworker is intentionally abridged as it relates to history and policy, because that has been well documented.[6] Unlike previous works, the voices of Black women play a central role in this book, those who have worked within the system and those who have been affected by the system. My aim is to galvanize child welfare professionals who are stuck between what the system requires of them and what humanity deserves from them. I constantly found myself in the middle of that dilemma—failing at balancing both. It is clear to me that if professionals continue with this balancing act, the workforce will suffer, and poor outcomes for families will persist.

• • •

I created a framework that maps my evolution through the field of child welfare. The framework starts with being an **Agent** of the state, then an **Advocate** for change, then an **Activist** toward equity and justice. For me, my development through these phases was facilitated by *questions*. When I was in the agent phase, all of my questions were directed to families. I rarely thought to question myself or the system that governed my work. As an investigator of child abuse, all of my questions were focused on uncovering parental failures. But in the advocate phase, my awareness deepened, and I started considering hard questions and tracking down answers. Questions like: *Why are Black families overrepresented in the child welfare system? Why are some families reported for child abuse at higher rates than other families? Since poverty is so similar to neglect, how can the system be more effective in extricating them? Why do the courts mandate virtually the same requirements for all families?* When I was able to answer those questions honestly, the resistance that carried me into the last phase—activist toward equity and justice—was ignited. At this point, all of the questions from my advocate phase were directed at the child welfare system as a whole.

To expound, agents of the state carry out procedures and requirements, always hiding behind the bureaucratic shield. They see it as their civic and professional duty to investigate families. They embrace the imbalance of power, and they wield it to secure compliance. Policy and procedure drive the actions of the agent, and vulnerable families suffer because of it. They carry out the most disturbing of routines and the most invasive of procedures, even if unwarranted. More times than not, they're unwarranted. Agents of the state are driven by the urge to find a guilty and offending parent and punish them. This sort of professional makes all-encompassing judgment calls that usurp any nuance or individuality. Agents rarely take time to acknowledge structural, systemic, and community factors that affect families. They operate as if they have the solutions to problems that they haven't even taken time to understand. This is known as a segregationist mindset,[7] where professionals see the families they serve as categorically inferior to them. There is a deep and never-ending chasm between an agent of the state and the families they serve. Due to that chasm, they are void of empathy and hope, and their actions reinforce the "othering" of families.[8] At the start of my career, I was an agent of the state, and I describe several cases that ran concurrently during that phase.

In the advocate phase, professionals are clear that inequity and injustice are marring the child welfare system in various ways. This phase is a time of self-awareness, a time to pursue answers to tough questions, and to advocate for change. Advocates recognize the power dynamics within their work and pursue a negotiation of power with families. This negotiation of power allows families to share their perspectives, thoughts, and feelings (known as their lived experience),[9] though the true impact of their voice on the case outcomes is limited and inconsistent. Most social workers are educated and trained to be advocates, and although it has potential for positive influence, this phase is considered the *safe zone*. During this phase, social workers embody their professional code of ethics—social justice, dignity and worth of the person, and importance of human relationships[10]—but they are still tightly woven into the status quo. Scholars recognize the person in this position as being an assimilationist,[11] which is a person, in contrast with the agent of the state, who has hope for families. With that hope, they work to save families through rehabilitation. That road to rehabilitation is littered with tasks and mandates that are informed by heteronormative white values. Advocates may not seek to punish parents like agents do, but they are still committed to *saving* families. And the savior mentality creates a dehumanizing chain of events because it doesn't allow for professionals to see the inherent strength of families.[12] It was during this phase that I pursued a PhD, leaned into my social work values, and fiercely advocated for change. But I didn't rock any boats. Much of that advocacy was facilitated by researching, writing articles, and delivering expert testimony in child welfare trials.

Activism was the next phase of my development. I believe that the beginning of true change is developing the questions. The resistance begins when child welfare professionals ask themselves the hard questions. Then the revolution is activated when they speak up and ask others to embrace discomfort. In this phase, child welfare activists are challenging the mindsets and antiquated behaviors of those around them. And once they start asking others the same hard questions—*Why are Black families overrepresented in the child welfare system? Why are some families reported for child abuse at higher rates than other families? Since poverty is so similar to neglect, how can the system be more effective in extricating them? Why do the courts mandate virtually the same requirements for all families?*—they finally see that this system is functioning in blissful and willful ignorance. No one is willing to answer those questions because the answers point directly to an incredibly flawed system that lacks the capacity to protect or strengthen anything, let alone a family.

Becoming an activist meant a new lens of bravery and courage for me. It pushed me beyond social work values and made me pick a side from the line that I had been straddling. A child welfare activist is someone who doesn't lead with punishment (Agent), but they also don't rely on their education and training (Advocate). An activist has an antiracist mindset and is led by a sense of ethics and the pursuit of equity and liberation. Activists are determined to free families from the harmful systems that surround them. The forefront of activism is the value of humanity, and activists operate with the belief that compassion and empathy can lead the way to a new child welfare paradigm. An activist stands up and says the hard thing; they push themselves beyond comfort and lay a lot on the line. In this book, I describe a case that catapulted me into activism and into a space where it was impossible to see the depths of harm inflicted by child welfare and remain standing still.

The intentional development of the child welfare workforce could be an incredible lever toward true change. Professionals in this field should be your partners in transformation. These are the people who have direct contact with families in our communities, and the voices of families must be prioritized with any change efforts. Child welfare professionals need to see their role in the paradigm shift toward the empowerment of families. These professionals must have the safety and support to acknowledge culpability, take responsibility, and seek accountability. With all this talk about changing the system, I take some solace in reminding folks that the system is made up of people. Those people are human beings who have solidified value sets yet malleable hearts that can be shaped toward justice.

The workforce is bound by ethics to promote safety, permanency, and family well-being. With that ethical charge, child welfare professionals can make a huge difference in transforming the system. They are the most proximal to what families are facing and the barriers that exist to providing for their needs. For a shift to occur, there has to be a commitment to reimagining how the system operates and then work toward reconciliation with and healing of the community through rebuilding trust.[13] A big step toward building trust starts with an admission that our system has lost its way.[14]

I believe that there is power in the people. Which includes families, child welfare professionals, policy makers, and community partners such as educators, physicians, mental health providers, and law enforcement. Child protective services can't do it alone, but they also cannot wait for everyone else to change before they do. In order to begin a redesign process for a new system, which is equitable and family centered, child welfare needs to take an honest and brave look at who they really are, who they are serving, and what truly is best for children and families.

WHAT I KNOW FOR SURE

I GREW UP IN A TOWN WITH ONE TRAFFIC LIGHT. THERE ARE A few more there now but it's still a tiny town. We called our community Fruitland Park, because most of the streets were named after fruit—Orange Street, Grapefruit Street, Lemon Avenue. I learned later than I'd like to admit that Fruitland Park was actually called Highlands Community. It was a small suburb in central Florida. My neighborhood was made up of about four blocks. It seemed like my mother could call for me from our house, and I could hear her no matter where I was in our neighborhood. Fruitland Park was a predominantly Black community. Our local church was nestled in the center of those four Fruitland blocks. We only had to take a short stroll on Sunday mornings to get there. The church was painted white in some century before I was born. It sported a rusted marquee on the front lawn that listed service times. The sign also alternated uplifting spiritual phrases like "Jesus Loves You" or "God Is Good."

Everybody knew everybody in Fruitland Park. We were invested in caring for one another. The children of one family were loved and cared for by other families without question. A neighbor would call on another neighbor for more than forgotten ingredients to a recipe.

Neighbors looked after each other's kids outside and inside our little collection of worn-down houses. A single mother could count on neighbors to take care of her children if she had to pick up another shift at work. An elderly widow knew that her lawn would be cut each week by someone with a riding mower. Somebody would return an empty trash can after trash pick-up or run an errand to a grocery store for someone who wasn't feeling so well.

Our close-knit community also came in handy if unwanted insects made their way into your home. One night I heard my dad rummaging around the house to get dressed. I was bleary eyed and barely done dreaming. I was twelve. I went to see what the commotion was and saw my dad shuffling down the hallway putting on his shoes.

"What's happened?" I asked him.

"Sister Henrietta has another lizard in the house," he said on his way out the door.

"Oh, okay." I went back to bed.

My father, the neighborhood lizard-slayer, emigrated from Jamaica at age seventeen. He was not formally educated but he could build anything. He was a carpenter without a union. He spent his days working at a nearby construction company and weekends helping repair our neighbors' homes. My mother, born and raised in Hurtsboro, Alabama, worked as a certified nursing assistant for my entire childhood. They raised me and my two sisters, one older, Rachel, and one younger, Coretta. We each had our own rooms with a TV and posters on the wall of our favorite singers and celebrities. We had a bulky desktop computer that we all had to share. My parents were married. They both worked full-time, and they both cooked dinner for us. It just depended on who was home at dinnertime. In our eyes our mom was a southern soul food and pastry chef who forbade us from entering the kitchen until she was done baking. My dad was an expert in currying goat, and he made meals while belting out songs, never finishing a song before starting another one. He usually made too much but I loved the leftovers and so did the neighborhood. My sisters and I had a chore chart that hung on the front of our refrigerator. We spent hours and hours negotiating the terms.

"If you do the dishes for me tonight, I'll vacuum for you all week," I said to my older sister, Rachel.

"Hell, no," she said. "I hate dishes."

Fruitland Park was insular, and its insularity made it all the more intimate. I had a family at home, a church that felt like a second home, and a community that was fully present in the lives of its children—all of its children. I had people all around me who I trusted and who cared for my sisters and me. In youth, you're often unsure and constantly figuring things out as you grow. But what I knew for sure was that Fruitland Park was where I belonged. I could not fathom being taken away from any of it.

• • •

I went to college in a city adjacent to mine. I still drove to my neighborhood church every Sunday. I decided to study criminology and sociology. These were interesting disciplines, but not very practical in terms of the job market. During my last year, I took an elective course on grief and loss. Our professor asked us to call him Bruce. The course met every Thursday evening for three hours. Bruce was a tall African American man with a bald head and a graying stubble beard. He told us that he was a licensed clinical social worker (LCSW). I had never heard of this before. He explained to us that he worked with children during the day and taught college courses at night as an adjunct professor. His work was therapeutic; he helped children cope with loss. Bruce took a practical approach to the material from our textbooks. He would add context from his work in the field and gave us knowledge we could use. It was real to me because I had already experienced grief in an indelible way. My father had died during my junior year of high school; I had no words for that loss, until that course with Bruce. The course even broadened my understanding of grief.

"We are all at varying stages of grief. Usually, grief is only associated with death, but I want folks to understand that grief and loss can also happen even outside of someone dying," he told us. Although it made sense that you could grieve someone who was not dead, I had never considered that. I had attributed all grief to mourning the loss of someone through the finality of death.

After taking his course, I knew I wanted to become a social worker. I wanted to work directly with children but I also wanted to share what I was learning in an educational setting like Bruce. I applied and was accepted into a social work master's program at Florida State University (FSU), the same place where Bruce received his social work degree. I was headed to Florida's capital city, Tallahassee, four hours north of my hometown.

• • •

At twenty-two, I moved into my first apartment not too far from FSU's campus. Social work was a broad discipline; there were many career options that a social worker could pursue—therapeutic practice, medical social work, veterans' affairs, public health, and policy work. Sometimes having too many options is tough. When I met with our internship counselor during my first year of grad school, I was presented with an opportunity to receive a scholarship that would cover my full tuition along with a stipend to cover housing costs. It sounded too good to be true. The catch was I would need to complete an internship in child protective services and commit to working in that job for at least one year after graduation. I wasn't convinced that this was the right career path, but the counselor explained that an internship was a great way to find out.[1]

"So, you want to take people's kids away?" my classmate asked me after I told her about my internship. She made a face that was half disgust and half worry.

"Of course not. But a part of the job will be making sure that kids are safe."

"Well, good luck," she said, "because nobody likes those CPS people."

CHAPTER 1

DO BETTER

ON THE FIRST DAY OF MY GRADUATE SCHOOL INTERNSHIP, I AR-
rived at the child protective services office dressed in black slacks, a
white collared blouse, and a single-breasted gray blazer. I wore a nice
pair of black shoes that pinched my toes whenever I took a step. The
lobby was spacious with black and silver chairs lined in rows facing
each other. A wide aisle separating the rows of chairs led up to a receptionist's desk. The lobby had beige walls and worn white ceramic
floors. It was an airy but also eerie atmosphere.

According to her nameplate the receptionist was Shelley Irving.
Shelley was petite. She sat behind a desk with a protective glass shield.
The small rectangular opening was not big enough for anything larger
than a piece of paper or a small notebook. Her computer was off to her
left side, and she was gazing toward it. Her cell phone was lying next to
her keyboard and someone's voice was blaring from its speaker.

"Good morning, my name is Jessica Pryce, I'm an intern from FSU
and this is my first day." The person on the phone quieted at the sound
of my voice.

"Hold on one second," Shelly said toward her cell phone, tapping
the screen quickly to place it on mute. She turned her chair toward
me. "Good morning. Do you know who your supervisor is?" she asked.

"Lydia Davis."

"Lydia works in Unit 6. Walk through this door." She pointed toward her right side while pressing a button to buzz me in. "Go straight back and to the left."

I thanked her and walked through. There were identical charcoal-colored cubicles on both sides of the hallway, which was lined with gray carpet. It was so thin, it felt like old hardwood under my feet. Sounds rang out around me: various pockets of chatter, the hum of papers sliding through copy machines, and phones ringing. Periodic spurts of laughter bounced off the partially enclosed walls. I turned into an enclave of cubicles, after seeing a small placard that read: Unit 6.

As I walked in, there was only one woman there; she seemed antsy leaning over the back of her desk chair typing with purposeful and rapid keystrokes. She had to stand on her tiptoes to type over her chair. She was African American and wore a more casual outfit: black capri pants, gold top, and fabric flats. Long black braids hung to one side, hiding her face from my view. Before I said a word, she paused her typing and slightly whipped her braids to look at me.

"Are you my intern?"

"Good morning, yes, I believe so. I'm Jessica." I hesitated before confirming her identity. "Are you Ms. Davis?"

In a seamless motion, she stood upright, picked up a large black tote, and slipped it over her shoulder.

"Yep, and we have a case. Let's go."

• • •

I was several inches taller than Lydia and had longer strides, but she marched far ahead of me, leading the way through the same door I had just entered. Feeling the sting of each step, I questioned my choice of footwear. Lydia acknowledged Shelley at the reception desk with a quick head nod as we exited.

"We'll use the state car today. We have to drive out to Woodville Highway," Lydia announced. Neither of us slowed our stride until we reached an old Ford Taurus covered in rusted gray paint. The state car, I assumed. "And none of that 'Ms. Davis,'" she said, unlocking the driver's side. "Just call me Lydia."

I nodded and climbed into the passenger side. Although I had been in Tallahassee for about a year, I did not venture out much, so I wasn't sure how near or far Woodville Highway was. Lydia pulled a GPS out of her tote and attached it to the mount on the front window. I adjusted my seat to get more comfortable. Once I got settled, I glanced in the back and noticed two car seats. One standard seat for a small infant and then a booster seat that could be for a toddler. Lydia placed her bag, stuffed with a thick manila folder, near my feet. Everything was seamless in the way Lydia moved from typing in the address on the GPS to situating herself in the driver's seat. When she was done, the GPS displayed an estimated thirty-five-minute drive to our destination.

At first, I was worried about what we'd talk about, but it turned out, there was a lot to discuss.

"I graduated from Florida State, six years ago," she said. "And I've been working as an investigator ever since." I guessed her age was about twenty-eight, about five years older than me.

"Do you like it?" I asked.

"Some days. Some cases are so bad and they stick with you, and the long hours are rough. My mom helps with my three kids. I don't know what I would do without her. 'Sorry I'm late' is like my catchphrase these days."

Lydia took a deep breath as she drove. "But you know what? This job is important, and my kids are at the age where they understand what I do, they know that I work to keep kids safe."

I smiled. "You must be a superhero in their eyes."

"I don't know about that," she said. Still driving with one hand, Lydia reached over and pulled the folder out of her tote and handed it to me, never taking her eyes off the road. "Here's the case, you should review it. When you finish, let's call the reporter."

As I'd learn that first day, some states require all people to report concerns for child abuse, but most designate particular professionals as mandated reporters.[1] Those mandated reporters include social workers, medical personnel, teachers, mental health professionals, childcare providers, and law enforcement officers. When someone calls in a suspicion of abuse toward a child, they call a hotline. As they speak to a hotline operator, the reporter is asked a series of questions in order to determine if the call will be "screened in" as an investigation or not. Sometimes cases are "screened out," which means they are not accepted, meaning there wasn't enough information to justify opening an investigation. This is the process of how a case arrives on the desk of an investigator like Lydia. In that year, 2008, there were three million reports called in alleging child abuse, which accounted for six million children. Sixty-three percent of those reports were "screened in" for investigations, which means approximately two million reports spanning over three million children and their families underwent an investigation that year.[2] And Naomi Harden, the person we were on our way to see, was one of them. She was African American, a mother of three, and in her late twenties. I opened the folder and started to read through the pages that were fastened together by small, round metal prongs.

"Each report is classified under a specific maltreatment or abuse code," Lydia explained. This report was categorized as *Environmental Hazard*.

"What do they mean by 'environmental hazard'?" I asked.

"Basically, a dirty house."

"People are reported for having a dirty house?"

Lydia answered without missing a beat. "If there are young children and the house is really bad, yeah, we have to go out and investigate. How old are the kids? Their ages should be toward the middle of the page."

"Joshua, seven; Zoe, five. The youngest is Miles; he's two years old," I read aloud. The older children shared the same last name, and the youngest had a different last name. I continued to read over the file, taking in these new terms and details.

"Since you're an intern, you can't interview anyone in the family on your own. Just shadow me and observe. You understand?"

I nodded. I had no interest in interviewing anyone.

"But you can take notes for me in case I miss something," Lydia added. "You'll also help me with entering the notes in the system and submitting our reports. I usually have interns help pull criminal records and prepare court documents too. And you will handle all of the collateral contacts."

Lydia's brain seemed to move a mile per minute; she spoke with rapid-fire cadence, but everything was clear and coherent.

"Collateral contacts?"

Lydia explained that collateral contacts are interviews with people who are a part of the children's lives but not in their family. These could be neighbors, teachers, a therapist, or even pediatricians.

"You should also walk through the home noting any hazards while I talk to the mother. I'll need you to check the kitchen and cabinets to see if there is sufficient food in the home. Walk through each bedroom to note anything you think might be harmful for young kids. Read page two and the criminal history is toward the back."

Allegation Narrative: The three children are living in squalor. Home not cleaned in months. Children arrive at school in the same clothes, un-washed, day after day. There are dirty diapers all over the home. There is a roach infestation, some coming out of children's backpacks in class. Teachers noted fleas on the children and ringworms in their hair. Multiple animals on the property, unknown if they are family pets. Children spend hours outside until dark. Hard to reach mother. Whereabouts of the children's father is unknown.[3]

None of what I read felt like we were headed to a real home that housed children. The GPS alerted us that we were getting closer to our destination. As we drove, Lydia made a phone call, and I gathered from the conversation she was speaking to whoever had called the abuse hotline to report Naomi.

When she hung up, Lydia confirmed my thoughts before I could ask. "Before you go out to meet the alleged perpetrators, always call the reporter. They can give you important information you might need that wasn't included in the report."

"Alleged perpetrators?" I asked.

"Yes, the parents. Always remember, these are just allegations. It's our job to go out and investigate to find out what actually happened."

I nodded as I continued to go through the case file. The case packet included a current child maltreatment report and all past reports with CPS, if there are any. Naomi had a previous case about a year ago, a domestic violence incident with the father of her youngest son, Miles. The report stated that she called the police to her home because Miles's father was physically abusive. As I read on, the report indicated that he was arrested for the abuse, but by the end of that case, Miles's father was back in the home living with the family.

Lydia slowed down and made a measured turn onto a narrow dirt path. Thick trees lined both sides of the dirt road as we continued inching along. Eventually, we approached a series of mobile homes with electrical power lines streaming from pole to pole. We pulled to a stop in front of the last mobile home on the lot, toward the back of the community. Every part of me tensed up. I almost asked Lydia if I could just observe from the car. But it was my first day and retreating wouldn't bode well for an initial impression.

Lydia held a clipboard under her arm and a pen in her hand; her photo ID and cellphone hung alongside a badge around her neck. I got out of the car with my purse around my arm but turned back to toss it back in the car when I saw that Lydia had left her tote. I needed to do something with my hands, so I grabbed a notepad and a pen and hurried to catch up. The steps of the small wooden porch creaked. There were children's clothes hanging on the side of the porch and a few bowls of water on the ground nearby. I recalled the mention of animals in the report but did not see any.

"And, Jessica." Lydia looked at me as she knocked on the door. "I don't think you're going to want to dress like that for this internship."

I looked down at my clothes.

"What? Did you think this was an office job?"

• • •

In 2008, the population of Tallahassee was around 180,000 people. That might not count as a big city, but I grew up in a town of 5,000 people and I lived in a very small neighborhood. Demographically, white people comprised a 55 percent majority of the inhabitants of Tallahassee, followed by 35 percent Black residents, 7 percent Hispanic residents, and 4 percent Asian residents, with the remaining percentage categorized as mixed race.[4] Coming from Lakeland, where the population was 80 percent white and less than 19 percent Black, Tallahassee felt like a bastion of diversity. The city had a Black mayor, John Marks, whose policies and values leaned progressive. But, not unlike other cities in Florida and around the country, segregation in Tallahassee still reigned. Communities remained stratified and segregated according to income and race. During this time, Black people more than likely lived near Florida A&M University, a historically Black college on the city's southside, or in the predominantly Black Frenchtown neighborhood. There were a few Black families in pockets near the northwestern part of the city. There were also large communities in Tallahassee that had no Black people at all.[5]

The concentration of Black families in certain areas can be attributed to many things, including the low-income public housing units situated in certain parts of the city. In 2008, the Census Bureau released its data on median income for families. For Tallahassee, Black people had a median income of $39,879, and over 35 percent were living below the federal poverty line.[6] Affordable housing accessibility was constantly at play, and the reality is that people live where they can afford to. The data on families in poverty and unstable housing wasn't real to me until I started working in CPS. Everything I learned about poverty and income inequality in my social work courses was on display during that internship. There were glaring differences across communities and neighborhoods, according to income and racial makeup. And in some neighborhoods, CPS had a constant presence. In others, we rarely ever set foot.

• • •

The yard outside of Naomi's mobile home was littered with food containers and dirty diapers ripped open and scattered. There was a large trash can off to the side of the mobile home filled so high that the lid could not shut. Lydia told me that I should record these things later, so for now I made mental notes.

Naomi answered the door, just enough for me to see her face and an ensconced little boy straddling her hip. A foul odor met us; it was thick and pungent like a mix of spoiled milk and mildew.

That must be Miles. I peered at the little boy. Miles looked at Lydia and then at me, then buried his face in his mom's shoulder. He only wore a diaper. Even from the narrow view from the porch, the interior of the mobile home was in visible disarray. A TV blared loudly with cartoons that I couldn't recognize. Naomi was wearing a long black spaghetti strap dress; Miles's little hand clutched the strap. She had a small afro that was matted on one side of her head. She was not expecting us (or anybody); she looked like she had just woken up. Lydia held her badge out for Naomi.

"Good morning, I'm Lydia Davis, we're from the Department of Children and Families. Are you Naomi Harden?"

Naomi's expression shifted from indifference to a wry curiosity. She looked over Lydia's head toward me. I wondered if I ought to say something or introduce myself. But I kept quiet and averted my eyes to my notepad.

"What's this about?" Naomi asked.

Lydia was straightforward, well-versed in this kind of introduction. "We've received a report about you and your children, and I need to ask you a few questions. I also need to see your children—"

"My kids are at school," Naomi interrupted. "Who reported me and what for?"

"Ma'am, we need to come in. I need to see your home, and I can explain everything to you." Lydia's voice remained steady.

Naomi didn't move an inch for a while. It felt like a standoff and Lydia had settled into her stance like she had all day to be there. I was surprised when Naomi slowly backed up to open the door wider for us. I followed Lydia inside, still not daring to say a word.

"This is Jessica Pryce," Lydia finally announced. "She's an intern, and she will be observing me. She needs to walk through the home and take some notes. While she is doing that, we can talk."

"Notes?" Naomi looked directly at me; her curiosity was turning into defiance. "Don't walk through my house taking notes about shit."

I froze and looked to Lydia for direction.

"It won't take long," Lydia said assertively, and then she nodded me toward the hallway. The interview continued as I moved through Naomi's home. I overheard Naomi's clipped responses to Lydia's questions. I looked around, recalling the report's mention of dirty diapers, bug infestation, and fleas. Dirty diapers were overflowing from the kitchen trash can. Laundry was piled up haphazardly all over the floor of the adjacent hallway, and dirty dishes filled the sink and much of the small kitchen counter.

I took notes about the things I saw. The interview between Lydia and Naomi sounded like it was escalating. The mobile home had an open layout where the kitchen and living area were all combined. The only way to tell the difference between the living room and the kitchen was the linoleum tile on the kitchen floor versus the dreary carpet in the living room. Naomi's voice grew louder and louder. I slowly opened the kitchen cabinets and drawers. I remembered Lydia's instructions from the car. *Make sure to check the kitchen to see if they have food.*

"What the fuck is she looking for?" Naomi asked Lydia.

There were empty fast-food containers in the trash, but not much food in the cabinets or refrigerator besides milk and cereal.

"How much longer is this going to take?"

I left the kitchen. I wanted to escape the sting of Naomi's glare. I made my way down the hallway to the bedrooms, stepping over piles of dirty clothes along the way. I slowly pushed open a door to a bedroom, but something was in the way. I stuck my neck through the small opening and looked in the room, immediately wishing I hadn't. Clothes were everywhere, and mounds of them were blocking the door from opening all the way. That's when Naomi yelled at me to get out of her kids' room.

This is insane, I thought to myself. *How does a place get like this? Couldn't this woman do better than this?* The entire experience was making me queasy. The carpet that lined the floor was stained and frayed at the edges where it met the wall. I felt righteous indignation well up inside me because children were living like this. I knew about personal bias. It was one of the more interesting concepts I learned while studying social work. I knew that in this kind of work—where we enter people's personal and private spaces—we had to try to minimize how much our own biases shaped our opinions (and judgments) of clients. I knew all of this at that moment, but my frame of reference was how and where I grew up. I could not imagine growing up in a home like this, and I also couldn't fathom how anyone could let it get this bad. I wasn't sure what the best course of action was, but this place did not seem like a safe place for Miles or his siblings.

"Don't go near my kids! And don't come back to my damn house!" Naomi's yelling jarred me from where I was, so I headed back toward the living room.

Lydia motioned for me to join her as she made her exit. Still holding tightly to her baby, Naomi flailed her free arm toward the door as if we did not know the way out. Once we were in the car and pulling away, I inhaled a deep breath through my nose and slowly exhaled through my mouth in an attempt to calm my nervous system. Eventually, I looked over at Lydia, who seemed unphased. Resolute. As if an angry woman, holding a baby, throwing us out of her house was a common occurrence.

Lydia handed me the case file and started the car. "Go ahead and get the kids' school address and type it into the GPS," she instructed. I found the address as Lydia pulled out her phone, all while she was coasting the car slowly back down the dirt road. I quickly cued up the GPS for navigation to the school.

"Hi, this is Lydia Davis from the Department of Children and Families calling about Naomi Harden's children. We have contacted the mother and are heading over, can you bring them up to the office?"

As we left the lot of mobile homes, Lydia began forecasting the next steps. "When we get there, we have to see each child and talk to them and their teachers about what's going on."

After some silence, and just the Taurus's labored car sounds, Lydia asked: "What did you see in the house?"

"Well . . ." I was still taking in everything that happened and didn't really know how to describe everything I had seen, or what I felt. After a few seconds I settled on, "The report was pretty accurate."

"I figured as much," Lydia said. "She would not let go of the baby, so I didn't get a good look at him. But his diaper was old, probably the same one he slept in. You should add that to the notes."

"Okay," I said softly and added this to the notepad on my lap, even though I had not noticed his diaper. "So, what happens after we see the kids?"

"Naomi's not going to like it, but those kids aren't going back there tonight." Lydia, impervious to her own declaration, kept her eyes fixed on the road. I was stunned by what she said but also by how she said it. It was so piercing and matter-of-fact. As if she had said that sentence a hundred times before.

CHAPTER 2

EVICTED

2008

AS AN INTERN, I LACKED THE CONFIDENCE TO SPEAK UP, AND I rarely had to take the lead, but I always felt useful. After my first day, I dressed more casually for work and wore more comfortable shoes. My cubicle was an arm's length away from Lydia's desk, which was convenient since she would regularly reach over to hand me files to review, court documents to sort through, and notes to put in the system. I spent my days listening, observing, and trying to make Lydia's life easier.

One of my tasks was to look up the criminal and child welfare history of families before Lydia and I went to visit them. These tasks were considered precommencement activities, things that took place before we met a family, which constituted commencing a case. Lydia seemed to appreciate that I handled that part and filled her in on the case in the car. After we finished commencing a case and interviewing all family members, we were responsible for assessing present danger and imminent risk. We completed a risk assessment that was detailed through notes and metrics in the system. A part of every risk assessment was to look at the history of the family to identify any patterns or risk factors. I spent time going through criminal histories, 911 call records to the family home, and any prior history with CPS. We were armed with a trove of information before we went to meet a family.

The quality of my notetaking improved pretty quickly. If I typed that the alleged perpetrator had a history of criminal drug charges, Lydia wanted me to go through their criminal record and write how many times they were arrested and distinguish if it was for drug manufacturing, distributing, possession, or use. I had heard horror stories from interns who had supervisors who wanted a coffee concierge and/ or a designated notetaker. Those kinds of internships were not learning experiences. But I could tell early on that Lydia wanted me to learn the job. She was patient when she explained new concepts, procedures, and decisions, and I grew to love working with her. Instead of her being annoyed with all of my questions, my curiosity fueled her confidence in her own work. She was comfortable in her command of the complicated situations we investigated during my internship.

In addition to my internship, which was unpaid, I was a full-time student and worked part-time at a call center. As I worked to make ends meet, I did not have much free time. The free time I did have, I spent with close friends, namely, Erica Gaines. Although we shared a couple other good friends, she became my closest friend in Tallahassee. When Erica and I weren't together, we talked on the phone almost constantly—between classes, running errands, while we were cooking or cleaning. Erica inquired about how my internship was going. I would share what I could about cases, which wasn't very much due to confidentiality. I also shared with Erica how much I was learning from Lydia.

Erica had transferred to Florida State from a community college in Jacksonville, which was her hometown. We met on campus. She was working on her undergraduate degree, I was in graduate school, but we were the same age. Erica had taken an alternate path so she could work and save money. Back home, she had spent much of her time providing support to her goddaughter, Madisen. Madisen was a bright, inquisitive, and energetic toddler. If you knew Erica, then you knew Madisen and saw instantly that she was the apple of Erica's eye. Even while studying at Florida State, Erica made frequent trips back to Jacksonville to pick Madisen up for a weekend visit in Tallahassee.

When I first met Madisen, she was about two years old, with her legs wrapped around Erica's waist, clinging to her as though she might vanish at any moment. Their bond was clear and beautiful. Madisen called Erica "Gigi." On weekends, Erica would host potlucks, and our other friends would join. Madisen loved those weekends because she was the star of the potluck. She would sing, dance, and twirl around the apartment. Those nights, we would all bring a dish to share and spend time together talking, laughing, and pseudo-studying. Our laptops and books would be out and open in the living room, but the laughter and chatter overshadowed our term papers. Long after Madisen went to bed, and our other friends left, Erica and I spent time talking and deepening our friendship. During those late-night conversations, I learned more about Madisen.

$\cdots$

Madisen's mother was Diedre "Didi" Lott, a resident of Jacksonville, Florida, about 160 miles east of Tallahassee. Jacksonville had experienced an uptick of 56 percent in the number of families who were living below the poverty line in 2008. That was the year I began my internship with CPS, and that was a harried time for Didi and her children as they endured multiple evictions.

In 2008, there were 664,000 people nationwide who experienced homelessness on a given night.[1] Florida was one of five states that had the most homeless, tallying over 50,000 per night.[2] Didi never imagined that she would become one of them. The concept of being on her own and struggling financially was not exactly foreign to her, but being evicted was a new experience. When she was growing up in Brooklyn, New York, she always had a roof over her head. She was raised by her single mother, Beverly, who was among the growing legion of single women raising families in the city that never sleeps. Didi was born in the early 1970s, and the years that followed her birth were marred by high poverty rates and persistent crime in Brooklyn. Beverly never intended to raise her children alone. She spent years married to Franklin Lott, a man she had adored for a decade prior to their nuptials. Beverly went into labor with Didi on February 4. On that same day, he moved his belongings out of their Brooklyn apartment. By the time Beverly brought Didi home, snow coated the ground, and Franklin was long gone. His abandonment was acute. Beverly fell into a deep depression that would turn out to be unrelenting, mostly untreated, and decades long.

Most people celebrate their birthdays, but Didi always felt conflicted about hers. She has never gotten over the fact that her own father refused to even meet her. She has a disturbing perspective on this that she often shared with others. For Didi, her father's *abandonment was her birthright*. She did not know much about her father except that he was a member of the Nation of Islam and that he introduced the religion to her mother. Beverly insisted on maintaining their Muslim practices: daily prayer times, dietary restrictions, and general modesty in their attire. Beverly never formally divorced her husband, but she had relationships with other men after he disappeared from their lives. Didi was joined by seven siblings over the next decade.

Being the eldest came with an innate desire to protect her siblings, and in many ways, Didi was their co-parent. Beverly worked tirelessly as a housekeeper for families on the Upper West Side. She also worked a part-time job cleaning office buildings, leaving Didi to provide care for her siblings. There were many days when Didi, a preteen, would cook, clean, and care for her toddler siblings, usually with the youngest attached to her hip. She spent many evenings braiding her little sister's hair and helping her other siblings do their homework. The apartment that Beverly and her children lived in was secured through an affordable housing program that required annual verification of income.

Beverly would jokingly tell Didi, "I'll be back later, I have to go down to the housing authority to prove we are still poor."

As the family grew and finances became tighter, Beverly decided to ask an extended family member, Barry, to move in to help. The decision seemed prudent at the time, but it changed Didi's life forever. When she was twelve years old, Barry began sexually abusing her. Beverly began taking on even more jobs. She had to leave the home early in the mornings. This turned out to be the window within which Barry would violate Didi. She shared a room with her siblings, so he would wake her up and guide her into his room. When he was finished, he would instruct her to go shower and then wake up her sisters and brothers for school. He would then ask normal things like, "Do you all want cereal today or I can scramble up some eggs?"

"Cereal is fine," she would answer, and then chide herself for participating in this faux exchange.

With each passing day, Didi felt like she was losing more and more of herself, while her mother was seemingly happier with her new bona fide au pair. Now that Beverly's days began much earlier, her evenings became more open and flexible. Usually, Barry cooked dinner, and Beverly even sat down to eat with them, a rare occurrence before he moved in. Before, Beverly would leave cooking instructions for Didi because she would have to work through the evening.

As Didi approached her teen years, the abuse continued; she developed a dull ache that seemed to radiate from her chest whenever she was near Barry. She became withdrawn and depressed. The emotional dissonance that Didi experienced was exhausting. She hated Barry, yet he was an integral member of their household.

Didi began to resent her mother and became fixated on staying away from the apartment as much as possible. Her best friend, Jeffrey Lawson, sort of a latchkey kid himself, welcomed her newly minted freedom, and they roamed the streets of New York together. She eventually went home, but she waited until it was so late that her mother was surely back home and everyone else was asleep. She became even more clever in the morning; she would rise at four, alongside her mother, under the guise that she had to study before school. When her mother left around five, so did Didi. She got dressed and went to school, meeting up with Jeffrey, and waiting until the school day began. During those mornings, sometimes Didi and Jeffrey were quiet. Talking was never necessary for them. At several moments, Didi thought she might tell Jeffrey about Barry, but she felt embarrassed and dirty. The silence became safety and solace. She experienced very few quiet moments at home, so she relished those mornings.

On the nights that she stayed out late, she simply told Jeffrey that she was at odds with her mother and needed space. But the sight of Barry repulsed her. The prospect of him asking her to do innocuous tasks like clean up, or wash clothes, or run an errand, was something she could no longer bear. Jeffrey never had any issue with spending time with Didi. He also lived in Brooklyn, with his father, and although his father claimed residency, he was seldom home. His father spent most of his time in Washington Heights dealing drugs, but also getting high on his own supply. An imposing figure, Jeffrey's dad was six foot six inches tall and had a deep caramel complexion. Jeffrey's mother, Janet, fell head over heels in love with him, but his addictions and drug dealing ravaged their marriage. Eventually, Janet left Jeffrey's father and moved to Jacksonville, Florida. Jeffrey developed a deep resentment of his father, and he was adamant that he would never let drugs ruin his life. With his mother gone, and his father virtually absent, Jeffrey was essentially on his own.

Didi and Jeffrey had many things in common: the longevity of their friendship and collective memories from childhood, the painful absence of their fathers, and the yearning to reach for something outside of New York. Didi and Jeffrey's bond grew stronger while her relationship with her mother became strained. To Beverly, Didi's behavior was selfish, disrespectful, and downright dangerous.

"Something could happen to you out there, Didi. It's not safe." Not knowing the danger within their own home, Beverly tried to alert Didi to the dangers outside. But Didi left her mother's warnings largely ignored.

"I'm going to call the police and put you in juvenile detention!" Beverly's fear turned into threats to make Didi fall in line. "If you don't come home right now, I will throw all of your shit on the side of the road!"

Didi's evenings out with Jeffrey were her only solace, and she started to look forward to their early mornings too. But, within a few weeks, Jeffrey dropped a bomb: he was moving to Jacksonville to be with his mother. Didi was devastated. Although her mother often mentioned how dangerous it was for them to be out so late, Didi felt shielded from the NYC realities because Jeffrey was by her side. A week later Jeffrey was gone; a subdued Didi started to spend more time at home.

The abuse continued, and Didi's unremitting rage and despair were back and potent. Seeing Barry walk around, laugh with her mother, or just seeing him breathe sent her into a storm of fury. She felt fueled by her rage but also imprisoned. Shortly after her sixteenth birthday, on an evening when Didi's darkness was too heavy, she went into her mother's bathroom and found prescription meds. Beyond her depression, Beverly also experienced back issues due to the strain of her work, so she had various pain medications. Didi pulled out three different bottles and swallowed all the pills in a few desperate, labored gulps.

After she swallowed them, Didi lay down across the bathroom floor. She started to panic and thought about making herself throw up. *What had she done?* But, Barry's face flashed in her mind. The image of him produced a flood of tears that fell down the sides of her face before she even knew she was crying. She never wanted to see him again.

Hours later, after her mother found her on the bathroom floor, Didi was surrounded by medical and mental health professionals in a cold hospital room. They were able to save her life, but now they needed to figure out why she tried to end it. Before long and after much prodding from the hospital social worker, she reluctantly disclosed the abuse.

The social worker, a mandated reporter, called the Administration for Children's Services (ACS)—the designated child protective agency in New York City. During that time, the methods of interviewing children were under intense public scrutiny due to the trauma inflicted on children during trial preparation. New protocols were established in which children who were victims of sexual abuse were interviewed by a forensic social worker at Children's Advocacy Centers, and all interviews were recorded. Didi gave a full forensic interview about what had transpired with Barry, but the social worker assured her that she would not be asked to recount the events again since the recording could be used in the court proceedings. It was not long before Barry was arrested and charged with sexual battery against a minor. Didi thought this would bring some relief, but the events that followed were constant reminders of what her disclosure set in motion. Child protective services visited their home frequently and interviewed all of Didi's siblings to make certain that they were not hurt by Barry. CPS also asked questions about Beverly. *Is your mother here most of the time? Who cooks dinner for you? What happens when you get in trouble?* Things were crystallizing for Didi. Although Barry was the perpetrator of the abuse, CPS was investigating her mother too. Didi couldn't know that eventually, fifteen years in the future, CPS would once again enter her life to interview her own children.

• • •

Not long after, Didi decided to leave New York City. This was unsurprising as she and Jeffrey had maintained contact; he consistently urged her to come to Florida. Beverly did not approve of the move, given Didi's age. She was seventeen and hadn't finished high school, but Didi went anyway. During the past year, she had gotten much closer to her mother following the horror of the abuse and the suicide attempt. But, Didi never really saw a future in New York. Too many painful memories lived in that city, in that apartment, and she was ready for something, anything different.

A year later, almost predictably when they both turned eighteen, Jeffrey and Didi got married. Their parents protested, but it didn't stop the two teens. Didi trusted Jeffrey. For her, it was an easy decision. Neither of their parents' marriages worked out, but Didi was determined to make hers different. Sometimes she missed the fast pace of New York and being close to her mother and siblings, but Didi embraced Jacksonville. It was her chance for a do-over. Almost mirroring her mother Beverly's birthing sequence, Didi had five children over the next ten years. Her first son was Jeffrey Jr., then James, next Trish, then Tiffany, and her youngest Laila. They eventually moved out of Jeffrey's mother's house and into their own apartment.

Didi had long since let go of the tenets of the Nation of Islam, and they joined a local Protestant church called Love's Chapel. This is when she met teenage Erica. The church was small, and it seemed like the congregation was one big family. The church was a haven for Didi, and she built a meaningful relationship with the pastors, Charlotte and James Gaines. The pastors had three children, a set of twin girls and their eldest daughter, Erica Gaines. The pangs of poverty within their city were of great concern to the Gaineses, so they were intentional about providing meals, housing, and even monetary resources to their church members in need, and other families within their community. To the Gaines couple, their community and church members were not "like family," they were *family*.

Didi's parental responsibilities grew by the day. Jeffrey worked all the time, odd jobs, but primarily double shifts as a dishwasher at a nearby restaurant. Neither Didi nor Jeffrey finished high school, so she began working toward her GED. She hoped that one day she could become a nurse. Financially, they were getting by and leaned on the church for help when they needed it. As Didi's children continued to grow, the church nurtured each of them.

Erica was just a teenager when she first met Didi. They formed a quick bond. Erica's light brown skin was clear with a smooth jewel undertone, and she had a bright smile. Didi always commented on Erica's smile—it seemed to light up rooms. Her near-perfect teeth were always attributed to braces, though she never had to wear them. Over the years, their relationship grew and deepened. With over a decade between their ages, Didi became like a surrogate older sister to Erica. Erica, being the eldest in her family, appreciated this new connection to Didi. Some gossipers in the church made comments about Didi and all of the children she had, but Erica loved them all. She never wanted Didi to feel like her children were a burden.

Didi became deeply involved in the church; she and Erica spent many evenings together, preparing for an event, rehearsing songs for the choir, or cleaning up. Didi's kids were always in tow, running up and down the aisles. Didi talked to Erica about her aspirations to become a nurse, and she also shared vulnerable admissions like her and Jeffrey's financial problems and the bills that were piling up. Most teens might not be interested in that sort of conversation, but Erica was mature and intuitive. Many people confided in her in that way.

In 2005, Erica had started taking classes at the local community college and Didi had given birth to her last child, Madisen. The new baby brought excitement, but the ongoing realities of life and family, including the overwhelming cost of growing a large family on one income, continued to weigh on Jeffrey and Didi. Within the first year of Madisen's life, Jeffrey and Didi were evicted twice. Didi and her family moved into the homes of church members. Although Didi was grateful, she worked tirelessly to secure an apartment for her family. She waited on hold for hours, added her name to wait lists, and tried to save everything she made from odd jobs like doing hair. Most of Didi's children were school age, but she struggled to keep up with Madisen.

Erica was devoted to looking after Madisen, and it was during this time that Didi asked her to formally become Madisen's godmother.

Madisen had an infectious personality as the baby of the bunch. She was spoiled by everyone, especially by Erica. Her dark bronze complexion made her honey-green eyes shine brightly. People would stop them on the street to comment on Madisen's eyes. Erica loved buying Madisen cute dresses and outfits with matching accessories for her hair. Didi never worried about Madisen when she was with Erica. She appreciated the support and desperately needed it. In the back of Didi's mind she knew that Erica wanted to eventually transfer to a larger university, and she was hoping to have her own place before then.

Within a few weeks, Didi was reported to CPS. Although mandated reporters remain anonymous, she believed it must have been her caseworker at the Jacksonville Housing Authority. Housing instability and evictions present unique and ongoing problems for parents who are in poverty,[3] and CPS is often the sought-after recourse for mandated reporters. When the CPS investigator came to commence Didi's case, they interviewed all of Didi's children about the housing situation. Didi tried to assure them that she and Jeffrey were working on a housing solution. Since they were able to stay with a member of the church, the investigator was somewhat appeased. But that did not stop her from calling regularly and making unannounced visits.

It is not uncommon that families who receive services from housing authorities have past CPS involvement as well as a current case.[4] CPS has a disappointing track record when it comes to providing quality and relevant services to the family or attempting to prevent future homelessness. Didi couldn't be sure if this CPS case would help her family or if they were there to monitor her shame in this embarrassing situation. Often homelessness and unstable housing experiences are generational. Homeless families are also struggling through financial hardship, facing mental health challenges and a range of other adversities. This was especially true for Didi. She remembers her own mother coaxing through their housing authority program year after year. Her mother worked multiple jobs to make ends meet, and Didi had found herself in the same cycle.

Another generational cycle was unfolding at the same time. Unbeknownst to Didi, Jeffrey had begun dealing and using drugs. Didi only found out because he was arrested. She was in disbelief as she could never forget Jeffrey's vehement disdain for how his father turned out. He did not spend very long in jail, but his court fees were substantial, and he was sentenced to five years' probation. Their housing prospects were still rocky, and the open child protective services case was a looming threat. Under all that pressure, Didi's marriage disintegrated. Through the years, it seemed the only connection she and Jeffrey shared was physical. It became clear to her that the merging of their lives was not about a true romantic connection. It was driven by loyalty and a chance at some healing from their painful pasts with the only person they loved and trusted. Building their family was something they were both very proud of, but their relationship was not able to withstand the weight of the challenges they faced. Jeffrey moved out.

Losing him was bad enough, but it also worsened her childcare, housing, and financial burdens. She was devastated and out of options. Despite the love the church offered to her and her kids, it was time she made a new plan. Didi decided to go back to Brooklyn. She called her mother.

"I think we have to come back home," Didi said flatly. "Jeffrey's gone and I can't find anywhere to live."

"You and the kids are always welcome here. I knew you were having trouble but I had no idea that Jeffrey had left."

"Yeah, well," Didi replied. "It's my birthright."

CHAPTER 3

THE LIFE-CHANGING MAGIC OF TIDYING UP
2008

YOU'RE THE BEST INTERN I'VE EVER HAD," LYDIA SAID. "SOME IN-terns cannot do anything without me holding their hand. You will be good at this job if you decide to come on board."

I was glad to know that Lydia saw potential in me becoming a full-time investigator. It was hard to imagine handling cases on my own, though. I had grown accustomed to Lydia's certainty with every deci-sion. I became anxious at the thought of doing anything without her co-signing it. Spending so much time with Lydia created a dynamic where I began to understand her thought process and her tactical approach to investigations. Learning how she operated helped me stay a few steps ahead. I could literally finish her sentences. One day, we returned to the office after a case, and she was a bit flustered because Shelley had placed another case on her desk chair. That's how Shelley did it if you weren't around. She never put it on your desk, always on your chair.

"We need to head out soon," Lydia began. "But for now, we need to—"

"Request medical records for the ten-year-old and make collateral contact with the previous case manager," I finished for her. Lydia chuck-led at my accuracy.

Our camaraderie bred inside jokes, communication through imperceptible eye contact, and long car rides where we were so tired we were seeing double. We established a private call and response between us. When there was a situation that was clearly innocuous but not exactly by the book, Lydia would say: "Unasked." And I would aptly reply: "Unanswered." Which essentially meant, if no one asks about this, it never happened. This was similar to the reasoning behind the saying that it's better to ask for forgiveness than ask for permission. I once asked Lydia if she wanted me to report to the office every morning at eight, which was technically when my internship hours began.

"Girl, no. I'm not here at eight." Lydia grimaced. "Just be where you are supposed to be when I need you to be." Somehow, I knew what she meant.

"Unasked," she said.

"Unanswered," I finished.

Lydia also left notes for me on my desk. Her calligraphy was unique, a mixture of cursive and standard script letters. Her written instructions were often worded in short, incomplete sentences indicating her mind was moving faster than her hand. To this day, I'd know Lydia's handwriting and shorthand anywhere.

When she started to feel more confident in my abilities, she permitted me to conduct follow-up home visits with families on my own. The first follow-up visit that Lydia assigned to me was back to Naomi Harden's house.

"We need to close this case soon, so go check to see if she has cleaned up the place. And don't tell her you're coming."

In the CPS world, making unannounced visits to families was customary. Lydia explained that the obvious reason was that we didn't want people to prepare for our visit by hiding things, hiding people, or rapidly cleaning up. We arrived unannounced so that we could see if they were complying with the court-ordered mandates.

It had been three weeks since we removed Naomi's children from her home due to an environmental hazard. I knew she did not want to see me.

• • •

Three weeks earlier, when Lydia and I arrived at the school to interview Naomi's children, they were waiting up front in the office. First, we spoke with the school counselor, who had called in the report.

"Please tell me you all are going to do something. These kids need help and their mother refuses to do anything. They both have ringworm and rashes all over their scalps. Our school nurse has tried to treat it here in the clinic, but it just keeps coming back," she said.

I stood behind Lydia and wrote down what she said in my notes.

"I just can't keep looking the other way. These kids are basically taking care of themselves." The counselor's eyes filled with tears, but she kept them at bay with a series of deep breaths and rapid blinking. "I hate that I had to file this report."

"I understand," Lydia assured her. "Thank you for calling us; we will do all that we can. Will you please print out their attendance record for me?"

Like Lydia, I found myself sympathizing with the counselor. She obviously cared very much for these kids.

Joshua and Zoe sat across from us at a small table, and Lydia introduced herself. They were seven and five years old, respectively. Through the low cut of his hair, I looked for the ringworm/rash that was mentioned earlier and saw it tracing the back of Joshua's neck. They wore school uniforms: khaki pants and a red shirt with the school's logo. For the most part, their appearance looked fine to me. Zoe's shoes were dirty and so were her pants, but I had nieces and nephews, and they generally came home from school with some level of dirt on their clothing. If anything, Zoe and Joshua's demeanor was more telling. They seemed tired and sad. They also had a clear dependence on each other; Zoe's arms were wrapped around Joshua's elbow throughout the interview.

It was clear that Joshua was leery of us and only answered our questions with short responses. Joshua made cereal for his sister every morning; sometimes he changed Miles's diaper before catching the bus, if he had time. His mom was usually still asleep when he and Zoe walked down the road to the bus stop. The bus stop wasn't far, Joshua added. He told us that things at home were fine and that he makes sure that his siblings have dinner in the evening.

"Tell me about your dad, Joshua. Does he help your mom take care of you?" Lydia gently asked.

"No," he answered.

"What about other family? Does anyone help your mom?" I chimed in, hoping that was okay. Lydia gave a quick nod of approval.

"Me." Joshua pointed to himself.

Every question Lydia posed was said softly and kindly, and she kept her eyes on both Joshua and Zoe the whole time. When asked about the house, Joshua responded nonchalantly, as if it was more of a nuisance than an actual problem.

After the interview with Naomi's children, we spoke with the principal and both kids' teachers before we returned to the car in silence.

"It's a damn shame," Lydia muttered under her breath. "These children deserve better."

Lydia called the CPS attorney who was back at our office, leaving the call on speaker as we drove off.

"I need to find placement for three kids until we can figure out what's really going on with this mom," Lydia said into the speakerphone.

"Tell me more, and I can tell you if we have enough probable cause to petition the court," the attorney, Terri, replied.

From that conversation in the car, I learned about how all the pieces came together for removals. Investigators made the decision to remove a child from their parents; however, if there was not enough probable cause to do so, a judge could dismiss the petition and send them back home. The CPS attorneys were there to work with us to create a viable petition to present to the judge. So, technically, children were taken from their parents prior to a final ruling of approval.

Lydia ran down the details of our rationale for removal. She rattled off every observation like a list. "Two teachers, the principal, and the school counselor, they all have concerns for the kids. They both have ringworm, so we need to add medical neglect as a maltreatment code to the case. The school staff report making active efforts to work with her, but the mom is unresponsive. The oldest son is taking care of the other kids. I can't send those kids back there."

"Do they attend school regularly?" Terri asked.

"Yes, they have perfect attendance," Lydia answered.

"How was the mom when you met her?" the attorney asked. I started to catch on to how they identified parents. "The mom." "The dad." Common CPS lingo.

"She was angry and didn't seem to think anything was wrong with her place," Lydia said. Then she glanced at me. "I have an intern with me. Jessica, what do you think?"

"About Naomi?" I asked hesitantly, unsure how much my words would or should weigh at this moment.

"Yes. You were there," she said, still looking over at me. Lydia really knew how to throw someone into the deep end. An awkward silence stretched between us as Lydia and the attorney waited for me to speak.

"Um, I agree," I finally answered, adding to the probable cause. Recalling the state of Naomi's home and Joshua's somewhat despondent nature I backed up my statement. "I don't think the kids should have that much responsibility. Seems like the kids need help."

"Alright then," the attorney said, "I'll start compiling the paperwork."

The next steps in the process moved quickly. Lydia called law enforcement to request that an officer meet us at Naomi's house to assist in the removal.

"The police come too?" I asked.

"I always call them when I'm removing kids. Parents lose their shit. It's just a precaution."

I nodded. These early days in my internship cemented new rules in my mind. Law enforcement were our partners. Parents, apparently, were not.

When we returned to Naomi's home, Lydia and I stood near the car and waited for law enforcement to arrive. Naomi must have heard our car or anticipated our return because she opened the door still holding Miles. She had changed into a different dress and removed the clothes that were drying outside. She had also brushed her hair up into a small afro puff with a blue scarf wrapped around the bun.

Once the police car pulled in behind us, Naomi did not hide her mirth. She started to laugh. "You have got to be kidding me!"

"Naomi, I'm back to get Miles," Lydia said. The whole scene intensified when a tall, white male police officer came over to stand beside me and Lydia. Still, I felt a little better having this person form a wall of authority between us and the Black woman whose children we'd come to take. In that moment alone it was clear that we had a lot of authority, including the power of the police at our immediate disposal. His uniform and weapon were the only distinguishable traits separating me from this officer.

Lydia walked toward Naomi while I stayed back beside the officer. At first, I couldn't hear what was said between them, but soon enough Naomi became agitated and defensive. Naomi was holding on to Miles while gesturing with her free arm as she spoke to Lydia. The exchange between Lydia and Naomi continued, and then, after more than a few minutes, Naomi suddenly acquiesced and detached Miles from her hip, passing him to Lydia. Miles showed his allegiance by gripping tightly to the strap of his mother's dress. Naomi just stood there not even attempting to remove Miles's hand. Miles started to scream for his mom and struggled as Lydia gathered him in her arms then walked back to the car. Naomi's expression was almost unreadable, but she was seemingly exhausted as she clasped her fingers together and placed them behind her head. That's when I saw her break and start to cry.

"Well, that went well," the officer said, somewhat jovially.

"It's my first day," I announced. "What's an example of this not going well?"

"The parents refuse to give up their kids and then we have to step in. Sometimes it gets ugly," he answered before heading back to his car.

"Good luck with the job," he said to me. Then he gave a quick nod to Lydia as she settled Miles into the patiently waiting booster seat.

By the time the officer drove off, we were back in the car with the toddler strapped in. As I got settled in the front seat, through my window I heard Naomi talking to Miles. She had walked down to the car and was near our window. He began screaming and reaching toward her. "It's okay, baby. I love you. Don't cry," Naomi said in a soothing tone. I did not anticipate how tender her voice would sound. She spewed so much anger at Lydia and me but she had met her match . . . her baby's tears. Naively, I thought even at two years of age Miles would come quietly with us, without distress or alarm. But, no matter our good intentions, we were strangers to him, and he was being taken away from what he knew: his mother and home.

Lydia twisted in the driver's seat to reverse out of the lot. I kept staring at Naomi, who was now gesticulating wildly and talking on her cell phone. The whole drive back down Woodville Highway, Miles's shrieks bounced off of every surface of the car. It was going to be a long ride back into town.

• • •

As I made my way over to Naomi's house for the follow-up visit, I fidgeted in the driver's seat. I was getting more anxious as I retraced the same route Lydia and I had taken on my first day. This time, I was driving alone and in my personal vehicle. After removing Naomi's children, we had a hearing set for the following day. At the hearing, Naomi appeared apathetic while the concerns of the court were explained to her. She stood in front of a judge alone in the very same dress that Miles had clung to the previous day. Lydia whispered to me, "She didn't even change clothes," as if her repeated outfit was even more rationale for removing her kids.

The hearing lasted approximately fifteen minutes. That's all it took to change her life and the lives of her children. The judge asked Naomi a few questions, and she answered them curtly. The petition to place the children in their maternal grandmother's custody was supported by the courts. Lydia was lauded for finding a kinship placement for the children, a loving grandmother, who lived nearly an hour away in Gadsden County.

"Ms. Harden, your children will remain in the care of your mother until child protective services finds that your home is a safe place for the children to return," the judge began. "You are able to visit your children as much as you would like."

"This is ideal" is what Lydia said to me as we walked out of the courtroom. *Ideal*. "We got the kids placed with family. The mom will get some help now and she can visit her kids whenever she wants. Now we can get this case closed."

At that time in Florida, the investigation portion of a case conducted by CPS was to be completed within forty-five to sixty days. If children are removed, or the court is involved, the family's case is transferred to a privatized community-based care (CBC) agency for ongoing case management services. Naomi and her mother were assigned a CBC case manager who would work directly with them over the next year to help reunify the family. To Lydia's point, this outcome seemed like it was the best-case scenario for this family. It was still early in my internship, but I was already feeling the exhilaration from being able to help those children.

At the close of an investigation, we have to include a finding or conclusion for the alleged abuse. At that time, the categories for investigative findings varied. *Substantiated/Verified* was used when there was a preponderance—or majority—of credible evidence that showed harm or threat of harm. *Unsubstantiated/Unverified* was used when the evidence did not meet the standard of preponderance to prove harm or threat of harm. Sometimes, there was a finding of *Inconclusive*, and Lydia explained that this meant that the investigator wasn't able to come to a provable conclusion. Lydia instructed me to close Naomi's case with verified findings of Environmental Hazard and Medical Neglect.

When I arrived at Naomi's house, someone else was already there. A white woman, dressed comfortably in jeans and a light sweater, introduced herself to me as Naomi's new case manager, Caroline. I was thrilled to not be alone.

"Nice to meet you," I said, shaking Caroline's hand. "I'm an intern, I work with the lead investigator and I'm just here to check in before we close the case." We stood outside in front of the worn wooden steps to the porch.

"I'm just on my way out," Caroline said. "I came to meet Naomi and explain the process she's got ahead of her."

"How is she?" I asked, hoping to gauge how my encounter would go.

"She's still angry. Apparently, there are issues with the kids at her mom's. Her mom doesn't drive long distances, so the kids aren't going to school. The bus comes out here to pick up the kids, but their school bus doesn't go to Gadsden County for pickups." Of course, it doesn't. "I'm looking into another placement, one that's closer to their school."

"You need to move the kids again?" I had thought that our "ideal" placement had solved the main problem; instead, it created a whole new set.

"I don't see how I can get around it." Caroline glanced at the file. "The alternative is changing their school. And we don't like to do that. If I can find a placement closer to the school, it will also be easier for Naomi to see them."

Caroline and I spoke for several more minutes. She mentioned that she had been in communication with the children's grandmother, and that she was overwhelmed with everything that was going on. The grandmother told Caroline that she couldn't believe that Naomi had gotten those "welfare people" involved. Apparently, Naomi had always held down a job, but after some issues with domestic violence, she quit her job and became estranged from her family. After Miles's birth and the separation from his father, she completely shut everyone out.

"Wow. I had no idea." And clearly Lydia did not either.

"I'm working on getting some mental health evaluations set up for Naomi. She's clearly got something going on." Caroline climbed into her car and drove away.

My solo visit with Naomi was brief. The home environment was largely unchanged. This perplexed me. We removed Naomi's kids because this home was unlivable. I could not understand why Naomi would not at least clean up as a first step to show the courts that she wanted her kids back. I knew that simply cleaning up would not magically change Naomi's life, but it sure seemed like a good start.

Nevertheless, it was now Caroline's job to help figure out what exactly was going on with Naomi—my job, which I was eager to complete, was to tell Naomi about our case findings and leave. I explained to Naomi that this visit meant her case was closed and CPS was verifying all of the allegations. My words didn't seem to affect her; she simply stared at me, waiting for me to go.

As I was heading back to my car, Naomi, still standing on her porch, asked me a question. "Do you have children?" This was the first time I was asked this question as an intern, but over time it would become frequent ammunition for parents. I was twenty-three and childless, and Lydia advised me to never divulge any personal information to clients. But for some reason with Naomi, I felt like I should.

Even though there was distance between us, I felt cornered and exposed when I replied, "No. I don't."

Naomi scoffed. "I knew it." Then she stood there staring at me from her tiny little porch as I drove away.

CHAPTER 4

ATLAS OF THE HEART
2016

JATOIA POTTS WAS BORN AND RAISED IN GEORGIA, SPLITTING time between her mother Margaret's home and her grandparents'.[1] She was the only child and the only grandchild, so although attending college was exciting, she was also nervous to be moving away from home. She was looking forward to studying marketing and accounting at Tennessee State University.

Jatoia's family was close, but it wasn't large. She had an abiding desire to build a big family and become a mother. Although being an only child made her the family's magnum opus, the recipient of loads of love, it also felt lonely, and growing up she longed for siblings. Jatoia often thought of the joy of having children and watching them fuse together through sibling attachment and love.

She shared these hopes with her best friend, Rosalyn, who made her promise to travel the world with her before starting a family. They made a plan that once they graduated college, they would travel and live in several different cities. They were not sure where they would end up, but they planned to follow their heart. They considered places like New York, Los Angeles, Houston, and beyond. Shortly after graduation, Jatoia and Rosalyn started their trek with Florida. They moved to Jacksonville.

In Jacksonville, there is an annual festival called "One Spark." It's a community-led experience for entrepreneurs to showcase their work. There are art vendors, food trucks, and music, and this event draws upwards of ten thousand people. Jatoia always had an interest in entrepreneurship, so she decided to attend the event with Rosalyn. That is where she met Lawrence Daniels, and the spark was instant.

Their love grew into a connection that Jatoia had only dreamed about. They were both vegetarians and had similar dreams of building their own businesses and raising a family. Lawrence was interested in photography and shared his future plans with Jatoia. Lawrence's parents lived in Jacksonville, and Jatoia became very close to them. Before long, Jatoia was pregnant. As excited as she and Lawrence were, she was nervous to tell her mother and grandparents. She and Lawrence were not married, and she had always been told to be careful of unplanned pregnancies. But when she told her family, they were ecstatic about the new baby.

The next year, life came at Jatoia and Lawrence fast. Her mother was diagnosed with breast cancer. She and Lawrence moved back to Georgia, and then she gave birth at home surrounded by her family. They named the baby boy Lawrence Daniels Jr., and they started calling him LJ. He was born January 4, 2016. He was healthy and happy, and he smiled all the time. The entire family converged on this little boy like he was next in line to the family throne. Jatoia felt an overwhelming sense that this was the realization of what she had always wanted. She was a mother. And at that moment, that was all that mattered.

That first year of LJ's life seemed to fly by. Jatoia loved him more and more as time went on. "You would think," Jatoia said, "your love is at its peak when you see your baby for the first time at birth. But my love has grown and continues to intensify." When LJ turned one, Margaret went into remission, and Jatoia found out that she would be welcoming a second child.

Her mother had since relocated to Durham, North Carolina, with her husband, Richard, but she kept in close touch with Jatoia and the family. Six months later, Margaret's cancer was back and had spread to her lungs. Her health began to rapidly decline, and she was placed in hospice care. In July 2017, at about six months pregnant with her second child, Jatoia, Lawrence, and LJ headed to Durham for an extended stay. Jatoia wanted to be close to her mother during this time, so they rented an Airbnb not too far from Margaret's apartment.

Jatoia was thankful to be with her mother on a daily basis, and Margaret was able to spend precious time with her only grandchild. It was hard for Jatoia to imagine her mother being gone, so she dismissed the thought and put effort into being present. Even through the beautiful moments with her mom, Jatoia was stressed, and it was affecting her pregnancy. Weeks later, Jatoia's placenta ruptured, sending her into labor; she was only twenty-eight weeks along. Within moments, she, Lawrence, and LJ were arriving at the labor and delivery wing of Duke University Hospital. Jatoia felt scared and heartbroken. She had every intention of birthing her baby, at full term, at home like she did with LJ.

Although being in Durham created the opportunity for Jatoia to be closer to her mother and stepfather, her support network was back in Georgia. With her stepfather by her mom's side, there was no one to take LJ. So Lawrence and LJ sat in the lobby while Jatoia got settled into her hospital room. The physician explained that her placenta had detached, and they were going to have to get the baby out as soon as possible.

Jatoia was in a hospital room without any of her family, and she was surrounded by doctors and nurses she did not know. As the labor intensified, one nurse held Jatoia's right leg, and another nurse her left leg, and Jatoia wished that Lawrence was holding her hand. After a few pushes, a tiny three-pound baby came into the world, another son. They named him Kenneth, and he would become known as simply

"Kenny." Jatoia's relief at his arrival was overtaken by fear as the nurses immediately took him away to assess his vitals.

"I didn't even get a chance to hold him," she said. Two nurses followed the doctor with Kenny to the Pediatric Intensive Care Unit (PICU) where he was fitted for the incubator that he would remain in for the next ninety days.

• • •

Kenny had a host of medical issues. He needed multiple blood transfusions. He was also diagnosed with osteopenia, a condition that results in a loss of or limited amount of bone density. This was likely due to his premature birth, which affected the architectural integrity of his skeleton. Kenny also experienced prolonged gastroesophageal reflux disease, known as GERD. He would struggle with GERD for many months.

When it came to vaccinations, Jatoia and Lawrence had questions and preferences. What they did not anticipate was the pushback and the glaring eyes from the medical team at their inquiries. She and Lawrence always took time to study and ask questions of the staff. They wanted to know what they were doing to Kenny and what medications they were putting inside him. After Jatoia was discharged, the couple found an apartment at Duke Manor, a location very close to the hospital, so that they could see Kenny as much as possible and stay updated on his condition. When Jatoia visited Kenny, she insisted on skin-to-skin contact because she knew how important it was for bonding, attachment, and security for newborns, though that was not always allowed. The hospital was often short-staffed, and some visits consisted of Jatoia staring into the incubator, watching Kenny's chest go up and down.

Lawrence's parents visited from Florida and Jatoia's grandparents traveled from Georgia to visit with Kenny while he was in the PICU, and miraculously, Margaret was still hanging on. She was even able to visit with Kenny, though it was not as frequently as she would have liked. Margaret was now back home with in-home hospice care, and she carried around a mobile oxygen machine. She spent time with LJ while Jatoia and Lawrence visited Kenny. Now that they were living in Durham, Lawrence's photography business started to pick up with locals for pictures and events. Jatoia started offering hair and makeup as a part of Lawrence's photography package. They were finally building the business they always wanted.

After three months, Kenny weighed five pounds, and he was discharged, though he was still having digestive issues. The physician told Jatoia to try not to worry and that Kenny was likely a "happy spitter," which meant he regularly spits up after meals without a big fuss. Jatoia had never heard of that before, but she felt relieved. She was thrilled to have him home, but her nerves were on edge and she worried about him all the time. He was still small and feeding time made her anxious. Was he getting enough to eat? He spat up after every meal; how much was he digesting?

She took her time when feeding him his bottle, only fifteen milliliters and then a break. The formula was recommended by the physician, and it was supposed to help with digestive discomfort. After the break in feeding, she would try to give Kenny a little more to eat, then she waited. He always spat up the milk, though she reminded herself that the doctors told her it was not something to worry about.

Even though she had visited with Kenny regularly over the course of the three months in the PICU, Jatoia felt like she had missed so much. She wanted to bond with her son and get to know him. She didn't get the chance to breastfeed him. She remembered how she bonded with LJ during his breastfeeding stage. During the weeks that followed Kenny's hospital discharge, Jatoia exclusively worked from home. In the past, she would go to a client's home and do their hair and makeup as they prepared for a photography session with Lawrence. Now she asked clients to come to her home. She was apprehensive about having the baby out and about as she still saw him as fragile. Her mother came over to visit, although infrequently due to her health issues. But they spoke every day. Within three weeks, Kenny had gone to see his pediatrician and his ophthalmologist. Jatoia would call her mother after each visit and explain how it had gone. The first set of wellness checks were all fine. Jatoia felt relieved.

During the time Kenny had been home, the weather was growing colder. Jatoia opted to stay in as much as possible. She spent her waking hours methodically feeding Kenny and watching him sleep. Going out into the world with or without Kenny was unnerving. One evening, Lawrence had a photography event, and the clients also invited the entire family. Jatoia decided to bring LJ and Kenny, and Lawrence even took a few pictures of Jatoia and the boys. There were very few pictures of Jatoia out with both of her kids, so she cherished those pictures. She made sure to share those photos with her family back in Georgia and Florida.

After Kenny had been home for a little over three weeks, Jatoia had a client over to do her makeup. As usual, she swaddled Kenny and draped him over her chest in an infant sling. LJ sat nearby on the floor, tossing around his Transformer toys, caught up in his own little world. Although Jatoia had grown accustomed to Kenny spitting up, that day the volume had increased and he began projectile vomiting. After she cleaned him up, a frightened Jatoia put him down for a nap and then finished up with her client, trying to hide the worried look on her face. Soon, it was time for him to eat again, but she felt apprehensive because of his earlier episode. She started slowly with less milk than normal. Unfortunately, Kenny was so lethargic that he didn't consume any of it. Jatoia called her mother as she had been doing over the past few weeks. Each day was nerve-racking as she tried to stay vigilant and care for him.

"I don't know what's going on with Kenny. He vomited earlier and now he seems so tired. And, he didn't eat this evening."

Margaret did not seem too concerned, but she told Jatoia to write down exactly how much he'd eaten during the feeding times and to keep a log of any other things that were unusual. That way, they had details to share with his pediatrician.

"Keep an eye on him," her mother instructed before ending the call.

Jatoia tried not to overthink it. She didn't want to panic. She reminded herself that Kenny still had digestive issues, and that might be the reason he vomited. Maybe he was just tired. He had a medical appointment just last week and the doctor had no concerns. Jatoia watched Kenny like a hawk when he went to bed that night. Kenny's nighttime routine was like clockwork, and he would wake up for a feeding at least twice. That night he didn't wake from his sleep to eat. She noted that he did not eat overnight.

The next morning when she went to change his diaper, it was only slightly wet. This wasn't normal for Kenny. Jatoia's heart started to race, her hands started to shake, and she began taking deep breaths to steady herself. As much as she tried not to panic, she could not control it. She called Margaret again.

"His diaper is not wet. There are too many things happening all at once. Can you come over to watch LJ so me and Lawrence can take the baby to the ER?" Margaret agreed without hesitation. While she waited for her mother to arrive, Jatoia gathered the things that she would need for the baby and got LJ settled in for the day. She had no idea how long this would take.

She put a new onesie on Kenny and began to re-swaddle him. His leg started to twitch erratically. She had never seen that before. Then she noticed that his eyes flushed left and did not move. It was as if his eyes were frozen and staring off into space. She called her mother back.

"Momma, where are you? I need to go now! We will just bring LJ with us."

CHAPTER 5

ALL ABOUT LOVE
2009

IT HAD BEEN TWENTY YEARS SINCE DIDI HAD LIVED IN NEW York. The readjustment period was bewildering. Didi was thirty-seven years old. The New York of 2009 was radically different from the New York of 1989. Gentrification had transformed her neighborhood, but she still felt like she had traveled back in time. She and her children were back in that Brooklyn apartment on Lincoln Avenue with her mom. She had time-warped back to the most horrible and traumatic time of her life.

Didi's first few weeks in New York had her going from agency to agency to request resources. She went to the Department of Social Services and applied for public housing assistance and cash assistance through TANF (Temporary Assistance for Needy Families). As a part of the process for public assistance, Didi was assigned a social worker, Luis, who called her each week. He even came by for periodic visits.

Before Didi left Florida, she called on Erica for help. She asked if Erica could keep Madisen in Tallahassee, temporarily, while she got her other children enrolled in school and found a place to stay. Erica obliged the request and Madisen stayed in Florida. Didi explained to Luis that her youngest daughter was in Florida with family. She considered Erica family. She asked him if there would be help with daycare once Madisen came to New York. Luis explained that there were support programs, but that subsidized daycare resources in NYC require proof of employment. Didi was already depending on her mother for housing and did not want to overburden her by asking her to take care of Madisen, too. She decided to focus on getting a job as she waited on her housing applications to be reviewed.

In addition to Luis's involvement, a local CPS investigator, a young Latinx woman named Gabrielle, also visited Didi and the children. She would inspect Beverly's apartment and talk to everyone in the home since there was an open case from Florida. When a parent has an open investigation in one state and they relocate, typically the home state will inform the new state of the case involvement. As a rule, a courtesy home visit is requested and a decision is made as to whether the initial allegations have been resolved. In Florida, the issue facing Didi was housing, and that issue persisted in New York.

As Gabrielle walked through Beverly's home, she brought up the issue of space at the apartment. There had never been enough room in her mom's three-bedroom apartment, even when Didi was a child. She and her siblings shared rooms and clothes and everything in between. Currently, Beverly had a room, the girls had the second room, Didi took the third room, and the boys were on the couch and floor pallets. Eight people living in a three-bedroom apartment wasn't ideal, but they were family. For months while in Florida, Didi had to hear she wasn't doing enough and that her standards were not up to CPS standards. Didi had been evicted, reported, and saw her husband jailed all while trying to take care of her kids and take care of her bills with little money in her bank account. The thought that CPS was finding yet another issue with her parenting was overwhelming and debilitating for Didi.

Didi made daily calls to check on her application for housing assistance. She was repeatedly told: "It's a process, and we will call you when we have space." The person on the other end of the phone call seemed to be personally offended at Didi's persistent inquiries. Affordable housing programs are systemically underfunded. They always have been. According to the National Low Income Housing Coalition (NLIHC), there are just thirty-six affordable and available rental homes for every one hundred low-income renter households nationwide.[1]

Black women who apply to these agencies for support are exposed to a barrage of mandated reporters. They are also expected to reveal the interiority of their domestic lives to the system, which leaves them vulnerable to even more reports to CPS.[2] The stress of being dependent and wedded to these systems turned into apathy for Didi. She started to feel that familiar ache of despair and depression from her childhood. The pain felt irreversible. It was as if she felt nothing at all, except that ache.

Didi thought of Jeffrey often. She was still grieving the end of her relationship and the disconnection from her life in Florida. The church, Erica's family, the new life she'd created, and the home her children knew were far away. Every day in New York brought a new level of urgency in her life, yet she felt hopeless. She wasn't sleeping. Some nights Didi barely closed her eyes for a short nap before the thoughts of what she hadn't done, what she needed to do, and what she *wasn't* doing jolted her awake. CPS reports haunted her. Her days seemed to last forever. Small tasks, taking a shower, responding to her children, or replying to simple requests from her mother felt insurmountable. Didi was constantly on edge; her only reprieve was isolation, the minute or two when she could just sit alone in a quiet room. She only left the apartment if it was absolutely necessary. When Didi was younger, her one goal was to be in that apartment as little as possible. Now, she was so burdened that she had no interest in leaving.

Didi decided that a short-term solution for the sleeping arrangements would be for her to move out. She knew there were shelters available and she had a friend she could possibly stay with for a few weeks. Didi was certainly not alone in her quest for a stable home.

That year, 1.5 million people across the country were living in shelters or transitional housing,[3] which was a 30 percent increase from the year prior. The nationwide housing crisis was not remotely improving.[4]

Didi called the investigator, Gabrielle. "I'm moving out. Now the boys can get a room and the girls will be in the other room. No more sleeping on couches or pallets on the floor."

They had a brief discussion about how Didi would still meet her parental obligations and help Beverly with the children. Didi agreed that she would come over each morning to help the kids get ready for school and then come over in the evening to help with dinner and bedtime. This seemed to appease Gabrielle, and Didi started to pack her bags again.[5]

• • •

I heard the worry in Erica's voice. She explained to me that, after two months, no one was coming back for Madisen. When Erica finally got ahold of Didi, she learned that Didi was sleeping on the couch at a friend's house and still looking for a job. Didi said that she just couldn't bring Madisen back to New York yet and that Erica should call Jeffrey. But trying to get in touch with Jeffrey was futile—he was back in jail. There wasn't anything Erica wouldn't do for Madisen, even to her own detriment. In that moment, I decided to spare her the questions that whirled around in my head. How could she take on the full-time responsibility of a four-year-old while working and trying to finish college? But, Erica had been there for Madisen from the beginning. She watched her take her first steps and she heard Madisen speak her first words. This time was no different. And after all I'd seen Erica accomplish, I knew she was not the kind of person who got deterred easily when something needed to be done. It was all about love with Erica. Family always came first.

As the days went on, Erica heard a variation of unsolicited advice from everyone. People encouraged her to turn Madisen "over to the foster care system." Erica was adamant that she could never do that to Madisen. But she also knew that if she was going to keep Madisen indefinitely, she needed to drop some of her classes and try to work more hours at her job. I knew that decision would be a tough one for Erica. She already felt like she was playing catch-up with college, and she hoped to graduate by the end of the year.

The first thing that Erica did was identify any and all nearby support systems she could leverage to help with Madisen. She explored help through SNAP (food stamps) and applied for a subsidized daycare voucher so she could still work and go to school. In CPS, I had provided more daycare vouchers than I could count. When we received abuse reports, it was something we offered to parents who had limited resources. The logic was that families could benefit from having their children attend a fun and safe place during the day, which may decrease stress and minimize incidences of abuse. But when Erica applied, she was denied all benefits because she did not have a case with CPS and she was not related to Madisen in any way that the state recognized.

Erica persisted. She dropped half her classes so she could work full-time hours to pay for daycare herself. The person she spoke with at social services advised her to get Madisen's parents to assign her the power of attorney so that she could enroll Madisen in daycare and manage any potential medical needs. She was still having a hard time reaching Didi, but she only needed one parent's permission. Jeffrey was able to consent to the power of attorney from jail. This was a temporary agreement, and easily revocable by the parents, but it would give Erica the ability to make some time-sensitive decisions for Madisen. Mainly, a daycare.

After visiting several, Erica found the Children of Excellence Daycare; it was close by and they had a couple of openings. Erica enrolled Madisen at a cost of $700 per month. This was more than her portion of the rent for the off-campus apartment she shared with her room-mate, but she took a deep breath and filled out the enrollment paper-work. She still had no idea how long this arrangement would last and how long she would be able to carry the financial responsibility. Every time Erica tried to get help from Madisen's parents, she felt that Jeffrey and Didi would deflect and push the obligation onto the other parent.

The pressure Erica felt in this situation was intense but she still found joy in how much Madisen was growing and learning. Erica had always worked with Madisen on her reading. She placed post-it notes all around her apartment with words that described the object. Every-thing from "table" to "wall" to "door." Each night Erica, no matter how tired she was, read Madisen the book *Mommy's Little Girl*, writ-ten by Ronne Randall and Kristina Khrin, but Erica adjusted the story to Gigi's Little Girl, as Madisen still referred to her as "Gigi." They read the book so much that before Erica even turned the page, Mad-isen recited what was coming next.

By the fall semester, Madisen had become the apex of Erica's life. From my vantage point, Erica seemed to have planned everything out with expert precision. She managed to work full-time to cover day-care fees. Three days a week, she had classes in the middle of the day and was granted permission to leave her call center job to go to FSU. As soon as class was over, Erica returned to finish the workday. She left work around 6:30 p.m. and drove to pick up Madisen before the daycare closed at seven. By the time they got home, the two had just enough time for dinner, bath, a bedtime story, and then sleep. Once she put Madisen down for bed, Erica would do her coursework for several hours each night.

Erica's effort to make this work was heroic. As far as she was con-cerned, she had to make it work. But all of her effort and planning could not erase the precariousness of the situation. Soon, Madisen's be-havior started to change. She started to have angry, inconsolable out-bursts and sometimes full-blown tantrums at daycare. Her behavior was getting progressively worse as time went on, and it was negatively affecting the other children. Calls from the daycare center became a daily nuisance. Each time, they asked Erica to speak with Madisen in an effort to calm her outbursts. Erica would get on the phone and try to be as soothing as possible with Madisen. She tried to make her laugh or asked what was wrong, but her efforts could only settle Madisen for/in the moment. She was only four years old. She was still getting adjusted to her living situation. Erica had put together a schedule around her busy life, and the extra work that she had to do in order to support Madisen meant spending less quality time with her. She was facing what many single parents face—a conundrum of living costs, working schedules, and, for Erica, a college course load. Erica's efforts were a kind of crisis management of an unfortunate situation. She did all that she could but it simply was not a sustainable solution. Madisen's behavioral outbursts were a response to all that was happening around her (and to her) based on a complex collection of familial and socioeconomic circumstances beyond her capacity to understand.

One day the call to Erica wasn't a request to calm Madisen down, but to pick her up early. Madisen's behavior in daycare now disrupted the arrangement Erica had with her boss and professors. Whenever the daycare called, Erica was forced to either not attend class or shorten her workday. Her well-planned schedule that relied on order didn't consider the complex needs of a growing child, especially one at an age where they are unable to communicate needs and are facing feelings of loss, absence, and abandonment.

During the first weeks of the semester, Erica and I spoke every day. But after a while we were speaking multiple times a day. She and I called each other while we were in our cars. I was usually on a CPS case and she was always driving between the same three locations—the FSU campus, work, and Madisen's daycare. Erica loved Madisen, but she had to admit she didn't always know how to respond to her. It was hard for Erica to admit she didn't know what to do. On our calls,

I made sure to listen just like Erica listened when I talked about the eye-opening experiences I was having in the CPS world. We became inseparable in many ways. Even with everything she had going on, she was a great friend to me. Not only was she a great listener, but she could also be trusted and showed love and loyalty for those in her life, including Didi, who remained impossible to reach. Erica became compulsive in her attempts to contact Didi. She even had her parents and other church members try, but they were all unsuccessful.

The pressure intensified as Madisen's behavior continued to worsen and the calls to pick her up early from daycare increased. Friendly warnings became firmer, and Erica wasn't able to continue to juggle things as easily as she thought she could. Erica tried to get a handle on where Madisen's tantrums were coming from. Could it simply be mood swings because she was growing up? Was it mental health related? Was this situation taking more of a toll on Madisen than Erica imagined?

"Maybe she misses her mom, and this is a way of expressing her sadness. If Madisen could just talk to Didi, it might help," Erica told me one day over the phone.

Erica's theory seemed plausible to me considering Madisen's age and the fact that she had been away from her siblings and parents for months. Madisen loved Erica and enjoyed being with her but it seemed like this eruption was bound to happen.

"I can't get a handle on her behavior. The daycare director said that if this continues, she might have to suspend Madisen and eventually expel her." I pictured Erica pacing, which is something she did whenever she was worried. Expelling a four-year-old seemed like an extreme punishment. It took weeks for Erica to even find a spot in this daycare center.

Our group of friends tried to step up more to help so that Erica could get back in good standing in her classes and make up time at work. But most of our friends were navigating classes at different times of day. And I was busy at work most of the day. Altogether, our ability to ease the pressure was limited. Erica started to try different disciplinary practices with Madisen that she read about or heard about from other parents. She consistently redirected problem behavior, took away privileges, and used time-outs. Erica was also a patient communicator and spoke with Madisen at length about the behavior whenever it occurred.

On Saturdays, I would try to change the pace for them both and we would go to the park. She, Madisen, and I would regularly take a long walk around Lake Ella Park. There was a beautiful walking trail. Madisen enjoyed throwing some of her snacks for the geese to eat—despite the half dozen signs that read: Please do not feed the wildlife.

"Madisen, we're not supposed to feed them," I reminded her with a smile.

"That is so silly," Madisen replied. Erica and I shared a glance and laughed at her choice of words. "They look hungry, and I have extra."

Madisen was good at making valid points. We let this gray area of judgment pass. Every so often I'd see Erica implement the parenting skills she'd learned about. She had read tips online about how to promote good behavior in an effort to redirect Madisen's undesired behavior. So, Erica started to use this weekly outing to the park as a reward for a good week.

"If you do well at school this week, we will go to Lake Ella with Miss Jessica."

Even with the best of intentions, more often than not Madisen's behavior spiraled. When Erica consulted her own parents about this, they encouraged her to take a firmer approach. Erica and her siblings were raised by parents who believed that if you spare the rod, you spoil the child. Her parents spanked them as they grew up, as did most of the parents she knew. But godparenting didn't mean being a firm disciplinarian. Erica's role often meant helping Didi or Jeffrey when they needed it or entertaining Madisen. Erica enjoyed being the "fun one" more than the "firm one." The thought of having to bring the rod made her apprehensive, but she was exhausted. She couldn't reach

Didi and was trying to balance her classes and a full-time job, and had to weigh every penny she earned in order to pay bills and take care of Madisen.

Soon, she started using her hand to pop Madisen's hand and bottom when she misbehaved at school. It shocked Madisen, but it seemed to be working. She could look at Madisen and say sternly, "Do I need to pop you?" and Madisen would reorient herself almost immediately. The thing is, there are not many parents who started to lightly pop their children and managed to render that exact measure at that exact interval for very long. Often parents have to up the ante, as it relates to disciplinary action weighing in as proportional to the undesirable behavior. But it's hard for anyone to accurately monitor how quickly spankings change in volume and force.

CHAPTER 6

THE NEW JIM CROW
2009

ONCE I FINISHED MY INTERNSHIP AND GRADUATED, I WAS HIRED to work as a full-time child protective investigator. I was twenty-four. My annual salary was $34,000. Excited to get a place of my own, I rented a studio apartment ten minutes from the office. I wasn't sure what else I should do with my degree. Social work was an interesting discipline to pursue, but it was a broad field. My aspirations for studying social work were based on a genuine desire to help children in some way. I didn't envision doing it in this way. But, this position felt like the next logical step, and I had received feedback from many in upper management that I would be a good addition to the CPS team. Sometimes you accept a position because you have some experience, you are familiar with the job duties, and an opportunity presents itself.

The internship was a good preview of what the investigator job entailed, but I still had nine weeks of formal training to complete before I would be able to carry my own cases. Our trainer was Dan, a stout white man in his fifties with two decades of experience in child welfare. He wore a baseball cap every day, usually a different one. He led with his love for baseball and how much the game reminded him of child protective services. He explained that when it comes to baseball, much of the game is based on strategy, instinct, and focusing on the base ahead of you.

"Like baseball, child welfare requires that you remember rules and procedures. All of that is important, but you also have to trust your instincts because when seconds count, a child cannot wait." This is how Dan began our training, with charisma and passion.

He told us that the cases we would soon start receiving were "pitched" to us. We couldn't predict the type of pitch (child abuse) and we had no idea about the speed or direction, but we had to try our best to connect. Per Dan, connecting with the ball was a metaphor for connecting the dots within an investigation. He told us that every base was a decision-making point and a clue to advance an investigation.

"Child protection is not just one decision; your work is a series of decisions throughout the life of a case."

When it's time to sprint to first base, what is your decision? He explained that once we make a decision, it affects everyone around us and what they can do next. There will be many distractions in this work, he said, and multiple ways you can interpret facts, but making the best decision, sometimes with limited time and less than perfect information, was the core of what we had to do as caseworkers. This made sense to me—sort of. Katrina, one of my new colleagues, later told me that it sounded like gibberish to her and that he needed to leave his caps and metaphors at home. As my friendship with Katrina blossomed, I realized that she was a harsh critic when it came to the quality of metaphors.

There were four of us total in training, three Black women (me, Katrina, and Sandra) and one Black man (Patrick). We all bonded quickly. A small projector balanced on top of a couple of books illuminated Dan's PowerPoint slides from a portable screen that he rolled into the training room. The slides were all words—no images, except the infographic on the CPS logo. This was going to be a long nine weeks.

We started with the legal foundations of the child welfare system (largely policy-oriented), guiding principles for child protective work, and our role and responsibilities as investigators. Next, we covered the specific assessment protocols and how we determine child safety. The next week or so would be all about child development and trauma. Then we would learn about how to measure child and parent functioning, and lastly, safety planning for families. Our heads hurt and our eyes glazed over.

"Is this purgatory or hell?" Patrick asked us in a whisper.

We all stifled a laugh. Our eyes were still fixed on the wordy PowerPoint slides up front. Patrick remained our comedic relief throughout the nine weeks.

Dan threw a ton of information at us. But there was some dissonance between this introduction to CPS and my practical experience as a former intern. The cases that I worked with Lydia could not be captured by what I was seeing in these slide presentations. It was clear that much of the content boiled down to investigator interpretation. This made me nervous. Luckily, Dan explained that we would have field days where we would shadow other investigators. This also meant we would be able to escape this room at least once a week.

"CPS intervention should intrude as little as possible into the life of the family, be focused on clearly defined objectives, and take the most parsimonious path to remedy a family's problems." Dan was really good at reading from PowerPoint slides. But even this piece didn't make sense to me. The work is inherently intrusive and the remedial pathways we took often created more complications for families. If I had been more assertive and assured of myself in that training class, I would have shared my internship experience. Intrusion in a family's life seemed like a foundational pillar of our work. I had walked through Naomi Harden's house, opened her kitchen cabinets and bedroom doors while taking notes. I thought about how often we partnered with law enforcement and lawyers to move our agenda forward. Most of our training class was either finishing an internship, like me, or coming over to investigative work from private sector case management. We all shared a look of disbelief when he discussed these unobtrusive and ideal circumstances.

"And please remember that child abuse is a crime. So, you are more than welcome to ask for law enforcement to accompany you on calls. Don't ever feel like you're alone in this work." He continued clicking through his slides.

During the next set of slides, we learned about physical child abuse indicators and medical neglect. We discussed the process of having a child examined by our physician and documenting their recommendation. That year, 2009, after years of child advocates working to establish specialized physicians, the American Board of Medical Specialties granted this designation. Nearly two hundred physicians sat for a certification exam about *child abuse pediatrics*. Advocates wanted physicians to be specially trained so they could distinguish between injuries that were abusive versus those that were accidental. Dan explained to us that our cases that required a medical exam had to be taken to the Child Protective Team (CPT), and a specialized child abuse pediatrician would examine the child. In Tallahassee, it was Dr. Tess Mahoney, someone I had already met during my internship. Dr. Tess was known to be persnickety and dispassionate about child abuse. Once she came to a medical conclusion, there wasn't much else she wanted to consider about the situation. Lydia once asked her a question and she replied: "Everything you need is in the file that I've already given you." And one of the other CPS investigators once told Lydia and me that after they questioned a medical recommendation, the doctor rhetorically asked, "Are you a doctor or am I?"

I cannot be sure how much I retained from training. The dull didactic classroom setting made everything harder to absorb. I appreciated the field days because I am a hands-on learner. On our field days, the lead investigator we worked with did not treat us like interns, they treated us like co-workers. Now that I was an employed trainee, I was able to interview children and their parents. Then the investigator gave me real-time feedback.

Armed with the procedures and policies that would inform my daily work, I completed my training; in week ten I became an official child protective investigator. I wish I could say that after a master's degree, a yearlong internship, and nine weeks of training, I felt ready for the job. But I did not feel ready, and I still had questions, and I was a bundle of nerves. The others from my training class felt the same way. This transition from training felt like it was going to be rocky.[1]

"You're going to be fine," Lydia reassured me. I wasn't convinced, but I appreciated her vote of confidence and her presence as a mentor. I decided to embrace the experience, and I leaned into the camaraderie of my new colleagues. We were told that for the first month, we would start to receive cases gradually. The Monday after my last day of training, Shelley handed me my first case.

• • •

Throughout your time as a CPS investigator, you see many different variations of trauma, distress, and pain. Some cases you struggle to remember the details of when you reflect back on your time in the field, but others are seared in your mind, and in your heart, forever. For me, one of those cases involved a four-year-old boy named Ryan. When I first encountered Ryan, he was in the ICU buried under an intubation tube, IVs, and hospital monitors that beeped in concert with his mother's sobs.

I was about five weeks out from training and cases were flying in. Lydia wasn't holding my hand anymore. The moment I walked into the office lobby at 8:30 a.m., Shelley was sitting at her desk holding out a case for me.

"Good morning," she said with a hint of sarcasm. Then she went back to typing on her computer as I headed down the hallway. I pulled out my phone to text Katrina.

Just got a case.

Damn. Need help? she texted back.

I'll keep you posted.

When I headed to my cubicle, I passed backpacks sprawled over what felt like every inch of the floor, limiting the walkway. It was definitely Back-to-School Week. And this was confirmed by a sign that rested atop an easel, in bold lettering: BACKPACKS FOR FOSTER CHILDREN! This was typical, though there seemed to be more bags this year than last year.

When I got to my desk, I sat down to read the case file. The child was in the ICU at Tallahassee Memorial Hospital (TMH), and I needed to head over there. I was exhilarated to have a new case but became terrified as I read the details:

> Ryan, age 4, was at home with father last night. The child was reported to be lying in front of a TV that was mounted on the wall. The TV fell off the wall onto Ryan, fracturing his skull and several bones in his face. His mother was not home during the incident. Child is currently in the ICU at TMH. Father reported to have been under the influence.

My whole body shuddered as my mind replayed what happened to Ryan. I started my precommencement activities, including reviewing the entire file, looking up family CPS history as well as any criminal history. Typically, no one was in this early unless they were preparing for court. I'd glance over at Lydia's desk periodically, willing her to appear, so I could ask for help. Lydia was my supervisor during my internship, but she wasn't my supervisor anymore. She was my colleague now. I tried to remember this when I had the impulse to call her. Before I left, I decided to call my actual supervisor, LeAnn. LeAnn was a white woman in her forties, and though married, she had no children. She was even-tempered in a way that was helpful for this kind of work. She listened intently before responding to my queries. She wasn't in the office yet but she could access the case file from her home.

"Have you had a chance to review the previous history?" she asked.

"I did. I plan to head over to the hospital. Just wanted to check with you before I left." I had had about five cases between the end of training class and this case. Those cases, I was either talking to folks in their home or to children at their school. A hospital was new territory. Since I was still new to carrying cases on my own, LeAnn often pulled up the case too and reviewed it. There was silence on her end, so I assumed she was reading.

"Looks like two years ago, the dad was involved in a domestic disturbance. Police were called to their home," LeAnn began. "The domestic disturbance was with his brother, the child's uncle. The uncle lives in the home with the family."

I had read the same criminal history but wasn't sure how that disturbance might play into the current situation. I also wasn't sure what I could do if the child was in the hospital. "Well, Ryan is in the ICU, so what exactly should be done when I get there?" I asked.

"Lay eyes on Ryan. Talk to the parents. Ask what happened. If the father was drinking or doing drugs, we need to know that. The police officer who called in this report should be there to meet you. Do you have any drug tests in your car?"

I didn't. But I knew where to find them. There was a file cabinet filled with them at the office. I grabbed one and headed out to my car. I hated the idea of giving people drug tests. I had watched Lydia test countless parents while I dutifully stood outside their bathroom with the door ajar as they urinated into the cup that I had just handed them. It all felt intrusive and awkward—which clashed significantly with what Dan taught us in training class about how this work should be carried out. It was a battle that persisted throughout my time in the field: *ideal* circumstances versus *real-life* situations. When real-life children experienced life-threatening injuries (even accidental), we were required to turn every stone to determine how the injuries could have been prevented. Once we found out how it could have been prevented, it was time to hold someone accountable for failing to prevent it.

When I arrived at the ICU, I showed my badge and without delay was led back to Ryan's room. I stopped outside Ryan's door when I saw his mother sitting by his bedside; she was holding his hand and crying. Hospital machines thumped, chirped, and beeped in a cacophonous rhythm as they kept Ryan stabilized. I remembered her name from the case file. It was Natasha; Ryan's father was Matthew. I presumed Matthew was the tall Black man sitting a few feet from me in the hallway, head in his hands.

Despite my internship experience and training, I felt unsure of how to begin. This was never the easy part. I decided it was best to start with Matthew, but considering how badly his son was injured, it did not seem like the right time for a CPS encounter. Regardless, I tamped down my nerves and proceeded in the way I'd been trained.

"Hi, are you Matthew?" He looked up at me and nodded. "I'm Jessica Pryce, I work for the Department of Children and Families. I'm so sorry for what happened to your son. But we received a report about the incident, and I need to talk with you and ask a few questions."

Before Matthew said anything, I heard Natasha behind me. She overheard my introduction. Her pain was raw, real, and at the ready when she asked, "Who sent you? My baby is in a damn hospital, and somebody sent CPS?"

Natasha was wearing a hair bonnet that covered half of her hair. Some braids peeked out and fell down her back. Clearly, she had not left here since last night.

"I'm sorry, the reporter has to remain anonymous." I answered Natasha's question in the same way I had seen Lydia answer this question from parents about who reported them.

Natasha said that she had nothing to say to me and went back to her son's side. Matthew told me that he would answer whatever questions I had. I made a mental note to document the mother's refusal and then sat down beside Matthew.

"I'm sorry," Matthew apologized. "She's just upset and worried."

"Can you tell me what happened?" I had my pen steady in my hand as he began. Later I'd learn that it was better not to actively take notes during an interview. Lydia never did but I was afraid I'd forget something.

He explained that last night, he and Ryan were at home preparing for a movie night. His wife and younger daughter were visiting grandparents nearby. Matthew and Ryan settled on the couch. Matthew dozed off during the movie and Ryan left the couch to lie down in front of the television. This was not uncommon, he told me. Ryan loved the big-screen TV and enjoyed lying down on the floor in front of it. Usually, he did this with his little sister without incident.

Remembering the conversation with LeAnn, I asked him, "Matthew, had you been drinking or . . . doing anything else?" I let my question trail off. He broke down in tears. Between his sobs, he told me that he had drunk a few beers and had fallen asleep. Matthew woke up when he heard the loud crash of the TV and Ryan screaming. I asked him if he would take a drug test and he said that he would.

I was at the hospital for the next few hours. Matthew's drug test came back negative for all substances. I spoke with the attending physician and nurses.

"How is he? Is Ryan making any progress?" I asked a nurse.

"Yes, but he's still critical. We don't know yet about any cognitive damage. It's going to be a long journey for him."

Natasha still wouldn't talk with me. Throughout my time there,

I watched family members check in on Ryan and sit with Matthew and Natasha. I looked around at this Black family and their extended family and wished to God that I could tell them they would not see me again. But I knew better. I would be back, and I would also need to go to their home. Training content rushed to my memory. My job was to ensure safety measures had been taken to decrease the likelihood of this happening again. There were many steps to take in the CPS process, and this could take weeks, months, and for the unluckiest, even years.

I prepared to head back to the office to work on my notes and submit the risk assessment. There was no reason to stick around at the hospital. While I was interning, Lydia explained that there were some instances when waiting around wasn't the best use of time. A big part of our job was child safety, but sometimes children were as safe as they were going to be at that moment. If a child was in school for an entire day, we could devise a plan before the child went home. If a child was in the ICU, we could move on with planning the rest of our case because they were surrounded by physicians and nurses.

On my way out, a police officer stopped me. He narrowed his eyes, looking at the badge that hung around my neck, registering that I was with CPS. He was a white guy who looked very young and carried himself in a way that exuded the essence of someone who had recently received his badge. He seemed a little green, like me. He explained that he was the responding officer last night to this family's home alongside EMS.

"All done?" he asked.

"Yes. I spoke with the father and I will go talk with my supervisor about next steps and follow up."

"Yeah, I just spoke with my sergeant too." He *was* new. For the next few minutes we spoke about the case; it became even more clear that he was as inexperienced as me. He even asked if I would be placing the child in foster care soon, to which I replied, "He's in the ICU."

"I'm sure you're aware of the father's history," he continued. "He was in a state last night; there is no way he only had three beers. We are working on a warrant so we can take him in. So, we would appreciate any information you compile."

Was there really no way that he had only three beers? I believed Matthew, but I was well aware of my novice credulity. It was stunning to me that Matthew could be arrested. It seemed like this accident could happen to any family, from any community. But just like what happens in CPS cases depends largely on the investigator, the pursuit of an arrest is often entirely up to the responding police officer. And in this case, my partner in crime—this rookie cop—was ready to brandish handcuffs. My own role slid into focus. While Ryan lay in the intensive care unit of Tallahassee Memorial Hospital, they were going to arrest his father. And apparently, I was going to help.

CHAPTER 7

NO WAY TO TREAT A CHILD

2017

ON DECEMBER 3, 2017, JATOIA AND LAWRENCE ARRIVED AT DUKE Hospital's emergency room with Kenny. A place their newborn had just left twenty-six days earlier. Their nerves were frayed. The medical staff immediately began examining the baby while asking Jatoia questions: *When was the last time he ate? He's so small, why is he so small? How long has he been behaving this way?* Jatoia answered, stumbling over some words but mostly getting her thoughts across.

The physicians told Jatoia and Lawrence that Kenny was actively having "silent seizures" and they needed to get him on antiseizure medication. But after they administered the medicine, they saw on the hospital monitor that the seizures persisted. As the physicians regrouped to begin a different and stronger antiseizure medication, Kenny needed help with breathing, so he was intubated. As they began adding a breathing tube, the physicians explained to Jatoia and Lawrence that they needed to run several tests.

When Jatoia and Lawrence reached the lobby, Jatoia's mother had arrived, an oxygen machine draped around her shoulder, sitting with LJ. Margaret pulled Jatoia into the seat next to her. LJ climbed into his mother's lap and laid his head on her shoulder. Jatoia placed her cheek on top of his head.

"He's going to be okay. I just know it," Margaret said out loud to no one in particular.

After a couple of hours, LJ had fallen asleep. Lawrence and Jatoia refused to leave until they heard more about Kenny, so they asked Margaret to take their eldest child home to get some rest. Jatoia assured her mother that she would call with updates. But as Margaret gathered herself, her oxygen tank, and her grandson, a Black man walked over to the family and introduced himself as Joseph.

"Jatoia Potts?" He made eye contact with each of them, waiting for someone to respond.

"I'm Jatoia." Jatoia stood up, which took some effort as her legs felt weak.

"Is this about my son?" Lawrence asked the question. Fear kept Jatoia quiet. She wanted to embrace the ignorance that she had settled into over the past couple of hours.

"Yes." Joseph stepped a bit closer, pulling paperwork out of his black satchel. "I'm with child protective services, and we received a report about your son Kenneth."

Jatoia could not process this information. She asked Joseph to repeat himself several times. Her baby was sick and needed help. When did someone think it was necessary to report her to child protective services?

"The report has allegations of medical neglect, due to malnutrition and also possible head trauma. It says here that the baby has fractures that are in multiple healing stages. Some of them are weeks old, but some are just a few days old. It says here that he is in critical condition and will be admitted. They are unsure if he will survive these injuries."

Jatoia's legs gave out. Lawrence caught her and gently guided her back into a seat. In the hours they'd sat and waited, running all kinds of scenarios in their heads, they had not received any updates on Kenny's condition. This information, delivered by a CPS worker, shocked them into total silence. Jatoia pulled herself together enough to walk with Lawrence to the intake desk to get information about their son from the medical professionals directly.

Dr. Lucas Scott was paged to the front and emerged fairly quickly. He had been anticipating this call. He introduced himself as the pediatric child and neglect physician, Duke's equivalent to Tallahassee's Dr. Tess.

"Mr. and Mrs. Daniels," Dr. Lucas began. Jatoia had no energy to correct him. She and Lawrence weren't married. "Your son Kenneth is quite a sick child. He has fractures on his skull and retinal hemorrhages in both of his eyes, in all four quadrants. His brain has been deprived of adequate oxygen, likely due to severe malnutrition. He's also *voiding*"—he paused, staring at both of them—"meaning that Kenneth's experiencing poor coordination between his bladder and his urethra, and there is difficulty emptying his body of the fluids. We are doing all that we can for him."

Jatoia heard the words, but everything Dr. Lucas said sounded garbled and ran together in a way she couldn't comprehend.

"What?" she asked Lawrence, not Dr. Lucas. Jatoia wrapped her arms around herself, trying to soothe her sadness about her baby boy's pain.

"The MRI on his brain, his skeletal survey, and head CT all are consistent with nonaccidental, inflicted trauma. We had to get CPS involved." Dr. Lucas expressed little emotion with his words, yet they sounded harsh to Jatoia. *Nonaccidental, inflicted trauma.*

"This is his hospital! He was born here!" Lawrence's voice elevated with every word. He was still holding on to Jatoia. "You should be able to look up his records to review all the complications he had at birth. There has to be some sort of explanation for this!"

The doctor took down a note, said a few more things about keeping the family posted, and then he turned to walk toward the staircase and left.

At that moment, Jatoia didn't care about the CPS investigator standing right behind her. She wasn't focused on Lawrence yelling at Dr. Lucas's shadow. She didn't care how loud she cried out Kenny's name as the tears fell. She was consumed with her reality. Kenny was fighting for his life . . . again.

• • •

"Record every conversation that you have. You have to keep records of everything that they say. They are clearly trying to blame you for this," Margaret instructed Jatoia the next morning as they spoke over the phone. They all had left, but Jatoia remained. She refused to leave Kenny's side and took intermittent naps as she sat perched by his bed. This is where she would be found for the next three weeks while Kenny was in the hospital. Lawrence came to visit, bringing her clothes to change into and food to eat. She never left the hospital, not even once.

Kenny continued to struggle with breathing. He remained intubated and endured more seizures. The hemorrhaging and the bleeding in his brain captured all of the physicians' attention. Throughout those weeks, Jatoia was inundated with CPS interviews and questions from law enforcement. She was asked the same question in different ways: *What happened during the week before you brought Kenneth into the ER? What details can you provide about the hours before your ER visit? Did anything out of the ordinary occur the day you brought him in? Was anyone else watching Kenneth during the week that led up to the ER visit?*

As the days went on, Jatoia endured the daily inquisitions, and she learned more about Kenny's condition. When she brought Kenny into the ER, he was hypoglycemic. He was experiencing an endocrine crisis, and he was in metabolic shock. None of this made sense, not because of the medical jargon, but because her kids were her entire world and she couldn't fathom how this all came to be. Just as her mother instructed, and unbeknownst to every person who spoke to her, Jatoia recorded the exchanges she had with hospital personnel on her phone.

A nurse or a social worker was in the room at all times. This, at first, seemed normal. Maybe they wanted extra oversight because of his condition. But eventually, Jatoia realized they were there to supervise her while she was with Kenny.

"I can't be alone with my baby?" Jatoia had overheard a conversation earlier about how they were short-staffed but needed to make sure that someone was able to stay there in the room.

"I'm so sorry," the nurse whispered. "I was instructed to stay with Kenneth as long as you are here. Any other questions, you will need to talk with the CPS investigator."

CPS explained that supervised visitation is the general rule if the state can't be certain that a parent is not a threat to their child. Once it was clear that they saw her as an abuser, Jatoia immediately wanted to change hospitals. There was nothing she could do to change anyone's mind, but she could transfer her son to UNC Hospital in Chapel Hill. CPS forbade it. Since there was an open investigation, the child had to remain at Duke. Besides, they felt that since Kenneth had spent so much time at Duke already, beginning with his volatile birth, it was in the best interest of his health to remain under their care.

Child protective services also decided that Jatoia should not be around LJ on her own. Her oldest son was then informally placed with his grandmother Margaret, pursuant to a safety plan that was signed by all parties.[1] After a couple of weeks, Kenneth was transferred from the ICU to a step-down wing of the hospital; this move signified that he was stable and improving. Jatoia let out a breath she felt like she had been holding for weeks. Her neck and shoulders loosened from their tight knots.

With the holidays in full swing, the hospital began decorating each door with small Christmas wreaths. They put up blinking lights and green and gold tinsel along the doorways. A tree erected in the corner of the lobby was on display, surrounded by faux gift boxes adorned with bows. The hospital provided a few toys for Kenny, and Margaret and LJ came up for a visit. They tried to make the best of the situation, but this was not what Jatoia had pictured for Kenny's first Christmas.

After the Christmas holiday, the hospital was finally preparing to discharge Kenny. He had improved enough to leave, though he was still underweight and needed special care in regard to feeding. He also had to continue medication for seizures. He had several follow-up appointments, the most important of which was with his ophthalmologist. But he was breathing on his own, smiling, laughing, which leveled Jatoia's axis.

Soon enough, things were upended again. The CPS investigator, Joseph, joined their discharge conference and reminded Jatoia that neither she nor Lawrence could be alone with the children. Their investigation was incomplete, and they needed to pinpoint the cause of Kenny's injuries. Since LJ was already staying with his grandmother, Joseph recommended that Kenneth be placed there as well. A decision was made to continue the safety plan, which required that Margaret or Jatoia's stepfather, Richard, supervise Jatoia's and Lawrence's time with the boys. Jatoia hated that her mother had to go through this—she was dealing with so much already—but Margaret agreed. Jatoia asked Joseph if it would be okay if she moved in with her mom to help care for the kids. He said that this was fine—as long as she was always supervised.

• • •

The investigation into how six-month-old Kenny became injured was underway. Law enforcement continued to interview Jatoia and Lawrence about the time lapse between Kenny's initial release from Duke Hospital's PICU (November 7, 2017) to an appointment with his ophthalmologist (November 30, 2017), where he presented no concerns, and then his emergency room visit with life-threatening injuries

(December 3, 2017). What exactly happened between November 30 and December 3?

The law enforcement officer was known as Detective Cross. He was a stout, middle-aged Black man dressed in a suit.

After all the interviews Jatoia was running out of ways to say, *I never hurt my child. I don't know anything about any fractures or injuries. He had been home for less than one month.*

Unlike the initial law enforcement officers Jatoia had met, Detective Cross was inquisitive but also kind. He expressed how sorry he was about Kenny's injuries. "I know that can't be easy for any parent to see," he empathized. "You both seem like good people." Detective Cross passed Jatoia his business card as he finished the interview and told her that he would be in touch.

Early in the new year, they got settled in at Margaret and Richard's one-bedroom apartment. There was limited space for the boys and hardly any space for Jatoia. She slept on an airbed in the living room that she inflated each evening and put away by dawn. She tried her best to keep the small space airy. This living arrangement—Jatoia staying with her mother and stepfather, and frequent visits from Lawrence—worked out for a while. But the state's involvement in her family changed the dynamics. Jatoia sensed that her stepfather didn't trust her or Lawrence with the kids. He was rigid about the supervised visitation. His rigidity upheld the CPS requirement but it alienated Jatoia and Lawrence. One morning, Jatoia picked up LJ to cuddle and kiss him like she did every morning. Richard watched her closely. When she tried to take LJ on a quick walk, her stepfather forbade it.

"I don't have time to go with you, so you can't do that," he said.

Jatoia tried to not upset her mother, who was still living with terminal cancer. When she decided to talk to her mom about her stepfather, Margaret insisted that Richard was doing his best to keep their family together. Jatoia did not belabor the point, but she felt more alone. Adding to all the tension were the frequent arguments between Lawrence and Richard. Jatoia was willing to put up with just about anything so that she could stay there with her kids. But Lawrence pushed back against Richard's intense oversight. Jatoia constantly mediated their heated exchanges.

The situation escalated when they all took Kenny to his first follow-up medical appointment. Richard was behaving as usual, over-protective of the children and acting as the primary discussant with the doctors and nurses. By shutting out Lawrence and Jatoia, Richard aggravated an already tense scenario. Another argument erupted and Richard demanded that Lawrence leave the appointment.

"These are my kids!" Lawrence's anger was explosive. Security was called and he was forced to leave.

Stuck in the middle, Jatoia remained frazzled hours later back at home. Although she appreciated her mother and stepfather helping out, she had no idea it would turn into this sort of situation. When Lawrence came over to the apartment that evening, his anger had not tempered at all. He was hostile and argumentative and made threats. As expected, Richard called law enforcement, who pulled in CPS. It was January 3, 2018. Everything came crashing down in less than four days.

By then, they had a new caseworker, a Black woman who deter-mined, due to the animosity among them, that the placement was no longer a viable option. She filed a court petition to move the boys into foster care. This devastated Jatoia in a way that she could not have anticipated. The sadness and grief settled right into her gut and she couldn't eat for days. Sleeping was so rare that when it happened, she jolted awake in a confused state, frantically searching for her kids. Some nights when she woke up, her face would be wet with new tears. Jatoia never knew that she could cry while she was sleeping. She tossed blame around from her stepfather, to Lawrence, back to her stepfather, and then to herself. Had she missed something? Did she get Kenny to the ER soon enough? She knew that she never hurt him, but what had she missed?

Then, Jatoia started to think of her eldest, LJ, and the day he was born. A home birth that still brought tears of joy to her eyes. Up until that point, LJ had never been to daycare and had rarely left her side. He reached for her when it was time for him to go with the CPS worker. The way he cried out to her was unbearable. To Jatoia, the thought of him being with total strangers felt cruel. How was that any way to treat a child?

CHAPTER 8

MY SISTER'S KEEPER

2009

GROWING UP, MY OLDER SISTER, RACHEL, WAS A HOPELESS RO-
mantic. Many people called her "boy-crazy," but from my perspective,
the boys were crazy over her. Her social butterfly personality always
took center stage. She was brave and fun, and it seemed like everyone
became a bit braver when they were around her. She loved to travel and
to explore fashion. Rachel enjoyed visiting restaurants whose meals
were described by numbered courses and whose waitstaff hovered
imperceptibly, anticipating her every move and need. We were quite
different from each other. I was an athlete, excelling in volleyball and
basketball. Boys saw me as an opponent, not someone to date. I was
also a bookworm and spent my weekends reading instead of socializ-
ing or shopping. When it came to clothing and fashion, I preferred to
wear the same outfit as many times as possible. As opposite as we were,
it was a joy to witness how Rachel lived her life.

I remember the day she brought her boyfriend Adam over to the
house to meet the family. She was just seventeen, but she declared her
love for Adam and the desire to move in with him. "He's the love of
my life," she said. And I thought, *What a thing to say at seventeen.* My
parents did not approve, but she moved in with him anyway. Not even
a year later, she was pregnant. The pregnancy really upset my parents,

but I was more concerned by how Rachel's once gregarious personality had changed in such a short time. The brave sister who I once knew had become a very different person. She did not exude the confidence that she once had. And she did not seem as carefree as she once was.

Over the next few years, she had three children. She loved her kids fiercely, but her love for Adam shifted into something toxic. They had been enthralled with each other since high school. Despite the toxicity, their long history seemed to keep them loyal to each other. I started to notice the many ways Adam began to control Rachel. Her instincts were to push back, but I watched her swallow her boldness.

My first exposure to domestic violence as a construct was through my college courses. I learned more about it while I was in graduate school studying social work. Our professors explored all aspects of intimate partner violence (IPV). My real-time, real-life exposure to IPV was witnessing Adam physically assault my sister. Learning about the intricacies of IPV in a classroom or from a book is one thing, but it's another thing to watch it play out in real life with your own family. The abuse continued intermittently over the years as they continued to raise their children. Some incidents resulted in law enforcement intervention. Unfortunately, our family seemed to passively accept the violent cycles of Adam and Rachel's relationship because my sister refused any interference. I have come to realize that domestic violence, to an onlooker, is clearly a dangerous and vile act. But to the person who deeply loves the abuser, the violence is often perceived as something to endure. Victims love their abusers so deeply, even from rock bottom—they remain a solid foundation for them.

When I became a CPS investigator, I started to take on cases of domestic violence and IPV. My disposition changed. I started to see my sister's situation in a new way. I realized that this sort of violence was not only an issue for the victim, but that it harmed children. All of this accelerated one night when I received a frantic call from Rachel. She and Adam were having another one of their altercations, and he was making threats. She told me that he accused her of cheating, and then he left the house with a vow to come back to kill her and "whoever she was sleeping with." I knew she must have been scared if she called me. For years, when they had violent episodes, she did not draw attention to it.

Those days, it was hard for me to take off my CPS investigator hat, so I went into precommencement activity mode. I reviewed their history in my head, remembering the years of law enforcement involvement and short stints of jail time for Adam. Then I thought of my two nephews and my niece.

"I think you should call the police," I said. The police had become a trusted resource for me in my work.

"Nah, you know how police are," Rachel said. "They will probably arrest him, and this whole thing is going to get even worse."

I instantly felt a combination of fury and pity. All of the years that she had been accepting this dynamic made me suddenly angry. *This man has a history of violent behavior, and he has threatened to kill you in the home where your three children are sleeping.* Yet, it appeared to me that her main concern was that he *might* get arrested. I lived four hours away from them and felt helpless. I could not let my sister's bizarre loyalty and protection of Adam affect the kids. As soon as we hung up, I decided to report the incident to child protective services.

"I work in child protective services in Tallahassee," I added—I guess—for credibility as I finished making the report. Some reports are not accepted by the abuse hotline. I knew that if the hotline operator knew I was an investigator, they would likely accept the case. "The children are at home and their father is threatening the mother with violence. She's my sister. And I want to make it clear that she and the kids are the victims of his threats."

At this point, I knew a great deal about child abuse because of my internship experience, the nine weeks of training with Dan, and then my recent experience of carrying my own cases. What I did not know was how specialized the approaches needed to be when investigating a domestic violence situation that involves children. Especially how unique the experience of domestic violence is for women who are on the margins of society.[1] Black women are 2.5 times more likely to experience domestic violence than their counterparts and are less likely to report this abuse.[2] There are various reasons why these Black women are apprehensive about seeking help. Some are: fear of retaliation, mistrust of law enforcement and CPS, and lack of access to resources.

The conclusion of "failure to protect" became an institutional condemnation when CPS found that parents, often mothers, did not adequately protect their children from potential harm.[3] This isn't as simple as neglecting to protect their children. The mothers suffering with IPV often feel powerless and struggle through mental health concerns. To a CPS investigator, the mother might seem like she's not prioritizing her children's safety, but in reality she's trying to survive from moment to moment. Finding the balance between parent support and child protection is complicated. Usually one takes precedence over the other. And if you're a CPS investigator, it's clear which one you're choosing.

When family violence occurred in a home, at that time the CPS maltreatment code was known as *Threatened Harm*. This is a general all-encompassing term that refers to situations/cases when children have the potential to be threatened with some sort of harm. Lydia and I had worked on many *Threatened Harm* cases, and I had a couple of my own since beginning my full-time role. Victim advocates have long criticized child protective services for minimizing the impact of IPV on victims and blaming battered women for neglecting their children's best interests.[4] Victim advocates do not excuse the burdens placed on mothers by child protective services. CPS attempts to rectify certain abusive situations, but the system doesn't seem to offer any assistance for addressing the problems that its presence creates. CPS investigators and caseworkers are encouraged to reconsider the term *victim*. For our cases, the children were the victims that we were tasked with protecting. But victim advocates see the parent who is being abused (overwhelmingly reported as women) as the priority. When there are two (or more) victims, who is responsible for protecting whom? What is the prioritization of which victim?

A couple of hours passed and my sister called me back. "Jessica, I know you did not send CPS to my house!" She was yelling. I told her that I only called them because I was afraid for the children. *And I wasn't sure she could assess the situation clearly due to her feelings for Adam.* She told me that the CPS investigator and law enforcement were there and talking to the kids. Her oldest was Tiara, age six; Lance was four; and the youngest, Ashton, was one. Rachel didn't say much for a moment. I could hear my nephew's soft and incoherent words. I pictured him at that moment. My nephew was usually content nestled around my sister's waist. He was the baby of the family, and he knew it.

My sister kept me on the phone while she spoke to the CPS investigator. I heard the investigator, a woman, and she sounded like me: *History of violence in this home. 911 call report was reviewed. No record of any restraining orders against him. Are you concerned for your children's safety in his care?*

They continued the process, and I remained on the phone as a listening observer. The investigator asked my sister if she would be willing to stay somewhere else for the next few days. Rachel said no.

I knew the CPS investigator was attempting to create a safety plan for my sister and the children. Law enforcement was in the process of locating Adam to deal with the threats directly. Until then, there was still the question of whether or not Rachel and the kids were safe in that apartment. There was no how-to manual on how to approach these sorts of situations. Each case was always vastly different from the others and involved many layers of connection between the abuser and the victim. I had learned from Lydia about the types of things that we can do to create a temporary safety plan. We are taught to encourage the nonoffending parent to (1) stop all contact with the offender and get restraining orders, (2) stay elsewhere, and (3) connect with family or close friends for ongoing support. Then we try to get the parent victim connected to community resources. It took a few hours, but Adam was found and arrested. This relieved the pressure on my sister to leave the apartment that night. But the CPS case was just getting started.

• • •

Over the next few weeks, my sister endured more visits from her investigator, and she was offered a slate of voluntary services. Those services consisted of a parenting course that was focused on training her to identify unsafe situations for her children and how to devise the best and most safe solutions. They also recommended a batterer's intervention course for Adam as a condition of his release. The investigator suggested that Rachel get some mental health services, therapy for the children, and family counseling. All of this was presented as voluntary, but Rachel did not feel she had a choice. It seemed like the custody of her children was being held hostage and the payment was completing as many of the voluntary services as possible.

This situation left me feeling uneasy. As a mandated reporter, I decided to call in this incident, but that was the extent of my direct involvement. I was not there to field the phone calls from CPS that Rachel had to handle each day or wait on hold when she was making appointments during her lunch break at work. I was not there to help her with childcare when she went to parenting classes or to be home when the CPS investigator made a visit. I was not around to assist her in her efforts to comply and show CPS that she was cooperative. A reporter's job ends when they finish making their report. But a report creates a level of intrusion into a family's life that I don't think mandated reporters fully grasp.

When I think about my sister, I consider that I must have known how this CPS situation would play out. I play the game every day. If I am being honest and reflective, I wanted CPS to somehow make my sister disown Adam. I wanted CPS to engage the police to arrest him. I also wanted to deploy CPS to finally address a situation that none of my family could. My sister was not reacting in a way that I felt was appropriate to the situation. She wasn't reacting the way that I would have. But that's CPS, isn't it? *Parent your children like we would, or else.* CPS workers hold families to certain standards of conduct, without acknowledging what informed the standards. These standards rarely leave room for nuance, compassion, or humanity.

• • •

Back at work, I processed my sister's situation with Lydia and Katrina. I felt horrible. Lydia lauded my decision. She knew it was complicated for me, but she felt it was the right thing to do. Katrina, on the other hand, derided me, "Damn, you reported your sister? To *us*?"

Katrina's response was disheartening, but I understood where she was coming from. Not many others would be as direct about my culpability. I was early in my career, but I knew the system had limitations and blind spots. I was overly focused on how to get my sister to care as much as I did about the safety of the kids. But, that narrow focus obscured too many other important factors—my sister's challenges as a victim of IPV and the awful history of Black people and law enforcement. And ultimately, the truth was, I put my sister's custody of her children in jeopardy. I couldn't take back what I had done, but I intended to consider these things on my next DV case.

Each week our office posts an on call schedule showing which investigator would respond to emergencies overnight. I noticed that Lydia was on call that night. As an intern, I had helped Lydia on her on call shift even though it was not allowed for my internship. Unasked. Unanswered.

Working on call is a whirlwind of people, details, and usually a sleep deprived investigator. During regular business hours, child abuse reports need to be commenced within twenty-four hours. This means that the investigator has to make contact with the child(ren) within that time frame and submit a formal risk assessment by the next day. The on call investigator is available for reports after business hours (5:00 p.m. to 8:00 a.m.), and any emergency reports received during that time must be commenced within two to three hours. There was also the possibility of receiving an emergency report (known as an "immediate") during normal business hours. And on this particular day, I received an *immediate* case at 4:30 p.m. Too early for Lydia to take it as an on call case. I drew in a breath and opened the file.

> 6-year-old boy had two large bruises on his neck. When his teacher asked his father about the bruises, he became irate and told the teacher that he was withdrawing his son from the school. Teacher has not seen or heard from the mother since the start of the school year, though it is believed that the mother lives at home with the son. Ivan told his teacher that his mother was recently in the hospital. Teacher concerned about child's safety, in light of father's threats to withdraw him. The family is Polish.

I started the precommencement work and saw that the family lived about thirty minutes away in an affluent neighborhood in South Tallahassee. The father was an architect. The family did not have a history with child protective services, but the law enforcement call-out report showed two 911 calls from their home in the last three months. Both calls were related to domestic disturbances. Since there had been a history of domestic issues, we were instructed to have law enforcement accompany us. I also noticed in the report that the child's mother was unemployed and had spent time in an inpatient mental health treatment facility. This was on the heels of my sister's situation, so I was especially unsure of myself with this initial assessment. I stood up and walked over to Katrina's cubicle. She was just down the hall near our attorney's offices.

I tapped lightly on her partial wall and started talking before she saw me. "Believe it or not . . ."

"You got a case," she finished for me. She had been reading something on her computer but quickly turned her chair around so I could see her roll her eyes in a display of sympathy. The dreaded case that falls in your lap right before you head home always draws pity. Katrina's petite frame sat comfortably in her desk chair with one leg tucked underneath and the other hanging down swinging just above the floor.

"Yep. And it's on southside."

"I can help you if you want. I have a home visit near there. Can you take me by my case when we finish yours?"

Leadership expressly stated that investigators should not go on calls with other investigators. If we needed support, we needed to call law enforcement. This rationale was due, in part, to the limited number of investigators relative to the bounty of incoming cases. But I wanted company so I nodded and she started to gather her things. Taking care of both of our cases sounded like a good way to justify doubling up.

Katrina was my closest friend on the job. We trained and we started together. There were four of us total in that training cohort, and by now we were all feeling more competent in what needed to be done within the plethora of time frames. It felt good to have a group who knew what it was like to work a job that was often fast paced, unpredictable, and demanding. I enjoyed talking to Katrina about the work because in many ways she was better at it than I was. She was an exceptional auditory learner. She only needed to hear something once to recall it later in notes. She absorbed everything and then connected the dots through quality reports.

I'm pretty keen and efficient when it comes to this work, but Katrina was intuitive. Her instincts were stellar, and I was always glad when we could work together on our cases. She was skilled at reading people and situations. We had worked on a case in the past in which we interviewed a man and his children in their apartment. The interview went off without any hitches, but on our way back to the car, Katrina asked me:

"Did you notice the smell?"

I told her that I hadn't. But then she started to explain the odors and a few other things she noticed when we walked through the house. She suspected that we had just visited a budding meth lab. Which turned out to be confirmed later by law enforcement.

I consider myself a type-A person when it comes to this job. I do not like to be late on deadlines or produce poor work. Each week investigators received an email reporting on who had overdue assessments with a list of the outstanding items. I was never on that list. These emails weren't necessarily intended to shame anyone; they served as a reminder to keep everything on track. But I still did not want to show up there. Paperwork and documentation were essential, and everything had to run like clockwork in CPS. Paperwork needed to be processed and filed, and follow-ups had to be completed and documented. There were more cases than caseworkers and every moment counted.

My efficiency boded well for the job, but not so much for my interactions with families. It created a scenario that lacked balance. I often put meeting timelines above all else. Though my work style made me a favorite with my supervisor, LeAnn, it did not translate well in the relationships with the parents from my cases. My hyperfocus on collecting the necessary information often came off to parents as hurried and detached. I was rarely late on anything and as often as possible, I closed my cases in advance of deadlines. My perfectionism in regard to timeliness created tension between sensitivity and depth in my investigations.

The job requirements, the procedures, and the deadlines that were drilled into us during training were there for a reason. When I traveled to homes to visit with families, I was already pretty clear on what information I needed, so that's what I zeroed in on. Like our trainer Dan said, *When seconds count, a child cannot wait.* I took that to heart, and I left very few stones unturned.

When Katrina and I pulled up to the house for my new case, we were awed by the size and style of the home. We exchanged looks as if to say, who in the hell can afford to live here? It was nearly six and the sky was quickly turning to dusk. Once again, I was happy to have Katrina with me. She had already called in a request to law enforcement to head over to meet us. But we didn't wait for them. This was something that I picked up on from Lydia. Often we started our cases and law enforcement would eventually show up.

The house had a sleek black shingled roof with overflowing gutters. The lawn was unkempt and empty flower boxes lined a stony walkway.

"Not big on landscaping, huh?" Katrina critiqued. I rang the doorbell, and within seconds someone responded, "Who is this?" Whoever was on the other side of the door had a thick Polish accent. They sounded defensive already.

"I'm Jessica Pryce and I'm from the Department of Children and Families." I recalled the name from the report. "Is Mr. or Mrs. Dima home?"

I heard the deadbolt turn and the door slowly opened. Andrew Dima was an imposing man, standing tall, stocky, and very pale. He wore brown slacks and a wrinkled white T-shirt. The glasses he wore made his eyes look small, and the lenses were smudged. His face held a mixture of confusion, annoyance, and suspicion.

We remained rooted in place and kept our respectful distance. He didn't invite us in; instead, he stared us down. "What is this about?" he asked.

"I need to talk with you about a report we received and I need to see your son Ivan."

Mr. Dima looked back down the hallway. He spoke in Polish, beckoning someone. A moment later, a little boy appeared. Ivan's blond hair was cut short. He stood, timidly, next to his father. Beyond where Ivan stood, I noticed there was a woman sitting very still in a chair in the living room.

"Hi Ivan, I'm Jessica. How are you?" I bent down a bit lower to be at his eye level. He looked quizzically from me to his father then back to me. "It's okay, I just want to talk for a few minutes." I stood back upright and asked Mr. Dima, "Can Ivan step out here for a moment with us?"

"No! I still don't understand why you are here!" he bellowed.

I glanced at Katrina, passing the baton. "How about my colleague talks with Ivan outside, and I can come inside and share with you everything that's in the report."

"No!" His voice was elevated with every new word he spoke. "I need to see your credentials, now!" I held up the badge attached to my keychain.

"I'm here because we received a report about bruises on Ivan. I thought it best to talk with you privately, but if you don't mind having Ivan with us, we can talk right here. Once we talk and gather the information we need, then we can get this process underway."

"What process?!" Every response came with more vitriol. His cheeks and neck grew red.

Katrina stood beside me, and she was as still as the woman sitting inside. I continued to speak calmly, enunciating every word. "We will need to see your home, talk to your wife, and possibly have Ivan examined by one of our physicians—"

"You're the KGB! Get off my property!" He pointed toward my car as an emphasis for us to be on our way.

"I think we should just go," Katrina whispered, already making her way down the stony walkway.

Instead of trying a different approach to my questioning, with hopes of de-escalating the situation, I said, "Mr. Dima, the police are already on their way. I suggest that you cooperate." The moment I said this I regretted it. Katrina returned to tug at my arm, but I stood firm.

I did not know what the KGB was, but apparently mentioning the police seemed to confirm something for him. He became even more angry. "I knew you were the gotdamn KGB! Get out!"

My response came out louder than intended. "I am not the KGB!" It didn't matter because he slammed the door shut. As soon as Katrina and I were back in the car, I called my supervisor, LeAnn, who immediately picked up and became my steady voice of reason. I placed my cell on the middle console and put her on speakerphone.

"I just commenced my case, and the dad would not let me in."

"Did you see the victim?"

"I saw him, but his father did not let me talk to him. The father exploded on us and started calling us the KGB. I told him that we were not the KGB!"

"Well, we might be," Katrina quipped while she looked it up on her cell phone.

"Remind me of the child's age and how he looked," LeAnn said.

"He's six. He looked okay, a bit timid. I didn't get a chance to really check for any marks or bruising. I saw his mother, but she didn't say or do anything. She seemed, sort of—catatonic."

"Was she okay?"

"I don't know. The whole thing was strange, and she never came over to even see what he was yelling about." There was silence on LeAnn's end.

I looked over at Katrina as she held up her phone screen: "Jessica, we're the KGB."

I grabbed the phone. The information on the page she had looked up said that the KGB were investigative state agents who worked for the Soviet Union. While we were not agents of the former Soviets, we were certainly agents for the great state of Florida. As I peered at her tiny phone screen, blue and red lights flashed around us as two law enforcement vehicles pulled up. If Mr. Dima only suspected we were KGB before, I'm sure he would be fully convinced now.

"The police just arrived," I announced to LeAnn.

"Do you think you can get the father to sign a safety plan?" she asked me.

Had she not just heard how this encounter had gone? Katrina raised her eyebrows, thinking the same thing.

"I doubt he will sign anything. I have a bad feeling about this guy and this kid. Can we talk to Terri about a petition to remove?"

The more I processed the interaction and spoke with LeAnn, the more I felt that the child and his mother were vulnerable. Mr. Dima was showing all the signs of an erratic and potentially dangerous temperament. The previous 911 calls from this address due to domestic issues did not surprise me at all. The police officer at my car window brought me back to the moment. I said hello and let him know I was on a call with my supervisor.

"We don't know that anything is going on," LeAnn replied. "And, if we talk to our attorney, she is going to ask if we made reasonable efforts to avoid removal. You need to go back and try to get the dad to sign a safety plan." The path to justifying the removal of a child was predictable. Removing a child from their family is never something to be taken lightly. But in this case, things seemed different; they *felt* different. What if this mother and her child really needed to get out of there? Katrina heard the instructions about the safety plan, and I saw her visibly deflate.

Minutes passed as I wrote up a safety plan. I checked in with the officer to update him on what was going on. I let him know that I was going to try to have the dad sign the plan for some modest assurance that he would act in good faith and not harm his son (or wife) in the foreseeable future. This safety plan essentially said that neither parent would take any behavioral altering substances around Ivan or physically discipline him until CPS had a chance to engage the family and provide some sort of assessment and service. Safety plans come in handy when you have concerns about the situation but things may not rise to the level of court intervention.

Katrina and I made our way back up to Mr. Dima's front door. The two officers stood back but remained in view. We were surprised when the door opened and Ivan's mother answered.

"Mrs. Dima?" She wore white flannel pants and a brown blouse. According to the report, she was in her early forties, but the lines on her face made her look older and frail. Her black hair was bobbed in a cut right at the bottom of her ears, giving her a severe look, though not as menacing as her husband's look. I felt like I was seeing a ghost. The school personnel reported that they had not seen or heard from her in months.

"I'm sure you mean well, but please leave," she said with resignation.

Katrina stayed a few steps behind me. She wanted a clear path to retreat.

"Mrs. Dima, can I talk with you about our report? We have concerns about Ivan."

Hearing her son's name seemed to pique her interest, but before she was even able to get another word out, Mr. Dima appeared, filling the doorway.

"Do not talk to them!" His voice was just as loud as before. "Go sit down," he told her, as he reached past her to close the door. I stopped the door with my foot.

"Mr. Dima, I have written up a safety plan for you to review and sign. Can you at least read it? Then I will leave." His answer was pushing the door shut so fast I was forced to do a quick hop out of the way so my foot wasn't crushed. Katrina and I heard the dead bolt slide back into place.

We got back inside my car and called LeAnn, who looped in our attorney, Terri, to discuss a possible removal. But just like Mr. Dima, they would not budge. Despite his hostility toward us, we did not have enough to petition for an emergency removal, or even entry into his home.

"But he wouldn't let me in. I never even saw the home. I didn't interview Ivan!" All of which, I was told, were mandatory for investigations.

"We can't force him to let us in without a court order and we currently do not have one or any grounds for one," LeAnn said. "Let's talk more tomorrow." We ended the call. I spoke briefly with the police officers and let them know that I would be meeting with my supervisor and attorney the next day. It was already eight and we still needed to go work on Katrina's case.

CHAPTER 9

THE COLOR PURPLE
2009

APPROXIMATELY 80 PERCENT OF SINGLE-PARENT HOUSEHOLDS are headed by women.[1] My mentor and colleague, Lydia, was one of them. She and her partner parted ways in 2007 when her kids were fairly young. She was working in CPS at the time and juggled this job while trying to be as present for her children as possible as they tried to understand why their father was moving out. She leaned on her mother for support during the long nights and weekends with the job. After a year, Lydia met Derek and they started dating.

When you are a CPS investigator, driving from house to house, school to hospital, and everywhere in between, you spend a lot of time on the phone. My go-to talking-while-driving partners were either Erica or Katrina. We all have our people who keep us sane. And Derek was Lydia's. Lydia talked to Derek while she was at her desk, while she stood at the copier, and while she made coffee in our office break-room. When I was her intern, it was not uncommon for us to climb into the car as her phone rang. "My day is going fine. Just getting in the car with Jessica to go work a case." Then a second later, "Derek says hey." I would say it back to him, through her, and then we would get our workday started. He was a steady presence during days that were incredibly unpredictable, and Lydia appreciated it. Since the first day I met Lydia, I was always amazed by how she managed everything. She worked incredibly hard, and there were countless days I watched her complete her case notes while she coordinated a school pickup for her kids. Watching Lydia multitask her work life and her childcare responsibilities deepened my respect for her. Working this job without children was hard, so I could only imagine how challenging it was for my colleagues with kids.

I hear their comments of frustration and see their stress when they are facing the choice between the children from their cases and the children they have at home. I saw humanity in my colleagues even in the face of difficult cases and complex circumstances. Watching Lydia, I realized, everyone just wanted to get home to their kids, their dogs, their lives, to find some way to override the stress of each day with some joy and solace.

It was Halloween, and our office manager, Shelley, decorated the cubicle walls with orange streamers and pumpkin posters. She always tried to be festive for every holiday with hopes it would cheer up the overtaxed and overextended staff and the reality of their work lives. It helped a little. Two large bowls of candy were placed up front in the lobby next to the visitation rooms that parents and kids used. That candy would be gone by midday.

After a long night on call, Lydia arrived at the office with a large court petition and a large coffee. When an investigator completes a night of on call, supervisors try to give them an easy day so they can catch up. Lydia mentioned that she and Derek were taking her kids out trick-or-treating later, so she was hoping for a short and quiet day.

I'm not sure if Halloween was to blame, but we were inundated with new reports. I was always told that cases spike around the holidays. Shelley was busy assigning cases based on who was up in the queue. She tried to consider how many cases we already had and balanced our loads the best she could. Shelley walked into our unit and handed two cases to me and one to Lydia. Lydia took it begrudgingly as Shelley said, "Sorry, girl. We are slammed."

I made a mental note that it was still morning, so I was hopeful that we could get these cases stabilized during business hours. Maybe we would have an evening free for once. After Lydia and I did our pre-commencement tasks, we went our separate ways into the field to work on our cases. I had no idea that the case Lydia had just received was on my friend Erica.

• • •

The child victim was four-year-old Madisen Lawson, located at a day-care center about twenty-five minutes away. Lydia was familiar with the owner and gave her a quick call.

"Brenda, I got the case you just called in. I'll head over now. Is it bad?"

"Hey, Lydia. This child got her ass beat," Brenda said. "There are marks and bruises on her legs and on her arm. You know I'm required to have you all check it out."

Brenda was a mandated reporter. By law, she had to call CPS whenever she saw or suspected incidences of child abuse. Once Lydia arrived at the childcare center, she sat in her car a bit to read the case more carefully.

Four-year-old Madisen Lawson came to daycare today with marks and bruises on her thighs and legs. She reported that her godmother, 23-year-old Erica Gaines, spanked her. Child's biological father is in jail and her biological mother lives in New York but is reportedly homeless and unemployed. Madisen has other siblings, some of which reportedly live in New York with their maternal grandmother. Madisen will be at daycare until 7 pm.

This case raised multiple alarms for Lydia. There was evidence of physical abuse, which meant that Madisen would need to be examined by Dr. Tess. Children under the age of five were considered more vulnerable due to limited visibility in their community—meaning many kids are not in daycare or school—and their limited language skills. Lydia went inside to meet Madisen. She had forgotten all about Halloween until she saw Madisen's purple dress. Madisen was all smiles when Lydia greeted her. "What are you for Halloween?"

"I'm a princess!" Madisen said with a look of *surely you know I'm a princess* beaming across her face.

Lydia and Madisen went down the hall into a small classroom to talk. Madisen didn't walk down the hall, she skipped. She seemed happy. Lydia took mental notes of the child's demeanor. Maybe it was Halloween excitement, but Lydia noted that Madisen was definitely in good spirits.

"What did you have for breakfast, Madisen?" Lydia asked.

Madisen made a face as if she were trying to remember something that happened a month ago, instead of three hours ago. "I had cereal."

Building a rapport with a child early on was critical to investigating cases. If children were uncomfortable or defensive, they were less likely to share important information. These were not meant to be interrogations. Investigators had to be especially careful with small children. Conversations usually began with some questions about lunch or the child's favorite teacher. This helped caseworkers observe how children recalled information and their overall verbal capabilities and style. Children often give the most honest and accurate information when they're just "chatting." Madisen expressed her excitement about the Halloween party and all of the candy she would eat. She also mentioned that she loved the costume that her "Gigi" bought for her.

"Who's Gigi?" Lydia asked.

"My Gigi . . . is my Gigi." Madisen shrugged. She looked confused that Lydia didn't understand. "My Gigi does not let me eat candy but she said I can eat a lot today!"

Lydia talked a bit more about Madisen's favorite candy and then tried to get closer to business. "Madisen, do you know why I'm here?"

Madisen shook her head.

"Your teacher noticed that you got hurt. What happened to your legs?"

Madisen shrugged her shoulders again and said, "I was being bad. My Gigi gave me a spanking."

A CPS investigator could take photos in physical abuse cases, but because Madisen would be examined by Dr. Tess, Lydia knew the medical team would take photos. Lydia explained to Madisen that she would take her to a doctor who would check her out and make sure she was okay. Madisen did not want to miss the party, but Lydia told her that she could bring her candy with her to the doctor's office. This seemed to work for Madisen.

Dr. Tess's team provided expert consultation on certain abuse cases, mostly cases that were alleging sexual or physical abuse, or medical neglect. The office consisted of medical exam rooms and also small rooms where forensic interviews were conducted behind a two-way mirror. The recording of these interviews was done in hopes of decreasing the trauma of disclosing painful experiences by only requiring the child to discuss it once.

Dr. Tess specializes in determining if abuse was accidental or nonaccidental. She sees some of the worst cases, and bringing children to see her is never pleasant, for anyone. Princess Madisen remained in good spirits, but the bruises on her body told a different story. I hadn't had too many cases like this back then, but it was clear Lydia's hope to have an easier day than the one before was not likely.

A few hours later, at around 3:30 p.m., Lydia and Madisen finished up at the doctor and began their journey back to the office. Lydia now had photos and various documents, including one in which the doctor rendered her medical conclusion about Madisen. The document was long, but the sentence that Lydia knew mattered was Dr. Tess's determination that this was, in fact, physical injury: *Nonaccidental and excessive physical injury to a child under the age of five.*

Lydia knew what a medical determination like that meant. Based on the bruises, the medical determination, and the age of the child, Madisen would likely be placed in foster care. Lydia was present during the examination, and the marks and bruises certainly looked bad. There were multiple bruises on her thighs and a bruise on her upper arm indicating that she was grabbed.

Lydia did the CPS math. Madisen was classified as an at-risk child. At-risk children, especially under five, who had this sort of medical determination, and two inaccessible biological parents, usually meant removing the child was the most viable route. Lydia studied the photos: What if she sent Madisen back with her godmother and something else happened? Placing Madisen in a safe place until the system could find her biological mother and sort things out seemed like the safest bet.[2]

The ride back to the office took fifteen minutes. Along the way, Lydia made several phone calls, one of which included sorting out childcare for her own kids. She asked her mother to pick up the kids and to tell them that she wasn't sure if she would make it to take them trick-or-treating. Lydia was exhausted, and she still hadn't caught up on her cases from last night. She called LeAnn, who was also her supervisor. LeAnn had already received the medical report and photos.

"I just saw the photos. She's only four years old. Jesus Christ," LeAnn said.

Madisen sat in the back seat, so they spoke discreetly and LeAnn instructed Lydia to notify the sheriff's office of the case details, another step in the protocol when there was physical injury to a child.

Madisen was quietly playing with the magic wand that came with her princess dress and unwrapping another piece of candy. She seemed unphased by what was happening and unaware of the ways her life was about to be completely changed. When Lydia finished speaking to LeAnn, she texted Derek an update, and then she called Erica.

"Hi, is this Erica Gaines?" Lydia began introducing herself and told

Erica that she needed to see her as soon as possible regarding a report on Madisen. Erica reacted with panic, asking if Madisen was okay.

"Is that my Gigi?! Is she coming to get me?" Madisen perked up with excitement as she realized Lydia was talking to her godmother.

Lydia assured Erica that Madisen was safe and reiterated that she needed to see her right away.

· · ·

Seventy percent of US adults use spanking to discipline their children. Research has found that if parents choose to spank their children, the likelihood that they will eventually become involved with CPS increases. Spanking is legal and a common practice that many parents turn to when children misbehave. Even when used infrequently, this form of discipline can be interpreted as abuse. The determination of the extent of the injury is often made by a physician. The process of distinguishing spanking from abuse or determining injury from spanking has proven to be complex and highly subjective. Research suggests that physicians are more likely to assume child abuse in Black children than white children, even though data has also shown that Black children have had fewer injuries than their white counterparts.[3] Once a physician has reported their findings on cases like this, the kids almost always face removal.

About 17 percent of the cases that come into the child protective services system are categorized as physical abuse,[4] yet it's important to note that physical abuse is most likely to occur during a disciplinary attempt. Some believe that physical abuse is most commonly an intentional and willful act, but on the contrary, it most often occurs when a parent is using their chosen form of discipline.[5]

I was already back at the office when Lydia returned. I didn't know how her day had gone or how close the case would hit home for me. As opposed to last night with Mr. Dima, my cases that day were straight-forward. I was typing up notes and had every intention of wrapping up and heading home.

But then I heard Lydia's voice. She was on the phone when she walked into our cubicle. She was talking fast and in a way that suggested she was conferring with Terri about a petition. *Dr. Tess. Child is four years old. Physical injury, nonaccidental. Parents unavailable.* So many conversations wafted through these partial walls. It sounded like Lydia was in for a long night.

All of a sudden, I felt someone playfully pulling at the top of my desk chair. I spun around to see Madisen in a sparkly purple dress. While she was excited to see me, I was in absolute shock to see her. A knot formed in the pit of my stomach. Usually when kids came here, they were being removed from their home. Madisen threw her arms around me in a hug. Lydia, still on the phone, observed Madisen's excitement to see me. With the recognition that I knew this child, Lydia informed LeAnn, who restricted my access to this case within the computer system. This is a common practice when there is a conflict of interest between a staff member and someone involved in a case. LeAnn told me that it was best to keep my distance from the case details and to try not to discuss the situation with Erica. Lydia got busy working at her desk, and Madisen did not leave my side. She asked me questions and told me about her day. While entertaining Madisen, I overheard Lydia's phone conversations; she mentioned marks and bruises. I did a quick scan of Madisen, but I saw no bruises because her dress fell down to her ankles.

Lydia explained to someone on the phone that Madisen's father was in jail, and her mother was AWOL, and she had no other family nearby. *Madisen had no other family nearby.* I wanted to speak up and say that Madisen *did* have family nearby. But I had already been told that I needed to keep my distance from this case. I handed Madisen some crayons and a coloring sheet from the stack we have on hand for whenever children are in the office.

I knew the steps involved for Lydia. The process was made up of a tedious but predictable set of events. Paperwork had to be gathered for Terri in order to draft a shelter petition to remove Madisen from Erica's home and place her into foster care. Lydia would give the photos and medical reports to Terri along with all of the evidence that would be presented to a judge the next morning, a Saturday.

While Madisen colored at my desk and Lydia initiated the removal petition process, my cell phone started buzzing. Erica was calling. I ignored it because I knew I couldn't talk to her right then. I walked over to Lydia's cubicle.

"How are you?" she asked me.

I glanced at Madisen, diligently coloring and still eating candy. "I think I'm in shock," I whispered.

"How well do you know Erica? Why would she do this?" Lydia asked as she pushed a camera toward me; I saw photos of Madisen's thighs and her upper arm. I knew I wasn't supposed to be seeing the photos, so after I looked, I quickly passed the camera back to Lydia. I couldn't believe it. Erica never even wanted to spank Madisen. But clearly something had pushed her to this point.

Before I could answer, Lydia's phone rang, and she stood up to walk up to the lobby. "Erica's here."

CHAPTER 10

THE THREE MOTHERS

2009

ONE OF THE MOST UNCOMFORTABLE PARTS OF BEING A CPS IN-vestigator is the interview with the alleged perpetrator of child abuse. The nature of the dialogue creates an atmosphere of distrust and defensiveness. Interviewing children isn't always straightforward either, but the dynamic between an investigator and accused parents is precarious.

Erica was in class when she received Lydia's call; she immediately made her way over to the CPS office. She was accompanied by one of our mutual friends, Shannon, who was also her roommate. Upon arrival, Erica and Lydia stepped into one of the visitation meeting rooms near the office entrance. Shannon waited in the empty lobby. Shelley watched from her desk.

Erica sat down, but Lydia remained standing near the door of the meeting room. Erica followed her lead and stood back up. Lydia generally conducted her interviews while standing. She felt that sitting down seemed informal and made interviews longer. If investigators were anything, they were efficient. The meeting room is small and typically used for parents who have visitation with their children, so there are toys, crayons, and toddler-size chairs in the corner. The walls are the same beige as the rest of the office. Along the back wall of the room there were framed portraits that had been drawn by children in foster care. The drawings were variations of families, houses, and out-of-scale pets. Lydia started her normal introductory statement; she and Erica were just a few feet apart.

"I'm Lydia Davis and I am an investigator with the Department of Children and Families. We received a report of physical abuse on Madisen. She was examined by our physician and found to have several marks and bruises. Can you tell me what happened?"

"*Abuse?*" was the only thing Erica heard. "I didn't—I've been taking care of Madisen for months and I can't get ahold of her parents. She's my goddaughter."

"Did you hit her?" Lydia asked bluntly. Lydia's interview style with parents was stern and direct compared to her approach with children. As an intern observing her, and now working with her as a colleague, I knew that Lydia rarely buried the lede. "Are you responsible for the marks and bruises on her legs?"

"I did spank Madisen, but I didn't know of any marks." Erica's whole body shook as she started to cry. Her tears almost made her confession inaudible. "Madisen was misbehaving. It's not against the law to discipline a child, is it?"

"No, but it is considered abuse to leave marks or bruises when you discipline a child. So, you didn't see the marks on her legs?"

Erica focused on her hands as she spoke, taking quick breaths, trying to subdue her frustration. "We are usually very rushed in the morning. She was so excited about Halloween. She put on her costume as soon as she woke up. I didn't notice anything."

Lydia listened intently, never taking her eyes off of Erica. Her body language gave nothing away. "We're going to take Madisen into state custody. She's been examined by our physician, and our legal team has compiled enough evidence to substantiate a removal. We need to get ahold of her parents and we also need to make sure that this doesn't happen again. There will be a hearing at 8:00 a.m." Lydia approached the table, closing the gap between her and Erica to show her paperwork. Sheet by sheet, Lydia laid out forms for Erica's review and signature.

"What?" Erica said in a panic as more papers appeared in a row. "Look. I'm so sorry about all of this. I never meant to hurt Madisen." Erica's voice got higher the more she attempted to explain herself. Lydia ignored the apology as she pulled a pen from her pocket. "Can she stay with my parents?" Erica continued: "They live in Jacksonville and they will come to pick her up. I don't want her to be in the system. I've been trying to avoid that all along."

Lydia pointed at the first paper in the row. "This document is for you to sign, which acknowledges that we have spoken, and you understand the next steps. This other form"—she tapped the sheet next to the first—"is a summary of—"

Erica stopped listening. She operated without thinking, still in a state of disbelief. Erica took the pen offered to her and signed each page.

"Can I see Madisen?" she asked.

"Visitation will be decided at the hearing tomorrow. You're not her biological mother, so you are not required to come. But if you would like to come, it will be at the courthouse downtown." Lydia bent toward the table to jot down details about the hearing. "For now, Madisen will be placed in a licensed foster home. She will be fine and safe there until we can figure out what's going on with her parents."

Lydia left the room. Erica forced her legs to move so she could follow her out. She slowly made her way to the lobby to meet Shannon. At that point, Erica must have started panic dialing me.

• • •

I was still sitting with Madisen at my desk so I ignored Erica's name flashing on my phone's screen. It was nearly 6:00 p.m. on a Friday, so most of our colleagues were gone. LeAnn had just left for the day. The office was nearly empty, though I still heard sporadic sounds, muffled chatter, printers pushing out documents, and beeps of paper jams. This was the chorus of sounds as caseworkers wrapped up their workweek.

"I am ready to go," Lydia announced when she returned from interviewing Erica. Her tone was one of exasperation. Lydia asked if there was anyone else who could transport Madisen to her foster placement. But I knew our transport team was either on other cases or on their way home.

"I can take Madisen," I offered.

"You know LeAnn would never let that happen," she replied as she stuffed papers, folders, and her laptop into her tote. A clear indication that she would be working on this case at home. She was right about LeAnn's preference that I keep my distance.

"But," she sighed, her eyes darting from her stuffed tote bag to Madisen, "I may not have a choice." Lydia acquiesced. "I'm not spending another night here and my kids are waiting for me."

She continued the process of shutting down for the day. She sorted and organized case files on her desk, gathered more documents to take home, and then pressed the "save" button at the bottom right of the computer screen—securing her notes. She clicked off the LED light strip that ran across the bottom of the cabinets within the cubicles and used her hip to push her chair underneath the desk. This exhilarating sequence of tasks typically ends with you heading home.

When CPS is looking for a placement for a child, the supervisors encourage family as an option, but this is not always a straightforward process. There are state standards of care that all adult relatives have to meet, and there are various steps to ensuring that a home meets those standards. Twenty states and the District of Columbia have statutes and regulations requiring relatives be licensed or certified as a foster family. Eight of those states allow for provisional approval, or immediate placement, while relatives fulfill the remaining requirements.[1] The process of establishing "goodness of fit" includes a criminal background check and child abuse histories on all adults in the home. In addition to this, a CPS professional has to go out to the relative's home to ensure suitability and provide a drug test to all adults. Not only do these requirements create barriers to placement, but they also take time. The cadre of licensed foster families that are readily available to CPS investigators tends to look more attractive. The path of least resistance was likely going to be Lydia's choice, especially after the week she'd had.

"You can take her," Lydia said as she handed me a document with the foster home details and address. "But, unasked . . ."

"Unanswered," I replied.

Lydia disappeared down the hallway. I started to gather my things and looked over at Madisen, who had fallen asleep at my desk.

"Madisen," I whispered, tapping her shoulder. "We're leaving now."

She rubbed her eyes, stretched her arms, and complained about being hungry.

"We'll stop and get food," I promised as I took her hand.

"McDonalds?"

"Yes, I'll take you to McDonalds."

Her smile was huge. It was the same one I had seen many times before in anticipation of a Happy Meal.

Moments later, Madisen was settled in the back seat of my car eating her dinner and oblivious to everything that was about to happen. I wanted to keep it that way. Since we left the office, my phone continued to buzz with calls and texts from Erica. I needed to answer her, but I was still unsure how to have that conversation. The investigator in me did not want to get involved and just wanted to get this child safely to her new foster home before LeAnn found out that I was transporting. But I also knew what the past several months had been like for Erica. I knew she must be beside herself with fear and worry. Erica and Madisen were not just names in a case file to me. I knew them. I loved them. And I knew what they were about to endure, because I had seen many families and children go through this ordeal.

In our training, we were taught to be decisive, dispassionate, and vigilant, with a focus on reducing the likelihood of additional harm. I believe that is what Lydia had done. Had this been a different family under the same circumstances, would I have made a different decision? Deep down I knew that I would accept Dr. Tess's recommendations, especially when it came to physical evidence of abuse.

Madisen had been in my car dozens of times before. We had been to the park and to different restaurants for lunch and dinner. A few times, I had picked her up from daycare and driven her home when Erica had to work late. Now, I was taking her to stay with people neither she nor I knew. A part of me wanted to just take her home with me.

Madisen was asleep by the time we arrived at the home of Patricia Lisbon, a middle-aged African American woman with two children of her own. I called her when I pulled up to the front gate at the entrance to her community. After I introduced myself, she opened the gate for us. Even though it was dark out, I could tell this was a pristine neighborhood with beautiful and mostly identical homes. After a few turns, I saw Ms. Lisbon standing outside her front door. She was dressed in a long skirt and a top with ruffles. She wore house slippers that loosely covered her toes. I turned the car off and woke Madisen up. After she looked outside her window, confusion slid across her face, and she asked me where we were.

"I'm going to drop you here so you can stay with this nice lady."

She jolted up as she realized what I said. "Why? Where is my Gigi?"

"Your Gigi is at home and hopefully you can see her soon." I practiced what I was taught about being as direct and clear as possible when talking with young children. I needed to be cognizant of what a child her age could understand. My training conflicted with my reality because I knew Madisen and no matter how I phrased it, none of this would make sense to her. Madisen was a four-year-old who had been abandoned by her parents, had been taken in by Erica, and was now entering foster care. She had a mother, Didi; a godmother, Erica; and now a foster mother, Ms. Lisbon. This was a lot to process for anyone, especially a four-year-old.

Madisen crossed her arms. Her stubbornness glowered. She was still wearing her purple princess dress, but it had become more crumpled throughout the day. She looked like an imperious little royal who would not suffer this inconvenience. She whined, "I don't want to be here. I want to go home."

The next fifteen minutes were some of the most difficult minutes in my early stint as an investigator. It was an emotional and physical struggle to get Madisen into that house. She cried and made her whole body go limp. Erica had talked to me about it, but I had never been privy to one of Madisen's meltdowns. Erica had told me about how she behaved in school and how disruptive she could be. Madisen flailed in my arms and screamed so loud that I was sure Ms. Lisbon's neighbors heard it. Witnessing how obstinate Madisen could be shook my resolve. Ms. Lisbon remained at her front door while I struggled with Madisen. She clearly had a lot of patience, which was essential in this role. After several minutes, she came over to help me, and we worked together to try to calm Madisen down with verbal assurances that everything would be all right.

"Gigi! Gigi!" she wailed. "I want to go home!"

I found myself apologizing to Ms. Lisbon. The effort and time required to coerce Madisen out of the car and into Ms. Lisbon's home felt like forever; it broke my heart to have to leave Madisen there. This is why investigators have to keep their distance from cases too close to home. And still the hard part wasn't done. Once we got Madisen in the house, she sat on the floor and screamed. It was a loud piercing sound that I couldn't believe came from a person so small. I reflexively covered my ears and then walked back outside. Ms. Lisbon was right behind me. Tears welled up in my eyes. I felt silly for being so emotional.

"It's okay," Ms. Lisbon said. Somehow this had turned into a situation where a foster parent was consoling me. "You're doing the right thing even though it is hard on children," she continued. "But they eventually calm down. It's what is best for them, and we know that." Madisen's wailing was still ringing in my ears as I got back into my car. And so were Ms. Lisbon's words. *It's what is best for them.* I felt exhausted and on edge. I took a deep breath and returned Erica's calls so I could find out what happened.

• • •

TWENTY-FOUR HOURS EARLIER

They sent Madisen home from school. Her teacher told Erica that they were giving her one more chance before expulsion.

"I'm sorry, Erica," Madisen's teacher said. The teacher understood the implications of the ultimatum.

Erica had to take a breath because she felt like someone had knocked the wind out of her. She was not surprised. This exact scenario had been keeping her up at night. Madisen's behavior had to change, otherwise Erica knew she would have to find another daycare that she could afford. She just wanted one thing to work, one thing to not fall apart in her fragile life.

"Don't they understand that she's going through a lot?" Erica asked rhetorically. Of course, they knew. She had explained everything about Didi to the daycare staff, but disruption was disruption and she'd been told, more than once, that they didn't have the capacity to control Madisen's behavior.

"Is she allowed to come back tomorrow?" Erica clarified.

"Oh yes. We are having a Halloween party so it will be mostly fun. Does she have a costume?"

Erica hesitated. "Yes, she does. But I'm wondering if it's best if I keep her home tomorrow. Isn't giving her a party rewarding bad behavior?"

"I see what you mean. But all the kids have been so excited."

Later after dinner, Erica began cleaning up the kitchen. Her roommate Shannon was working late so it was just she and Madisen. Erica washed dishes, wiped down the counters, and put away the leftovers. She felt numb and tired. Everything was a weary pantomime. She placed a sandwich and snacks in a lunch box for Madisen. She added a couple pieces of candy. This was rare, but it was Halloween tomorrow.

When she finished, Erica walked over to Madisen, who sat at the dining table playing with one of her dolls. It was just about 8:00 p.m.

"Madisen, how was school today?"

"Great! And tomorrow we get to wear our Halloween costumes for our party and have candy."

"Your teacher said that you had some bad behavior in school and threw toys at the other kids."

Madisen did not respond. Whenever she sensed a reprimand on the horizon, she remained as quiet as possible and tried to focus on something else, in this case her doll.

Erica spoke slowly and deliberately, "Madisen, you're getting a spanking tonight."

She started to cry prematurely. "No, Gigi. I'm sorry!"

Erica almost backed down but stayed the course. "Remember we talked about consequences to your behavior? I know there is a lot going on right now, but you just can't keep behaving like this."

Madisen pleaded for a pardon, but Erica reached for a belt that was hanging over the arm of the couch and wrapped the buckle around her palm. Then she hit Madisen across her bottom with the belt strap. Madisen jumped around erratically. Erica gripped Madisen by her upper arm, holding her firmly as she repeated the first motion across her bottom again. Madisen squealed louder, jumping and flailing her other arm and legs. Erica tried to steady her by holding her tighter. With deliberate swings, Erica repeated the motion, inadvertently hitting Madisen's legs. The spanking didn't last more than a minute, but this chaotic exchange left them both exhausted. Afterward, Erica carried Madisen up to her room and put her to bed. Madisen continued to wail from her room, only stopping briefly when she needed to take a breath.

Erica had to study, but before she settled at the dining table with her computer, she pulled out a piece of paper to write Madisen a note. She wrote that she loved her and wanted her to have fun at the party. Just as she did every day, she folded the note and placed it inside Madisen's lunch box. She hung the purple princess costume over the staircase railing, across from Madisen's bedroom, so that she could see it as soon as she woke up.

CHAPTER 11

THE AUDACITY OF HOPE
2018

CHILD PROTECTIVE SERVICES FORMALLY PLACED LJ AND KENNY in the home of an affluent Black couple, Mr. and Mrs. Sims. The couple were also fostering two other children and were highly regarded in the Durham community. Jatoia and Lawrence had a long road ahead, a path filled with court-ordered tasks and requirements that needed to be completed in order to get their children back.[1] Jatoia had contacted the "Safe Together Parenting Program," a preemptive attempt to move the process along more quickly. Her caseworker had already alerted her to the standard tasks that she would be required to complete. She and Lawrence were scheduled to begin the parenting course even before her court-ordered case plan was finalized.

Their sessions officially started in June 2018, and were scheduled for two sessions per week. Their parenting coach was Carol, and she was there to observe as well as coach them through the Safe Together Training curriculum. It was composed of three modules: safety, health, and parent-child interaction. All of the training is focused on equipping parents with the knowledge and skills for responding when a child is sick or hurt. It also advises parents on general ways to improve interactions with their children. Carol noted how Jatoia and Lawrence never missed a session. They asked questions throughout the training, particularly during the module on *health*.

"This information is helpful. Especially when you have a preemie who is still developing so much. I wish this could be given as a standard to all parents when they have a baby," Jatoia said to Carol.

After they finished their course, Carol would observe Jatoia and Lawrence with their children during visitations. Carol would also provide feedback on how they could childproof their new space. Jatoia was thrilled when Lawrence found a small apartment for them. Although a part of her wanted to leave North Carolina and go back home to Georgia, she knew she could not leave without both of her children.

They worked on safety measures in the kitchen, living room, and the children's bedrooms. Carol observed everything. She checked that all of the childproofing was accurate. During this part of the training, Jatoia felt a genuine excitement at the prospect of bringing her children back home. The idea of reunification is ethereal when you are working with CPS. Some days reunification feels possible and imminent but most days it feels like it is being held for ransom. Working with Carol and doing practical things to prepare her home brought Jatoia more and more hope. When she and Lawrence completed the parent training program, it was time to visit with the children and show what they had learned.

On the day of visitation, Jatoia's mind was vacant. She felt like she was outside of herself watching her hands prepare snacks for her boys. Lately she had been feeling like she was going through the motions of her day, just a few steps removed from actually being present. Her hands just knew what to do because she had fixed LJ snacks so many times. He loved Oreo cookies, so she made sure to pack them.

"Do we have the Transformers set that I bought for LJ?" Lawrence asked Jatoia, as she placed items into her tote. Carol told Jatoia that sometimes parents bring toys and snacks to their visit. Jatoia reminded Lawrence to pick up the cookies from the store on his way home.

"Please don't forget LJ's snacks," she texted him.

"I got 'em, Toia," he texted back.

She knew she was nagging him more these days. She constantly texted him reminders of CPS appointments: *We have parent training today, please don't be late. We need to get finger-printed today for background checks, do you have the address?*

When they arrived at the CPS office, they both looked visibly nervous. They knew that everything was being monitored and notes would be passed from here to their caseworker. When they went inside and saw the boys, all nerves and jitters evaporated. Their little eyes of recognition and hugs erased the tension in Jatoia's shoulders. LJ ran to his mother, throwing his arms around her neck, repeating "Mommy" until Lawrence playfully poked him asking for a hug. Then LJ embraced his father with ease and relief.

"How was your day, baby?" Jatoia asked LJ as she held Kenny in a cradled position. LJ grabbed for the Transformer toys that Lawrence presented. Jatoia peered down at Kenny as if he might disappear. LJ started to chatter about his day in between bites of his cookies. Lawrence sat next to him, tossing around the Transformer action figures. Carol sat in a chair nearby.

Carol observed Jatoia's and Lawrence's attentiveness to their boys. They showed affection, gave clear directions and instructions, soothed the children when they were upset, and seemed to genuinely enjoy each moment with their children. The visit was wrought with state intervention and observation, but it seemed that Jatoia and Lawrence put all of that out of their minds during those sixty minutes. They were natural in how they interacted with LJ and Kenny; they also gave reassurances to the boys that everything was going to be okay and they would soon be together.

Jatoia knew she needed to let Lawrence spend time with Kenny, but it was hard to let him go once she had him in her arms. He looked well and smiled all the time. He laughed when she rubbed the tip of his nose. When she finally passed the baby to him, Lawrence said, "'Bout time!" And they laughed. A sense of sadness swept over her as she thought about all that Kenny had gone through during this first year of life. If it were within her power, she would erase all of the pain that he ever felt.

As the visit was nearing an end, LJ became agitated. He started to whine that he wanted to go home with them. Jatoia hugged him.

"We will see you next week," Jatoia whispered. She kissed him in the middle of his palm then closed his hand. "And I want you to hold on to this kiss until then, okay, baby?" LJ nodded, wiping his tears with one hand, but keeping the hand that his mother kissed closed tightly in a fist.

• • •

After a few more sessions and observations from Carol, Jatoia and Lawrence completed the parenting program. They both received a glowing recommendation from Carol that she passed along to the CPS caseworker.

Ms. Potts and Mr. Daniels have demonstrated active and attentive parenting during our training program. Both have shown resilience and commitment. In particular, Ms. Potts has self-advocating and help-seeking behaviors. She has great coping skills and remains positive during this CPS process. She meditates, writes in a journal and is learning to prioritize her mental health. She knows deeply that she must remain as healthy as possible for her children. She has been incredibly receptive to the course content and engaged with questions. She has shown a strong attachment to her family, as evidenced by moving to a new city to take care of her terminally ill mother. When Kenny was born early, she visited him as much as the hospital would allow and she has remained in a city that is unknown to her so she is close to her children. She exhibited adequate insight and has the ability to consider multiple perspectives. The care that Ms. Potts has for her children is apparent and she is clearly committed to doing what it takes to reunify with her children and to keep them safe.

Following the parenting program, several court hearings were on the horizon. Jatoia started to keep her own impeccable notes about the process. At visitation, when LJ mentioned that he now eats meat, she wrote that down. LJ had always adhered to a vegetarian diet, yet the Sims family did not uphold that. Jatoia took notes when her new caseworker gave inaccurate details or statements. Jatoia started to read online about infant medical issues, and she ran across a story of a mother whose child was placed in foster care due to physical abuse. It was later confirmed that their child had osteopenia, a condition in which bones are weaker and more fragile than normal. Documentation showed that Kenny had that condition at birth.

"What if this is all due to his condition? Couldn't that explain why he was hurt?" Jatoia hypothesized to herself. She printed documents and showed them to her family. She also gave them to the caseworker. She requested all of Kenny's medical records from the hospital and went through them meticulously, highlighting them and making notes. Jatoia spent hours online reading and sharing with her mother, grandparents, and Lawrence. She was completely consumed and obsessive, but she felt she had to be. She devoured every relevant piece of information she could find. Between appointments she continued her frenetic research in the process of completing their case plan.

JATOIA AND LAWRENCE'S CASE PLAN TASKS

- The mother and father are ordered to complete a parenting class and demonstrate that the children are physically safe in their care.

- The mother and father are ordered to submit to a comprehensive parenting capacity assessment and follow the recommendations of the assessment.

- The mother and father are ordered to demonstrate what they learned in parenting classes during supervised visitation.

- The mother and father are ordered to submit to random drug screens.

- The mother and father are ordered to have a mental health assessment.

- The mother and father are ordered to engage in ongoing therapeutic services.

Instead of questioning any of the tasks, Jatoia threw herself into getting them started and finished. Surprisingly, she had found the parenting program helpful and decided to learn as much as she could so that she would be an even better mother once her kids came home. Although much of her attention was on CPS mandates, she also needed to meet with the police whenever they asked. Sometimes Jatoia would momentarily forget that law enforcement was involved with this case. It had been a while since she had heard from the initial officer, Detective Cross. When Jatoia received a call from a new officer, Detective Blake, it jerked her back to the reality of her situation.

"I'm taking over this case and need to see you both for some questions." Detective Blake spoke with deliberate and measured words. He didn't say anything other than what was needed. No pleasantries. No small talk. Soon, Jatoia and Lawrence were back at the police station talking about the case. Jatoia came prepared. She had a stack of documents of Kenny's medical records from Duke Hospital. Detective Blake seemed surprised by all that Jatoia presented to him. He was white, at least six feet tall, and he stood up during the entire interview.

"Detective Blake, I am a mother. I have scrutinized every inch of these records. Something isn't right and I think we need to consider that something happened to Kenny while in Duke Hospital's care." She had no other explanation. Child protective services continued to tell Jatoia that she needed to explain how Kenny was harmed. But all Jatoia could come up with was that Kenny must have had some condition that Duke missed or left untreated. Perhaps he experienced those fractures under their care? Detective Blake listened, but his face resembled the faces of others when she spoke about her concerns with the hospital. To them, Duke Hospital was unimpeachable.

"Your son was hurt so badly that I'm told that he nearly died. So, I'm going to need more information other than blaming the hospital. Was Kenny exposed to anyone who is violent?"

"No." Jatoia almost chuckled at the absurdity of this question, but then thought better of it, retracting the levity. She couldn't help but think about how her family poked fun at her and Lawrence because they barely let anyone babysit LJ. "Detective Blake, my older son has never even been to daycare. He's always been with us. Same for Kenny. We are not violent people."

• • •

For the previous detective, there was not enough compelling evidence to conclude that Kenny's parents hurt him. The new officer, Detective Blake, thought otherwise. He was not ready to close the case. The strange chronology of the following events mystified Jatoia. First, she learned that CPS was working to corroborate the alleged causes of Kenny's injuries. They began working with Dr. Lauren Bell, another child abuse physician who reviewed all of Kenny's hospital records and the documents from his emergency room visit. She agreed with the initial opinion of Dr. Lucas, the child and neglect physician who had examined Kenny at Duke Hospital that night.

Dr. Bell found that Kenneth Daniels did not have any underlying bone disorders or nutritional deficiency that would explain the multiple fractures. She agreed that the child was abused and medically neglected.

This additional medical report was added to a growing pile of ammunition for CPS, and it was sent to Detective Blake for his investigation. With each new development, Jatoia wanted to lean on Lawrence for support. But, she noticed that his mental state was deteriorating. He started to turn inward. He was more subdued. She knew that she could not help him. She knew that they couldn't heal each other if they were both being tormented by the same thing. Two drowning people can't save each other. Their family had been pulled apart and healing would be an inside job.

Jatoia found a therapist and had weekly sessions. Lawrence participated, but she could tell he was only doing it because of the CPS mandate. Their relationship became unhealthier as the days went on. If they did communicate, it was contentious and exclusively about the boys and the case. This new report from Dr. Bell was damning, but Jatoia tried to keep a level head. Somehow, she still had hope, and she felt that she owed it to her boys to never lose it.

"That doesn't mean anything. Of course, she agrees with the report. What doctor would go against the opinion of such a *big hospital*, like Duke?" she asked Lawrence almost rhetorically. He was angry, and sometimes she wasn't sure if he was angry at CPS or angry at her. She didn't know if he was clear about this distinction either. It wasn't long before Lawrence's repressed rage and emotions exploded. Jatoia was his closest target.

Days later, Jatoia and Lawrence were driving home from a CPS appointment. Jatoia had noticed Lawrence's indignant questions to the caseworkers. His voice was edgy and loud. It caused them to bristle, and it would derail the entire meeting. Jatoia became hypersensitive to all of their interactions with CPS. She knew the stakes and understood the intense scrutiny that CPS brings to bear on each proceeding. As she drove, she suggested that if they had any questions or any concerns about the case, she should be the one to take it to CPS. She felt they might receive the queries better from her, and maybe this could decrease the animosity that was disrupting their interactions. Lawrence took her suggestion as an insult; an argument ensued. It escalated so quickly that Jatoia decided to pull over to the side of the road.

Lately, when they had a heated argument, they were at home. At home, they were able to go to different rooms to cool off and give each other some space. At that moment, they were confined to a small car. Jatoia knew she needed to get out. Once she pulled the car to a stop, the volume of the argument reached an inflection point. They started to blame each other for their situation, hurling insults at each turn.

"Get out of this car!" Jatoia yelled. She felt lightheaded and exhausted. She was aware that this was out of character for her. She had managed to keep her cool in most situations, and even tried to shoulder many things on behalf of Lawrence. She tried to hold their grief and keep it at bay. But this was the moment that had lain dormant for months, brooding beneath every single CPS meeting and conversation. Now it was spilling out all around them.

Lawrence lunged at her. He pressed her against the car door, with both of his hands holding her by the shoulders. Then, somehow, his hands were around her neck. In that tight space, he shoved her and yelled in her face. Jatoia screamed so loudly that it disarmed him. Lawrence let her go. She scrambled out of the car. She struggled to breathe and had to steady herself by holding on to the car. A person who was witnessing the altercation must have called law enforcement, because a few minutes later a cop car pulled up behind them. Jatoia recognized the officer instantly; it was Detective Blake. She was in disbelief. How did a plainclothes detective, who was already investigating them, end up responding to this call?

Jatoia knew that Blake distrusted them based on what he had gathered from the CPS investigation. This was not going to help. Adrenaline drove Jatoia; she told the detective exactly what happened. He asked Jatoia if she needed to go to the hospital, but she declined. This fall from grace was steep. Detective Blake handcuffed Lawrence and read him his Miranda rights.

• • •

Jatoia was shaken up for days after that encounter. Lawrence spent some days in jail, but he was eventually released pending additional hearings. They kept their distance. Jatoia had already lost too much. Lawrence was the only other person on the planet who understood the pain of losing LJ and Kenny. Now he was gone too. She split time between her CPS case tasks and taking care of her mother. Her goal was to stay as busy as possible. Within weeks of the incident with Lawrence, her court-appointed attorney called to let her know that Detective Blake had issued a warrant for their arrests. They had decided to charge them both with felony child abuse and with child neglect for Kenny's injuries.

"How can we get arrested for something that we didn't do?!" Jatoia asked her attorney, as if she could offer anything except the obvious.

"An arrest warrant is issued when the state has probable cause that a person has committed a crime."

Jatoia heard the answer that her attorney provided, but she didn't need it to understand their predicament. She knew that Lawrence's physical attack was all the detective needed for probable cause. It was a public episode of domestic violence. She had spent hours at the police station talking to the detective, going through medical records, explaining how much they loved their kids, and emphasizing that they were not violent people, that they would never hurt Kenny. Yet, he had gotten a front-row seat to just how violent they could get.

Lawrence and Jatoia were arrested on November 7, 2018. All Jatoia could think about was that she was going to miss her visitation with the boys. It was scheduled for the very next day.

CHAPTER 12

TWICE AS HARD
2009

ERICA'S COURT HEARING WAS HELD ON A SATURDAY MORNING. Since it was a weekend hearing, they did not use the main courtroom. Lydia and the DCF attorney, Terri, were in a conference room, with Judge Dennis Willem seated at the head of a long rectangular table. Erica was there with her parents, Pastor Charlotte and Pastor James, who had driven over from Jacksonville the night before. Lining the walls were oversize pictures of previous judges, all white, mostly men. Lydia and Terri were indifferent to Erica. She was not obligated to come, as Lydia had told her. But Erica and her parents wanted to make it clear that they were Madisen's family and could be entrusted with her care.

The hearing was brief, and there were minimal questions posed to Erica. Lydia and Terri asked if she physically disciplined Madisen, and she answered honestly. They asked Erica if she knew how to get in touch with Madisen's mom; she answered no. Lydia and Terri presented the compendium of facts they'd acquired in less than twelve hours. Everything from how long Madisen Lawson had been in Erica Gaines's care, to how Madisen's biological parents were unreachable/unavailable, and about Didi's own history with CPS along with the reports that she had unstable, intermittent housing. Dr. Tess Mahoney's report was entered as evidence. It concluded that the physical abuse had been ongoing in the home. Erica denied any intentional abuse but reported that she had started spanking Madisen a few weeks prior.

Within fifteen minutes, the judge granted the petition and Madisen was remanded to state custody. Once the decision had been handed down, Erica was informed that the case would be turned over to the state attorney's office for review, and a criminal determination was pending. Erica was also required to complete a court-mandated case plan if she wanted to be considered for reunification, though the state's preference was to place Madisen back in the care of her mother, Didi.

Lydia closed her investigation with verified findings, which meant that physical abuse was proven and verified in this case. Any ongoing responsibilities were shifted to a private case management organization contracted through CPS. Erica would be assigned a new caseworker, Ariana Munoz, who would be her primary contact and would help set up visitation with Madisen. Lydia's investigative job was done, but things were just getting started for Erica.

Over the next few weeks, our friendship shifted. Erica explained the situation; she talked about the daycare threatening to expel Madisen and the subsequent spanking incident. Now, every discussion we had revolved around her CPS case. I became more reticent. I didn't know what to do or what was the appropriate advice or intervention for me to give/make. Erica questioned my loyalty. She called me out for being indifferent, which was how she interpreted my response to the entire ordeal. But indifference kept me safe. I wasn't condemning Erica, but I also didn't go against Lydia's perspective, judgment, and experience. The CPS process is more complex and more convoluted than a single investigator, and I knew that Lydia was Erica's easiest target. If I condemned Erica, I would be turning my back on a friend and discounting every single thing I ever knew about her character. But if I argued against Lydia, I'd be discounting many parts of her story too. My position was offensive to Erica, who was not an indifferent person. She did not reside on the fence about things. She picked a side, every time.

Erica's hate for Lydia became her fuel. She brought up Lydia in every conversation: *How could she just take Madisen without even talking to me first? She cannot possibly have any children or understand parenting! I cannot believe they have someone like her working for them!* I started to avoid Erica's calls. I didn't want to hear her trash Lydia. I went on with my work, picking up cases and doing what was required of me. Lydia never mentioned another word about the case. Sometimes I wanted to ask her: *Don't you realize how much damage you have caused?* But I never brought it up. This kind of question—the question of how much damage our work caused to some of the most vulnerable families— was a question that also applied to every case I worked. The harm and disruption our work causes became all too real because of how close I was to Erica and her family. So, if I was going to keep score on Lydia's damage, then I needed to tally up my own.

It was mid-November 2009, and our office was scrambling. The holidays were approaching. This meant that schools were preparing for closures, and reports were crippling our office. In the past two weeks, our office received some particularly difficult cases. I received a case with five children who had been sexually abused by their step-father. I sat on the other side of a two-way mirror as each girl came in, one by one, detailing the abuse. It was the most horrific thing I'd ever heard. After we completed all of the interviews, and their stepfather was arrested, I went home and slept the rest of the day.

We were trying our best to keep up with the influx of cases, and it wasn't long before it was my turn to be on call. It was after midnight when my work cell rang—pulling me out of the sleep that I desperately needed.

"Hello, this is Jessica Pryce," I said.

"This is Officer McCullough with the Tallahassee Police Department. We have a child, who looks to be around five, wandering around the Walmart parking lot."

I was on my feet before I knew it. Within thirty minutes, I was in my car. The Walmart was a ten-minute drive from my apartment. The officer gave me a few more details over the phone during the drive. The child had been spotted in the empty parking lot playing with a doll. Although he guessed the child was about five years old, she did not respond or speak to him when he approached her.

When I arrived, Walmart had long since closed. The parking lot was normally littered with cars and meandering shopping carts, but now it was a lone little Black girl with a cop. She looked aloof and listless. The broad-shouldered white male cop, Officer McCullough, was talking to someone on his radio. The little girl was wearing a striped candy cane nightgown. It was about 55 degrees outside, and she wasn't wearing shoes. I took a moment to think about all the things that had accumulated in my car while working this job, but I knew I did not have a pair of shoes or slippers for her. I did have a few jackets in my trunk, either accidently left behind by a child or left over from charitable clothing drives. I grabbed a jacket and walked over to where they stood. I acknowledged the officer and held up my badge as a formality. I squatted so I could be eye level with the child. I noticed her hair was braided down from a middle part toward her ears, with colorful beads hung on the end of each braid. Her hair looked like it had just been done. Her braids glistened from oil or pomade. Clearly someone cared for her.

"Hi there, I'm Jessica. What's your name?"

She averted her gaze and did not answer. "Can you tell me how you got here?" I rallied with another question, but she still did not answer. I held the jacket toward her, and she slipped her arms inside it. If she was five years old, she should be able to talk. But she was scared. She rubbed her eyes in the way that kids did when they were tired.

I had carried dozens of cases by this point. Still I hadn't experienced anything like this—a nonverbal child wandering around alone in the middle of the night.

"Will you please tell me your name?" I asked her again.

She wouldn't look at me. She said, "Mariah."

"It's nice to meet you, Mariah. What about your full name? Can you tell me your last name?" She shook her head. Mariah took a seat on the ground crossing her legs. She started to chew on the collar of her nightgown, still clutching her doll.

"Can I sit next to you?" I asked, sitting down before she could respond. I pulled out my phone to call about a potential placement. I did not know this child's parents or where she lived. I did not know if she came here on her own or if someone dropped her off. But I did know that she needed somewhere to go tonight.

"Anything you need from me?" Officer McCullough's question startled me. I was focused on Mariah and had forgotten he was standing just a few feet away. I was still in that in-between state of awareness that happens when you've been abruptly awakened from a deep sleep. I was awake but I was processing things more slowly than usual. Before I could answer him, his radio shrieked a signal. The voice on the radio was accompanied by static but was clear enough for us to hear. "Dispatch to deputy. We have a 911 call from a woman saying her autistic daughter is missing. The Haywood Manor area."

Officer McCullough and I exchanged looks of clarity and relief. I knew the Haywood area. I shut my eyes and exhaled. Maybe this night wasn't going to require me to work until daylight. Officer McCullough held the receiving button on the radio and quickly responded to the person on the other end. Within the next few moments, we received the address for who we believed to be Mariah's mom, Justine Atkins. We both headed in that direction, Mariah with me in my car, and the police officer leading the way. Pulling into the apartment enclave, Mariah perked up in the backseat. "Mommy," she whispered. We had found her home. Mariah and I ascended a steep set of stairs, and Justine Atkins met us at the top. Even after she had her daughter back in her arms, she remained hysterical with relief.

"Jesus. I was worried sick." She sobbed as she held Mariah in a tight embrace. Mariah seemed to melt into her mother's arms. Officer McCullough hung back near his patrol car.

"Ms. Atkins, I know this must have been very scary for you. But I need to talk with you for a bit before I leave. I'm from the Department of Children and Families."

"What?" Her face shifted. Her defense began. "Wait, I had no idea she had gotten out. I thought she was asleep! Who reported me?"

I slowly lifted my hands to protest her very accurate assumption. "Ms. Atkins, I am not accusing you of anything, I just need to know what happened."

With that, she led the way into her apartment and went toward the back with Mariah. I heard her tell Mariah that it was time to go to bed. Before I walked inside, I signaled to the officer that I had it under control, and he left. I had been to this apartment building before on many occasions for other cases. It was one of many low-income subsidized apartments in the city. I was familiar with the layout of the units. This one was a two-bedroom, one-bathroom with an open layout where I could see into the kitchen from the living room. It was the middle of the night, and I decided I did not want to open up this woman's cabinets. There wasn't much space, and she had a lot of furniture. It felt pretty tight inside the apartment. But there were no obvious concerns that I could see.

Ms. Atkins returned to the living room. We both sat down.

"Thanks for being willing to talk with me," I said to her, hoping to diffuse any tension. "So, this has never happened before?"

She went on to explain that Mariah had limited verbal skills. She confirmed that she was five years old and that she was homeschooled. After dinner earlier in the evening, she did Mariah's hair and then put her to bed. Around ten, she stepped outside to smoke a cigarette and then came back in to lock up the home before going to bed. When she got up around midnight to use the restroom, she peeked into Mariah's room as she usually did and realized that she was gone.

"She must have wandered outside, but I don't know why she would do that. I locked up. I'm sure I did." She was looking over at her front door, as if willing herself to remember.

"If it were locked, could she have unlocked it?" I asked.

"No," she said. "She would need some sort of chair or something to step on to reach it."

"Was there a chair near the door?" I probed.

She shook her head.

So, it wasn't locked. I wrote down a note on the notepad that was in my lap. Checking the time, I saw that it was nearly 3:00 a.m. I stepped outside to make a quick call to wake LeAnn up. When I returned, I explained to Ms. Atkins that after I walked through her home, I was going to head out.

"What happens now?" she asked me.

"Thankfully Mariah is okay, but this could have ended badly. We think that you could benefit from voluntary in-home services,[1] and a case manager should come out to visit you regularly to make sure you have everything you need to keep Mariah safe."

Reality was dawning on her face. I wasn't a woman who had found her daughter and graciously brought her home. I was not a heroine. I was there to document, track, and notate all that I could see.

"Am I in some sort of trouble?"

"We are recommending that the locks on your front door be changed, and you get a pair that locks automatically. I will probably be the person who will come back out and check in on the new locks."

She started to massage her temples. Every so often she opened her mouth but nothing came out. I could tell that she wanted to say more, but she was tired and so was I.

"I'll call you tomorrow," I said before leaving.

For the foreseeable future, she would have an open case with child protective services. She had a five-year-old special needs child who left her home and wandered for two miles in the middle of the night. Even in my sleep-deprived haze, I believed it was an honest mistake, but what if it hadn't been me or the officer who had found Mariah? Getting secure locks was important. I felt bad for Justine Atkins because over the next few weeks the system would be making requests of her that would be labeled as voluntary, but these requests wouldn't be optional. My sister Rachel knew that all too well. They really weren't requests at all. We might leave the courts out of this and merely recommend she change the locks, but CPS would come back to visit until it was done.

. . .

The experience of bad dreams/nightmares varies from person to person. For some people, nightmares are severe. They can generate distress that continues well into waking hours. The stress of my job had started to affect me in many ways. I started having nightmares, lucid dreams, and other anxiety-related sleep disturbances. Work was insurmountable, and the reality of what was happening with my sister and Erica only heightened my anxiety.

With everything that was happening at work over the past few months, I kept going back to my first day as an intern. I remembered Naomi's contorted angry face as we took away her children. I was haunted by the way her face relaxed into resignation and apathy. I thought having her children removed would ignite motivation within her, but it did the opposite. I never knew what happened to her and her family, and these days that bothered me. The last time I engaged with her, her children were in her grandmother's custody out of town, out of their school zone, and out of their community.

I also thought about my sister and fell into a sunken place of shame. I stood in the space of a mandated reporter and pulled my sister into the CPS system. It had been over three months since the incident, and she was still chasing down CPS tasks. She now had a history with CPS, which she found particularly disturbing. She wondered if it would affect her employment or future job opportunities. I didn't know if it would or not. At this point, my sister and I had limited communication. When we did talk to each other, we tried to keep it general and brief. It would not take very much for me to say something that triggered the mistrust that was so clearly wedged between us. Reporters generally remain anonymous, but Rachel knew instantly that I had made the call. She did not tell anyone else about what happened except me. I was afraid and helpless and thought it was a reasonable thing to do, but I would handle it differently if I could do it over. I would spare my sister the awful shock of having her parenting decisions scrutinized and objectified by total strangers. I would never bring the watchful eye of state agents into her home, which only added more stress to her already pressurized situation.

Mr. Dima and his family stood in stark contrast to my interconnected experiences with poor Black families. The Dimas will always be a defining case for me. Their case taught me that some parents had the privilege to assert their rights and manage or deflect the CPS process in ways that my sister or Erica could not. Every other family I encountered so far on this job had opened their doors when I arrived with my badge and law enforcement. Mr. Dima's refusal to engage with us shocked me. I was forced to realize that the power I wielded through CPS had a two-sided impact in the community within which I worked. CPS's intrusion into people's lives was apparently optional. I didn't know what was going on in the Dima home or if Ivan was safe or not, but he remained with his family. On the one side, law enforcement had little leverage over wealthy (or white) parents who knew their rights. Our CPS attorney, Terri, explained that Mr. Dima had hired an attorney who said that if CPS wanted to come back, they would need a court order. I thought about last night when I returned Mariah to her home. Her mother let me right in. I didn't have a court order. I'm sure Mariah's mother had no idea how vulnerable she became with that one decision to let me into her home. The truth is, parents have rights, but few of them know what they are.

Katrina and I became closer during this time because our workload had essentially doubled. Many of our colleagues had resigned. I wasn't the only one who was beaten down by the work. When someone leaves CPS, their cases are redistributed to those who remain. We were drowning. At the time, I had thirty-two cases. I was working around the clock. When you are in the thick of this work, it's almost impossible to connect with people who do not understand what CPS work is like. People who care about you provide a perfunctory: *Sounds like you need to take some time off.* I would do my best to mask my sarcasm in reply: *Yeah, sure thing.* Taking time off was not a simple solution. Taking a day or two would not move the needle on my levels of burnout.[2] I was emotionally and psychologically depleted. Who knew how much time I needed to debride the wounds of this work? I also knew what it was like to work a case that wasn't mine. Having others go out for you, gather the information, and then trust that they would do the work of the case accurately and in a timely manner was just too much to consider. Everyone had to pitch in because of the massive workforce exodus, and I didn't want to make it worse. I did what I always do. I kept going.

The day after my on call shift, Katrina and I decided to have lunch in the office kitchenette. I didn't have time to go out to get food that day. People walked in and out, heating up their lunch or grabbing their drinks out of the fridge, but we were the only two people sitting at the small circular table in the middle of the tiny space. I was telling her about the nightmare I had last night in which the children were lying dead on the lawn, and I continued commencing my case as normal. She pulled out her phone to look up the meaning.

"Don't bother looking it up. It's just stress," I said. "Mystery solved."

"No, it's more than that. This site says that when you see dead people in your dream, it means that you are feeling guilty and struggling with internal conflict."

"You don't say?!" I said. I was incredulous. She let out a long laugh.

"I know it's been weeks, but I still can't believe the Mr. Dima fiasco,"

I said. Katrina lifted her hands as if to say, *Please don't bring him up.* "And last night, I felt like some kind of apartment code enforcement operative. This woman has a child with severe autism and I'm in her face talking about, 'I'll be back to check in on you to see if you got new locks.'"

"Now she knows better than to leave that door unlocked in the hood!" Katrina chuckled.

"I think it was an honest mistake. How could she have known her daughter would leave?"

"Black people don't get to make mistakes like that because we will be at their door." Katrina meant this as a joke.

Some dark humor was common in our work. The joke didn't land for me the way these jokes usually did. I had heard similar jokes or comments like this before, but something in me was shifting. My allegiance to the principles of CPS was wearing thin, and these kinds of jokes-as-coping-mechanisms started to feel foreign. There used to be a conventional joke about a hospital social worker who only calls in reports on Black women with substance-exposed newborns. My colleagues would say, *Ms. Pat never calls in reports on white moms.* And everyone would nod in tacit agreement. A Black mother gives birth and tests positive for marijuana, and she becomes entangled in our system. She could possibly lose custody of her child. On the other hand, a white mother who tests positive for marijuana receives pamphlets on saying no to drugs and gets to take her baby home.

There was also a running joke in our office about the movie *Home Alone.* Eight-year-old Kevin McCallister is accidentally left home alone when his entire family flies to France for a holiday trip. Elitist neglect. When the family realizes this, they call the local police department. The call was sent to a crisis intervention line, essentially, a child abuse hotline. Kevin went about his Christmas vacation. He went grocery shopping and attended Christmas Mass. He earned a few raised eyebrows and even a question or two, but no one pursued this lone white boy. Of course, this is a movie. But the quips about what would happen if the *Home Alone* family was Black produced grave answers—if you understood the inner workings of CPS.

These jokes and comments were a way to cope with a complicated and often debilitating profession. For some reason though, they started to sound and feel like nails on a chalkboard to me. There were so many ways that the system humanized the struggles of white mothers and criminalized the struggles of Black ones. Some mothers had the privilege of making mistakes. Others did not.[3] I realized this implicitly over my time as a CPS worker, but the looping images of Black women in my personal and professional orbit—my sister, Naomi Harden, Didi, Erica, and Ms. Atkins—were an explicit realization of the rampant disparity. Katrina's words provided some emphasis in that loop: *Black people don't get to make mistakes like that.*

CHAPTER 13

THE GREAT ALONE

2009

ERICA PREPARED FOR HER SUPERVISED VISITATION WITH MAD-isen. Supervised visitation is the general rule if the state finds that the parent/caregiver poses a significant threat to the child. Ms. Lisbon agreed to supervise a visit at a nearby park. It was humiliating for Erica. She was hurt that the system deemed her a threat to Madisen, but she tried to push that out of her mind as she prepared for the visit. In preparation, Erica packed Madisen's favorite snacks and some of her favorite clothes. The temperature was dropping in Florida now as November carried on, so she brought along one of Madisen's jackets.

Erica arrived at the park early and waited in her car. There were several walking trails that outline the crowded playground equipment. This park was one that she had visited often with Madisen, but today it felt like a foreign place. She would see Madisen for one hour, under the close observation of a woman she did not know. Erica hadn't met Ms. Lisbon, but the two had talked over the phone. Madisen could have been in any/every car, and Erica eyed each one, waiting to catch a glimpse of her beaming face. The last conversation she had with Madisen was tough. Erica could hear Madisen's voice on the verge of break-ing, which made her even more eager to see her.

"Gigi, I want to come back home. When are you coming to get me?" Madisen demanded over the phone.

Fighting back her own tears, Erica tried to be honest. "You are going to have to stay there for a while. I'm sorry. But I want you to try to calm down."

Madisen said, "I apologize for my behavior." Erica smiled through tears. She could tell that Madisen was trying to be sincere and mature. She had taught Madisen to say these very words when she misbehaved. "I will not get into any more trouble," she said.

"Madisen, you don't have anything to be sorry about. I'll try my best to get you home. But I will see you this weekend."

Ms. Lisbon arrived a few minutes late in a black Honda. Once Ms. Lisbon opened the back car door to unbuckle Madisen, Erica perked up. Erica bolted out of the car as Madisen sprinted full speed toward her. Her little feet barely touched the ground as she ran. Erica picked Madisen up and bundled her into a tight hug. Despite her efforts to not cry, she was sobbing. She took a moment to survey Madisen's face, her smile triumphant. Madisen was thrilled to be back with her Gigi.

Ms. Lisbon hung back at the car for a bit before walking over to formally greet Erica. She offered her hand and the usual pleasantries. Erica shook her hand lightly. She was already aware of the time. She slowly lowered Madisen to the ground.

"I think we should play. What do you think?" Erica asked.

Madisen nodded with excitement. They both headed toward the playground, joining the other children and their parents. Erica wanted to camouflage her playtime with Madisen in the scrum of children playing and laughing with their parents. But a blanket of shame hung over her. She knew that Ms. Lisbon was observing her every move.

• • •

It had been one year since Didi returned to New York, and her housing challenges persisted. She left her mother's apartment and stayed with a friend for a few months, until she met William. They started to date. It wasn't long before he invited her to move in with him. She jumped at the opportunity. She didn't tell William what was going on with Madisen, or what the child protective services system was requiring of her. William, fifteen years older than Didi, had adult children. Didi wasn't sure how he would feel about her children stopping by or moving in, so she went over to her mother's apartment to visit them. She wanted to protect her living situation with William, so she never mentioned it to her mother. For the first time in a year, Didi was putting her clothes inside dresser drawers and leaving her toothbrush on the bathroom sink instead of in the side pocket of her duffel bag.

When the CPS caseworker, Gabrielle, came by for a visit, she inquired about Didi's plan for placement. "You don't have any of your children with you. Why would the courts send Madisen back here?"

The question hung in the air for a moment before Didi made an unsteady proposal: "Madisen can stay here with me and my boyfriend."

Her caseworker explained that she would need to talk with William first. They would need to get his fingerprints and run a criminal background check. She would also need to verify that she was employed and could care for Madisen. Didi would also need to complete a case plan of court requirements before reunification was considered. The case managers overseeing these plans describe their work as tracking the parent/caregiver's progress toward the case plan goals; that is not how most parents experience the process. Like many social services in the United States, case plans suggest support and reunification, but case management services are often viewed as rehabilitative, with heavy oversight and surveillance.

The case plan tasks focus on improving parental decisions and behavior. They are designed to assess any psychological deficits or problems through counseling and psychological evaluations. Although case plans include services that could meet family needs, there isn't consistent and intentional collaboration with parents to create a meaningful process that addresses the root causes of the issues. Despite the various paths of causality, when it comes to child abuse, the system generally places culpability on the parents. It is an undeniable fact that some parents willfully and brutally harm their children. Knowing that is not very helpful or useful within child protective services, where the overwhelming majority of child maltreatment cases are due to issues of *neglect*.

The court created identical case plans for Erica and Didi.

ERICA GAINES'S AND DIEDRE LAWSON'S CASE PLAN TASKS

- The parent/caregiver is ordered to complete parenting classes and demonstrate that the child is physically safe while in her care.

- The parent/caregiver is ordered to accept and act upon a referral to receive a psychological evaluation and follow through on any and all recommendations for further treatment.

- The parent/caregiver is ordered to attend anger management classes.

- The parent/caregiver is ordered to have six sessions of therapy with a community provider.

- The parent/caregiver is ordered to cooperate with the social worker, accepting and acting on all referrals for further services, meeting regularly and appraising the worker of any change in circumstances, housing, employment, therapy, etc.

- The parent/caregiver is ordered to undergo a bonding assessment with children to determine the quality of the relationship.

- The parent/caregiver is ordered to obtain and maintain a stable and suitable residence for herself and her children.

"I'm not doing any of that," Didi replied to the caseworker. "I never abused Madisen. Why does it feel like I'm being punished?"

"Since you've been absent from Madisen's life, your behavior is being viewed as abandonment. If you want Madisen to come back here, you're going to have to do what they ask." The caseworker was glib and uninterested. "I'll be back next week to see if you've made any progress with these tasks." And then she left.

Giving identical case plan tasks to Erica and Didi was counterintuitive to any true desire to help these mothers. Meaningful CPS case plans have to be customized to the parent, the child, and their particular situation. These two women faced different challenges; any plan that aimed to help them should've reflected their unique needs. But when there is an underlying assumption that *parents are the problem*, then assigning generic tasks becomes the modus operandi. The CPS system envelops parents into a binary with an anonymous label: *Abuser*. Some of the ways that this has become an acceptable, conventional practice dates back to the formulation of Mothers Anonymous (MA), founded in 1969.[1] MA became Parents Anonymous in 1970, a well-known child abuse prevention support group that popularized a misplaced response to child neglect and abuse. The goal of Parents Anonymous was to downplay any external social factors that could be at play when it came to child abuse and maltreatment. The founder, Jolly K, was likely well-intentioned and wanted to provide a safe and rehabilitative space for troubled parents. Jolly K was a young white woman who widely shared her personal experience of physically abusing her seven-year-old daughter. Jolly K believed that she and she alone was responsible for her behavior, saying that she "could not help herself." This rhetoric found its way into child welfare policy, the Child Abuse Prevention and Treatment Act of 1974 (CAPTA),[2] which endorsed Parents Anonymous and catapulted its growth. CAPTA is known as the foundation and cornerstone of the child welfare system and is highly pervasive in most of the system's operations. It has undoubtedly affected the public's view of parents over the past fifty years and made way for a focus on fixing individuals instead of exploring and addressing structural disadvantages.

Not only did CAPTA affect the view of parents, but it also created a reporting system that we have come to rely on. Mandated reporting requires that certain professionals are bound by law to report parents for suspected abuse and neglect. This policy largely pays for investigations and foster care, as opposed to paying for direct support to families who are being reported. An illusion evolved from Jolly K's experience: child abuse only occurs in families with troubled parents. The emphasis was placed on the parents' lack of growth, and the response centered on cookie-cutter, one-size-fits-all services. Jolly K emphasized that if parents worked hard at personal development and self-fulfillment, their abusive nature would cease.

The growing perception of "bad parents" led to the case planning process. Statutes may claim that court-ordered case plans were not an admission of guilt, but they certainly functioned that way. Case plans are rehabilitative in nature. They include tasks that a parent is required to complete in order to "improve themselves and their circumstances" before they can get their children back. I have observed and facilitated case planning for many parents and never thought about the legitimacy (or efficacy) of those requirements until they were mandated for Erica. At face value, the tasks seemed reasonable, but after Erica, I realized how presumptuous and generic they are.

Parents and caregivers are generally given twelve to fifteen months to complete their requirements. During that period, their time is not their own and is often usurped by the needs and requirements of their court-mandated case plan. Erica's only goal was to get Madisen back, so she immediately made appointments to complete her requirements. She found a therapist and began counseling and then got connected to a psychologist for a psychological evaluation. She had five weeks of parenting classes to attend, and she had to secure a bonding evaluation/

assessment for her and Madisen. She also had to do this during the holiday season.

Erica had to pay for these services out of her own pocket. Since she was not biologically related to Madisen, she did not qualify for any sort of subsidies. Despite the financial costs and poor timing, she was done within eight weeks. This was the fastest I had ever seen anyone do it. Depending on what the programs are, sometimes even biological parents are responsible for paying for their completion. Black women in particular were bewildered with the amount of time and money it took to complete the tasks, Erica included. Parenting classes are standard for case plans, and these being mandatory is problematic for many reasons. One being that they are often informed by heteronormative societal lenses. Also, it doesn't allow for partnering with parents in order to find out the root cause of the issue.

Erica's situation made me realize that every problem is not a parenting problem. To many people, including me, Erica was an excellent parent. There was also the dreaded psychological evaluation—another mandatory part of the compliance process that determines whether parents are mentally apt. In many cases, the results of parents' psychological assessments were likely coupled with the trauma inflicted by the CPS process, yet this wouldn't necessarily be considered or brought up in the evaluation itself. The psychologists and counselors who are completing the assessments are usually contracted through CPS, which could blur many lines. Everything that Erica and Didi were "ordered" to do was at the discretion of CPS workers, who carried out a set of standardized processes rather than working *with* parents on what *their* needs were so they and their children could be supported.

• • •

The week leading up to the Christmas holiday was pretty quiet. Everyone at my office learned not to relish it too much because at any moment an influx of cases could change the day. Christmas gifts lined the floors of our cubicles instead of the backpacks from the beginning of the school year. For the past month, gifts were donated and collected for foster children. This year some of these presents would go to Madisen.

Holidays were big for Erica and her family, but this holiday season, she was filled with angst and loneliness. Her parents and siblings gathered in Jacksonville for Christmas. Erica's family, nuclear and extended, knew that she had been caring for Madisen for the last few months. They knew of Didi's absence and Jeffrey's arrest. But how could she tell them that she had lost custody of Madisen due to child abuse? Her parents were aware of what was going on, but she wasn't sure if her other family members knew. With so many thoughts and emotions swirling in her mind, she couldn't bring herself to leave Madisen in Tallahassee without trying to spend Christmas with her.

On Christmas afternoon, Erica made her way over to the foster home with a bag filled with gifts. She'd bought as much as possible to try and make this day extra special. When she arrived at the house, cars lined the street. Ms. Lisbon had said that her family would be joining her for their holiday celebration. Erica's excitement to see Madisen deflated. How much would Ms. Lisbon's family know about her? She was already labeled by the state as an abuser. Would that label follow her everywhere she went? In the weeks since everything happened, Erica tried to go about her life not thinking, but doing. She went to work and school like usual, but she also fulfilled her case plan; her checking account dwindled from the costs of each action item. She was stressed in a new way, beyond carrying the weight of letting Madisen down. Erica wondered if this scarlet letter would ever fade.

Ms. Lisbon was polite as always as she invited Erica inside. The house was bustling with people. Erica fidgeted in place near the front door. Ms. Lisbon went toward the back of her home to gather Madisen, who was playing in the bedroom. Everyone wore festive clothing and talked loudly to one another while holding plates of food. Erica smiled politely to the folks sitting in the living room and thought of her own family, who were likely doing the same in Jacksonville. When Ms. Lisbon returned, Madisen appeared wearing a black dress with a red ribbon across the middle. She jumped into Erica's arms and squealed with excitement.

Erica was always on the verge of tears whenever she saw Madisen now. She had perfected the practice of blinking them back. "Merry Christmas, baby girl! I brought you some gifts."

"Gigi, thank you for my gifts, but we can't open them until after dinner." Madisen looked over at Ms. Lisbon who nodded in affirmation.

"Okay. Well, maybe we can spend a little time together?"

"Gigi, I really want to play with my sisters! Can you come back another time?" She hugged Erica and then took off toward the bedroom. Her sisters? After a moment, Ms. Lisbon walked Erica back outside. She explained that it was important to integrate the foster children within her own family, so Madisen had started to call Ms. Lisbon's children her sisters.

"I'll put your gifts under the tree and make sure she opens them later."

Madisen was always a social child. She loved interacting with other children. Erica knew she was thrilled to be in a home with other kids. This was what she'd been missing with her own brothers and sisters: playmates and family that extended beyond Erica. Erica tried not to take this personally, but she felt dejected. Madisen was just a child who was currently distracted by toys and Christmas activities, but Erica could not help how hurt she felt. These feelings always led her back to her anthem of hate for CPS. They had orchestrated this entire scenario—a scenario where she stayed in town so that Madisen did not feel that she was alone, but in actuality, Madisen wasn't alone. Erica was.

CHAPTER 14

THE WILL TO CHANGE
2009–2010

I HAD NOT SEEN MY SISTER RACHEL SINCE EVERYTHING HAP-pened, but I knew I would see her at home for Christmas. It's a four-hour drive from Tallahassee to my hometown, and I was actively trying not to think about my CPS cases as I made my way south. My only plan for the holidays was to rest as much as possible. That year (2009) Christmas fell on a Friday, so I'd be home just for the weekend and then I'd head back to Tallahassee on Sunday.

All weekend I couldn't help but consider what the holidays must be like for parents who have children in foster care. Erica had called me and explained what happened with Ms. Lisbon and Madisen. She was sad and angry, but mostly sad. Madisen had melded with Ms. Lisbon's family, and it seemed that there was no room for Erica. When your child is in foster care, Christmas must feel like some sort of hollow event. It's not the same for everyone, but most people center their holiday celebrations on family and children. My family certainly did.

At Christmas that year, as always, my mom cooked a delicious meal, and I sat watching my nieces and nephews tear open their gifts. They were thrilled, happy—safe. My sister and I did not speak of CPS; that would likely forever be taboo. The weekend was a reminder for me that children deserve to be in a place where they truly belong. It also wasn't lost on me that had CPS taken the kids into custody three months earlier, that holiday would have been drastically different, and the relationship between my sister and me would have likely never recovered.

• • •

After the new year, another slew of my colleagues resigned. Two of them were Patrick and Sandra, our friends from our training class. They had confided in Katrina and me about potentially quitting, so it was less of a shock and more of a sucker punch, because I enjoyed working with them. But the pressure from this job affects each person differently.

Sandra had two daughters, six and eight, and although she had co-parenting support from their father, she was growing tired of being the "absent parent." She regularly missed school and athletic events because she would need to work a CPS case. She also brought work home, so even when she was with her children, she was preoccupied. Her children were beginning to find her unreliable; they preferred that their father attend events because they assumed their mother would miss the event due to work.

Patrick was newly married and had a new baby. The desire to be present with his wife and their child was always at odds with CPS responsibilities. Patrick and I were having a conversation one day at work about the mounting stress. He had already been hinting at some marital strife. He shared that his wife was overwhelmed and resentful. He told me that he needed to focus on his family, and this job would not let him.

During that time, I had heard other complaints around the office. Corners of our little cubicles became nooks, safe places to vent with your most trusted colleagues. We had all been inundated with home visits, pressing deadlines, and heightened pressure to handle every new case with efficiency. It was late one evening when I overheard a colleague say: "I don't feel like chasing this parent tonight. She's never home. I don't want to drive all the way down Woodville Highway, and she will probably not even be there. I'm just going to write down that I did the visit, and then I'm going home."

This was such a stunning thing to me. This is known as "falsifying records," and although it was apparently a common practice,[1] I had never known anyone who did it, or would even mention it. It's not only a third-degree felony, which could result in criminal charges,[2] but it's also an incredibly dangerous practice. The work was unrelenting and the concept of falsification may be tantalizing, but it was also terrifying. Some child welfare professionals resort to fabricating their case notes in order to get everything done. Unlike them, I just sacrificed all else and ran myself into the ground to get everything done. What's worse?

"And then there were two," Katrina joked about Sandra and Patrick leaving our foursome. On Sandra's and Patrick's last day, the four of us met at TGI Friday's, a place where we had shared so many meals.

As was typical, their departure also exacerbated the stress of caseloads in the office. The departing staff's cases still need to be tended to; they are redistributed evenly among those left behind. From that wave of resignations, I received ten cases, which felt like an avalanche. These cases were not brand-new, so that did take away the initial pressure to commence and interview the family members. But catching up on each of the cases and figuring out what to do to bring them to closure was not an easy feat. Some days I wanted to tell our supervisor, LeAnn, that I needed help. With the staff shortage, LeAnn had decided to take on cases of her own. This was not the usual practice of a supervisor. Usually, supervisors provide direction and advice on their teams' cases, as opposed to carrying their own. Some days I wanted to confide in Lydia that I was overwhelmed, but like the rest of us, she was drowning too. Watching everyone around me barely hanging on made me wonder how long child welfare could maintain this dynamic.

Some of the hectic parts of the job were unavoidable, but some of it was due to functioning in archaic ways and an unwillingness to change.

During this time, I internalized the multi-meaning of carrying cases. As investigators and caseworkers, we carry cases physically. Some days we are literally holding the cases in our hands as we drive around the city. But there are multiple ways that we are carrying cases. And I believe that for the most part, we carry them morally, emotionally, and psychologically. As CPS workers, when we say that our caseloads are too large or unmanageable, the caseloads are heavy in various ways. Katrina and I started to discuss this in terms of "moral math." The cases became unmanageable—unbearable—because I did not see clearly how my presence was adding to the child's or their family's well-being or safety. CPS seemed to only manipulate, divide, or subtract. This realization added to my moral angst. And what came next for Erica showed me just how much CPS could derail a life.

On a sunny but very windy day in February, I got a call from Erica. I was standing outside of a house to make a home visit. I had ignored her first call, but she called right back.

"Hey, I'm working," I said, instead of hello.

She was crying and her voice was shaking. "I am being charged with *felony child abuse, cruelty towards a child*. There's been a warrant issued for my arrest."

Her words were muffled by tears, but I heard them. The phrase "cruelty towards a child" seemed incomprehensible. She could never be cruel to anyone, especially not Madisen. She asked me to come over; I quickly ended the call and walked up to the house to meet the family from my case.

A few hours later, I arrived at her apartment. Although Florida is notorious for short winters, or no winters at all, it was a fairly cold (low forties) night in Tallahassee. I pulled on my jacket as I walked over to the front door. Erica reached out to embrace me the moment I came through the door. Her eyes were red and her face flushed from crying.

I don't think I had ever seen someone so visibly despondent and de-moralized. Her parents and siblings were seated on the large sectional and regarded me solemnly.

What words of support could I possibly offer? Frozen in the gravity of the moment, I sat vigil with the rest of the family, while Erica showered and prepared herself for jail.

"If she were white, you know this would not have gone down like this!"

"She never meant to hurt Madisen; don't they see that?"

"Are they also going to arrest Didi? Isn't abandonment a crime too?"

I listened, mostly nodding quietly, as Erica's family swapped hypotheses and lamentations about this ordeal. After a few more minutes, we all went out to our cars. Erica rode with her family while I trailed them, driving alone over to the Leon County Jail. I was tired and my chest felt tight. And I still had more notes to type up for work.

We parked our cars and began walking toward the entrance of the jail. The industrial building sat behind high fences, and several police cars took up the limited parking spaces. We knew we needed to be here for Erica, and yet this was a hard moment to watch. Before long, a law enforcement officer walked over to meet us.

"My daughter is here to turn herself in," Erica's father, Pastor Gaines, spoke up.

"Name?" the officer asked as he pulled out his handcuffs.

"Erica Gaines," her mother answered. Erica didn't say a word, as if she was conserving her energy to withstand all that she was about to encounter.

"Do you have to handcuff her?" Erica's father asked as the officer locked them onto her wrists. With her arms latched behind her back, her shoulders slumped forward. Her parents hugged her tightly even though she couldn't reciprocate. She laid her head on her mother's shoulder and cried. When her mother released her, it was my turn. I walked over to say goodbye.

"Madisen has always been everything to me. I did not mean for any of this to happen," Erica said. I gave her a quick hug and said softly, "I know."

But as I stood there watching her escorted into the jail, I felt conflicted and confused; I wasn't sure what I knew.

Inside the jail, the police officer behind the glass shield gathered information from Erica and pulled together paperwork. Erica stood lifelessly still for her mug shot, an image that she feared would haunt her forever. Then, she was placed in a holding cell with a few others. The sound of the bolt slamming shut drove the point home—she was in jail. And even though she looked around the cell at other people chatting and pacing, she felt entirely alone.

Erica had not been sleeping well, and it was catching up to her, but she had doubted she would sleep that night. She was eventually permitted to call her parents. Their discussion was focused on the upcoming hearing, the judge setting bail and working with a bondsman to get Erica out. But the reality was, she would be there through the night. Erica's emotions were going from guilt, to regret, to anger, but always came back to sadness.

She regretted telling the truth. Should she have said that she had no idea how Madisen got the marks? A clean past with no CPS or criminal involvement was not enough. Trying to help Didi was not enough. Soliciting help early was not enough. Leaning on family and friends to help with Madisen wasn't enough. The veracity of her statements to CPS ended up hurting her in the end. She showed up for every visitation, every court hearing, every meeting, but none of it was enough. She completed everything asked of her from the courts, yet she was still sitting in jail.

Erica's hearing was the next morning. I made my way over to the courthouse before I headed in to work. Erica's parents; her attorney, Deborah; her roommate, Shannon; and I filed into the courtroom. Erica wasn't there. We were told that she would attend virtually from the jail. I had not slept much the night before. And by the looks of Erica as she appeared on the screen, neither had she. She was standing in full view wearing an orange jumpsuit. Her hands were cuffed in front of her. This hearing was known as a defendant's first appearance. This is when the defendant learns more about the charges against them, and a decision is made about bail. I had been to many hearings for my CPS cases, but never one for criminal proceedings. We were all anxious, and desperate to get Erica out. We talked about pitching in money and asking family and friends for help if necessary. I would have given anything to overcome my feelings of helplessness. The bail amount was set at $10,000. Her parents began working to get it sorted out. I was thankful that she was leaving jail that day, but no one was confident that she would not return. It would take several hours to process her release; her attorney was there to help with handling the logistics. I said goodbye to Erica's family and headed out to work.

• • •

A couple of weeks following Erica's arrest and her release, I woke up from a nightmare in a full-on panic attack. It was the first one I had ever experienced, so it terrified me. It went on for so long that I ended up passing out. When I woke up, I was inside the back of an ambulance. I realized that we were not moving, and the truck was parked in my apartment community. Lights were bright, two paramedics were sitting to my left, and to my right was Erica. This horrible CPS process had undeniably created tension and distance, but she was there. And as I peered out the open back door of the ambulance, I saw Katrina. Katrina's hair was wrapped up in the way she does before bed, and I realized it was the middle of the night. I had a cannula in my nose; it wrapped around my ears, and oxygen flowed through the device. A blood pressure band was wrapped around my arm, and one paramedic studied my vitals and the other spoke to me.

"We think you had a panic attack," the paramedic explained. "Do you have a history of anxiety? Are you in any pain?" I answered him as best I could by shaking my head or nodding my head. Yes, I had been experiencing anxiety. Yes, I was stressed with work. No, I'm not in pain. No, I don't want to go to the hospital. I was embarrassed, confused, and more tired than I'd ever been. I knew I had been under stress, but clearly much more was weighing on me than the day-to-day pressure of the job itself. That night I slept over at Katrina's apartment, at her request—I didn't have the energy to protest. Later, I was told that in the middle of my panic attack I had called Katrina, which started the sequence of events that led to the paramedics arriving.

I stayed home from work for the next week, and Lydia handled my cases for me. I was put in touch with a therapist who recommended medication to help with panic attacks. The moment I stepped back into the office, I heard the familiar sounds of everyone trying to get through the workday. I was hoping no one knew about my panic attack, but I couldn't be sure. I started to wonder if I was helping to keep anyone safe at all in my work. I couldn't even keep myself safe. I couldn't help Erica and I couldn't help Madisen, who was still in foster care. I was a week out from that terrifying panic attack when Shelley handed me a new case. At that moment, I knew I would leave that job.

CHAPTER 15

A LITTLE LIFE

2018–2019

JATOIA'S AND LAWRENCE'S ARREST CAME ALMOST A YEAR AFTER they took Kenny into the hospital emergency room. Jatoia didn't know what was worse, getting arrested right away or this delayed destruction of their lives. The yearlong paranoia, with a detective always in the wings, watching. Months passed and hope settled in, but then in an instant, their freedom was taken away. They took mug shots that will never leave the system, never disappear from the internet. A mug shot is a photo of your lowest moment for all the world to see.

Jatoia's bail was set at $250,000. She was a first-time offender, and the multiple injustices began to collide. In 2018, only 50 percent of defendants were able to post bail even when bail was set at $5,000 or less.[1] Jatoia wanted to believe that her family could figure out the bail through some sort of bail bond service, but she knew that amount was staggering for the financial situation of her family. Meanwhile, Lawrence and Jatoia were both offered a choice. They could go to trial to determine their innocence or plead guilty and receive four years of active jail time.

"I will not say that I am guilty of something that I know that I did not do," Jatoia told the attorney. "I will not become a felon just because it makes someone's job easier. They need to find out what really happened instead of asking me to take the blame." Lawrence and Jatoia maintained their innocence and were detained to await trial.

Jatoia Potts surveyed the pod; it was an open area surrounded by inmate cells. What could she do today to help pass the time? She knew she had to stay busy or she would not survive. She had signed up to take every class they offered, even sitting in on drug treatment programs, though she never used drugs.

"I just need to get out of that pod," she said, when her fellow inmates asked her why she joined them in drug treatment.

She also volunteered to help tutor inmates who were working on their GED. She had a bachelor's degree, and she was really pleased to help others who needed it. She offered to do the laundry for the pod. She washed, dried, and folded all the garments and then passed them out to each inmate. That took a lot of time, and that's what Jatoia needed. She needed to pass the time.

The only thing she had to look forward to was a visit from her oldest son, LJ. They wouldn't allow Kenny to see her since he was designated as the victim, but LJ could come. Knowing that she would see him each week gave Jatoia the strength to push through each day. Visitation was in a waiting room, filled with other people, and she and LJ had to talk to each other over the phone, through a glass partition. LJ was confused by the environment and became distressed at the end of the visits. Jatoia wanted him to continue visiting because he was the balm to the bitter existence back in her pod. But, for her son's sake, she knew she needed to stop visitation. She told her new CPS social worker, a Black woman named Valerie, that she didn't want LJ to come back to the jail for visits. She told Valerie that she would start visitation as soon as she was released from jail, which Jatoia hoped would be soon. The social worker wanted to make sure that Jatoia was aware of what she was asking.

"You're asking me to suspend your visitation?" Valerie wasn't accustomed to parents requesting this. If anything, parents rallied for more visitation. Even those in jail.

"Yes. It's just too much for him. I'm going to ask my family to send you photos you can show LJ, just so he will continue to see us." Valerie agreed to show LJ the photos.

As the days went on, Jatoia still advocated for her children to be placed with a family member. She made as many calls as she was allowed. She wrote letters and took visits from her family members. She spent their visitation time strategizing about potential placements for the children. Eventually, the CPS department initiated an Interstate Compact on the Placement of Children (ICPC) for each of Jatoia's children.[2] This law was enacted in fifty states. It provides for the protection of children who are placed across state lines.

The first ICPC was initiated with regard to the children's paternal grandfather, Samuel Adelson, Lawrence's father. He and his wife lived in Florida. Although the ICPC was approved, there were ongoing concerns about the grandparents' ability to protect the children from Lawrence. They would have to maintain supervised visitations, and there was some concern about how they would address Kenny's complex medical needs. The system did not consider that LJ had lived with his grandfather for several months while his family was residing in Florida or that they currently lived in Jacksonville, minutes from one of the most prestigious hospitals in the country, the Mayo Clinic.

There was also an ICPC done for consideration of placement with the paternal grandmother, but it was denied due to her criminal history (though nonviolent in nature). The next ICPC was done for Jatoia's grandfather, the children's great-grandfather. It was denied based on his perceived limited capacity to care for the children. An additional ICPC was initiated for a placement with Jatoia's maternal aunt, who was willing to move to Durham and care for the children. Her aunt would need to have a place to stay, so Jatoia suggested that she and Lawrence could give their aunt their apartment so she could care for the children. They would likely never live there together again. She was approved as a caregiver but the placement was denied by CPS due to ongoing concerns about the extended family's willingness to protect the children from Jatoia and Lawrence. CPS believed that because of Lawrence's previous aggression toward Jatoia's mother and stepfather, what would stop him from intimidating other kinship/family caregivers?

After a few weeks in jail, Jatoia's disappointment grew as each and every placement was denied. She struggled to maintain hope. She went through her days in a blur, doing exactly what was asked of her, but nothing more and nothing less. She was eventually placed in a single cell that had a firm metal bed and a toilet near the entrance. She was glad to be alone.

Her family continued to work on the bail situation, gathering donations and saving all the money they could to try to get her out. Her grandparents in Georgia regularly sent money to the jail so that she had money in her account to purchase feminine products, meals, and medicine if she needed it. The endless noise of the jail made Jatoia long for quiet. She developed a constant headache from the anxiety, and she couldn't shake it. Her emotions were erratic. Some days she was sad and exhausted, and spent time hiding the steady flow of tears. Other days she was so antsy she became obsessive about getting extra phone time to try to get things done for her case. And then there were angry days. These days she spent wallowing in her abject hatred of child protective services. With each passing day, she was losing more and more of her life. She had no job, no home, and she was facing up to twenty years in prison. She was grieving—her life and her emotions emanated from something deep inside her. Some days the grief was tangible, something she could touch and manipulate into hope and positivity. But when her grief ran deep, she couldn't connect to it or comprehend it. On these days she could barely lift her head.

• • •

After nine months of jail time, Jatoia and Lawrence were released to await their trial. Their pretrial release required them to wear an ankle bracelet for monitoring. Almost immediately, Jatoia pursued visitation with LJ. She was still not allowed to see Kenny due to the pending criminal charges. Months had passed since she had stopped the jail visitation with LJ. She felt nervous. But, seeing each other again was such a sweet reunion. On their first visit, LJ flew into his mother's arms. She held him for several minutes, until he finally wiggled free. They played together and talked. Jatoia kept hugging him. She was proud of how much he had grown, but she also felt cheated. Her sons were growing up without her.

After a few weeks of visits, LJ's foster parents reported that his behavior was becoming problematic. These episodes of poor behavior correlated with his visits with Jatoia. He was acting out in daycare—responding aggressively to the other children. His teachers sent daily notes home to his foster parents. LJ was very emotional in school. He had difficulty listening and following instructions. He hit other children and intentionally broke toys. He also started to choke a teddy bear at school and yelled at it, calling the stuffed animal "stupid." Some days LJ would cry and remain inconsolable for up to thirty minutes. When Jatoia heard about these behaviors from the social worker, she became worried. At their next visitation, she thought of her parent-coaching with Carol and initiated a discussion.

"LJ, what's going on in daycare?"

LJ didn't answer, but Jatoia could tell that he knew what she was talking about. She could tell from the look in his eyes.

"Did you break a toy? Did you hurt one of your toys?" she pressed him.

"Mommy, I was just playing around," he answered softly.

"Mommy wants you to try to play nicer with your toys. Some things are just not appropriate." She picked up a teddy bear from the pile of toys in the visitation room. She hugged it. "See? You need to be nice to it, hug it, and take good care of it."

Jatoia felt good about their talk. She was hoping it would help. But at the end of the visit, LJ erupted into tears and thrashed as the social worker carried him out to her car. Over the next few weeks, LJ's troubling behavior continued. When he visited his mother, the visits went well. He reacted positively to spending time with Jatoia. But at the end of the visit, he was distraught, and that mood and behavior stayed with him back at home with his foster parents and in school the next day. Jatoia tried to soothe him at the end of each visit. She reassured him that she would be back to see him the very next week.

Jatoia sensed that they were connecting his behavior to their visits. She understood the connection. By spending time with her, LJ realized their separation on some deeper level. But it wasn't fair to blame this on her. The behavior was not typical for LJ. All of their visits were supervised, and Jatoia knew she wasn't doing anything to instigate LJ's outbursts. She was also absolutely sure that LJ had never seen any violence between her and Lawrence. She wasn't aware of how the visits were going with Lawrence. They had separate visitation now. But his visits were also supervised. As LJ's bad behavior continued, the director of his daycare wrote a letter to the social worker outlining the challenges. In the letter, she made a point to include that none of those behaviors were occurring prior to him restarting visitation with his parents. After seeing the director's report, the caseworker sought clarity on the CPS permanency plan. If CPS was planning to reunify these children with their parents, then they should continue with the visitation as scheduled. But, if reunification was not the plan, then these visits were disruptive for LJ and the foster family and should be suspended. In the next permanency hearing, CPS stated that due to Jatoia's and Lawrence's pending criminal charges and the bond that had been established between the foster parents and the children, reunification was no longer the permanency plan. A month later, in September 2019, visitation was suspended, indefinitely.

Jatoia had already missed so much with her children. Now the system was taking away the one-hour weekly supervised visit. When they were arrested and jailed, Jatoia and Lawrence had lost their apartment, their car, and the business they had built. Jatoia was bartending during this period after her release and trying to save as much as possible. She needed help. She was currently living with a friend, and she tried to save to get her own place and her own car. She was required by the courts to pay child support to CPS, and although she tried, she wasn't always able to make the monthly payments. Rebuilding her life from scratch was challenging, and with this ongoing CPS battle it felt impossible. So, Jatoia decided to begin a GoFundMe account online where she outlined her story and asked for donations. There was collective outrage at what her family was going through, and the story was shared widely. Soon, she was invited to share her story at community events around Durham.

"I lost everything, and all I had to look forward to was seeing my son once per week. Then they stopped letting me visit him. It's starting to feel like a sick game, where they are doing everything they can to break me," Jatoia said at a community event in Durham.

It had been a year since she had last seen Kenny, and every day that went by, she knew that she was missing the little things that really matter in a child's life—her child's life. She continued to find support in the community.

"I'm missing very important parts of my children's lives and it hurts," Jatoia said. "I never saw Kenny take his first steps. I never heard his first words. The social worker told me that his foster parents recently gave him his first haircut, and I felt robbed. It seems small, but I wanted to be a part of that. I miss my little family. I miss our little life."

Jatoia was now on her fourth caseworker with CPS, another Black woman, who slowed this process down just by having to catch up. "I know they are playing catch-up, but these are my children's lives." She tried to be understanding when the new caseworker asked questions that she had answered many times before. When someone asked Jatoia about legal representation, she was honest: she never felt like her court-appointed attorney was in her corner and fighting for her family.

Her attorney regularly said things like: *We don't do that in this court.* Or: *This is just the way things are.* The CPS attorneys that are assigned to parents are the equivalent of public defenders in the criminal justice system. They have long lists of parents who they represent, and they stand around the courtroom all day, running through their docket. In her attorney's defense, they probably had no time to challenge CPS. There was no time to research how best to advocate for Jatoia's rights. This was also the reality for many other parents who were relying on court-appointed attorneys to proceed in their family's best interests.

Through the new connections Jatoia was making, she was soon introduced to an attorney, Elizabeth Simpson, who worked for Emancipate NC. Emancipate NC is an organization that focuses on dismantling structural racism and mass incarceration across North Carolina. They do this revolutionary work by engaging in community education, advocacy, and litigation. This organization would not require Jatoia to cover the costs of legal representation. Elizabeth agreed to observe Jatoia's next child welfare hearing, review the available documentation, and then decide if she could take the case. The hearing she observed was held in December 2019. Following that hearing, she was certain that she could provide more comprehensive counsel. Jatoia sent an email to her current attorney requesting this change, and Elizabeth aptly stepped into the process.

• • •

Elizabeth brought a perspective of justice to this case that was lacking. She was not afraid to disrupt the status quo in the child dependency court proceedings. The magnitude of the injustices of this case stunned Elizabeth.

"The impunity of the CPS system is appalling," Elizabeth said as she combed through Jatoia's case, piece by piece.

Working with Elizabeth exposed Jatoia to legal representation that actually tried to fight on a person's behalf. While Elizabeth began to work on the case, Jatoia continued seeing her therapist. Through therapy she realized that the circumstances surrounding Kenny's birth had made more of an impact on her than she understood at the time. Jatoia was a "helicopter mom." She breastfed LJ for much longer than most do, and she kept him at home with her since her work schedule was flexible. She spent most of her adult life thinking of everyone except herself. And she had many needs that went unmet. It took her too long to realize that she had needs too.

In therapy, she learned about postpartum depression. Depressed mood, crying spells, and withdrawal from family and social events were symptoms she experienced. Jatoia thought back to when Kenny came home, and how she just preferred to stay in with him. This feeling of withdrawal was so strong that she skipped Thanksgiving with her family. She was also able to discuss her relationship with Lawrence. Her therapist helped her to see that domestic violence isn't always physical. Although the day in the car was the first time Lawrence was physical with her, in therapy Jatoia noted the times where he was not just verbally aggressive, but controlling and manipulative.

When Jatoia was a child, she was sexually abused by a family member. She talked about it with her therapist, explaining that because she was violated at such a young age, she developed a distrust of men. In college she briefly dated a few people, but Lawrence was her first real boyfriend. Once she started dating him, she feared that she would not be able to find someone else she could trust. She was honest with her therapist about how much she still loved Lawrence, but she knew that she needed to distance herself and focus on getting her children back. Not only were Lawrence and she both facing criminal charges for felony child abuse, but Lawrence was also dealing with the domestic violence and strangulation charges.

Elizabeth asked Jatoia to consider initiating a no contact order against Lawrence. CPS had begun a narrative about Jatoia's capacity and willingness to protect her children from future domestic violence incidents. She knew that Lawrence would be hurt by this court order, but she also knew that she needed to make decisions that were in the best interests of her children.

As the holidays neared, Jatoia wanted to get the boys a few gifts for Christmas. She saved up to buy them some toys and a few pieces of clothing. Jatoia had to ask the social worker what her children's exact sizes were. Once she had the items chosen, and wrapped, she gave them to the social worker to take over to the foster home. This was the third consecutive Christmas without her family fully intact and at home. The first, they were all in a hospital with Kenny; the second, Jatoia was in jail; and now she was trying hard to have a presence in their lives, even though she had been completely shut out.

The year 2020 was approaching, a year that will always hold much grief for the world due to the coronavirus pandemic. But the pandemic was only one of many painful things for Jatoia. In 2020, her mother would die, she would find out the truth about how Kenny was injured, and the state would prepare to terminate her parental rights, clearing her boys for adoption.

CHAPTER 16

THE IMPOSSIBLE IMPERATIVE

2010

ARE YOU REALLY LEAVING ME WITH THESE CLOWNS?!" KATRINA texted me. I wasn't sure which clowns she was referring to, but I responded with: "YES!!"

"Another one bites the dust," was her reply.

After I told LeAnn about my resignation, I became laser focused on making sure that all of my cases were closed before I left. I knew how it felt to inherit cases when someone abruptly leaves. I wanted to do my best to close them all. It felt feasible since Shelley had me removed from rotation, so I had no incoming cases. What a novel idea. When the influx of cases slows down, a person has time to truly engage with families and find resolutions.

I was also preparing for another stint at school. I had applied to Howard University to pursue a PhD in social work. For my application, I had to articulate my research priorities. This turned out to be the easiest thing I'd done in a while. I wanted to research the child welfare workforce, to take a deeper look into how organizational culture affects turnover and retention. I was also curious about what goes into decision-making on child abuse cases and how the supervisory relationship affected certain decisions. In short, I wanted to learn everything I could about the inner workings—the machinery—of the CPS system. I needed to better understand what I had been through, and I knew that I could come to terms with some of what I was feeling about my experience by diving deeply into the culture of a system within which I had lost some part of myself.

Considering how much I relied on LeAnn and Lydia to guide and mentor me through my time at CPS, this was an interesting avenue for me. I wasn't even sure if a professional market existed for what I wanted to study, but I was genuinely curious about it. I had recently been instructed by a mentor to follow my curiosity, not necessarily my passion. When I became a CPS investigator, I was taking advantage of an opportunity that fit my education and training. My internship gave me the experiential learning that prepared me for the work. But it ultimately felt impossible,[1] and after doing the work, I was curious how someone could conduct child protective investigations while maintaining some sense of their own morality and wellness.[2]

As I prepared to close out my cases, I thought of Erica and Madisen. It made me sad that my friendship with Erica had become what it had. I understood the madness of what CPS had done to her life, but I didn't understand how our friendship had been dissolved in the process. We talked, but it always felt like something still needed to be said. That feeling percolated beneath every conversation we had. For a long time, I was conflicted about the spanking because I was opposed to it as a disciplinary practice. I blamed her just like the system had. My silence on this issue must have felt like friendly fire to Erica. But I didn't blame her anymore. There were other alternatives to placing Madisen in foster care and throwing Erica into jail, and I had always known that. I just never knew how to reconcile the requirements of my job with the impact of my job, until I saw how it devastated Erica. CPS comes between mothers and children, tears apart friendships, and drives wedges of mistrust between siblings. My own sister's case has since been closed, but the rift remains open.

It isn't fair to condemn parents based on a short scene in a very long movie. But that's what CPS does—by design. They receive a report describing a scene, and then opt out of viewing the entire movie. But I had seen the movie of Madisen's life. I saw all the sacrifices Erica made for Madisen. And beyond those sacrifices, I saw how deeply she cared for Madisen. The scene of Erica trying to discipline Madisen was a narrow, oversimplified view of a complex and desperate moment.

On a Sunday in late April 2010, after nearly seven months of Madisen being in foster care, Erica was now allowed by the courts to engage in unsupervised visits. Madisen was permitted to spend the entire weekend with Erica, and she called me to meet them at the park. I had not seen Madisen since I left her sprawled on her foster mother's floor, months earlier, so I was looking forward to it.

The last couple of months for Erica consisted of working with her lawyer on trying to sort out the criminal case that hung over her head. She was sure that after she was arrested, there was no chance CPS would consider her as an appropriate placement for Madisen. But for once in this case, Erica got lucky. The erratic nature of CPS decision-making made the once vilified Erica their only viable option. After several bonding assessments where a psychologist observed Erica and Madisen for hours across multiple visits, it was determined that their bond was as strong as ever.

We had not spoken much since the night of my panic attack, but I let Erica know that I was resigning from my job. She understood. She was excited for me to pursue a different avenue of child welfare.

At the park, Madisen hugged me with fervor. The pomade in her hair glistened in the sun. Her braids were pulled into a ponytail and fell out of the hair tie in bouncy ringlets.

"Gigi did my hair!" she said.

"It looks beautiful!" I said, looking directly at Erica.

Madisen sprinted ahead of us on the trail, sprinkling breadcrumbs for the geese. I smiled, taking in the moment. They were reunited, and their relationship was leveling back into place. The marks on Madisen's legs had long faded, but her love for Erica was even more pronounced. There are no perfect people, no perfect parents, but Erica was clearly Madisen's soft place to land. Unsupervised visitation was the precursor to reunification. I felt relief knowing that Madisen would soon be out of foster care. But I knew this wasn't the end for child protective services. After all, Erica had a verified case of child abuse on her record now, and Madisen was being placed *temporarily* back in her custody. A permanent plan was still unknown. Her caseworker would still be checking in and coming by. This was a pseudo-liberated life. These visits were meant to provide support, but they often felt more like surveillance. The visits were a form of benevolent harm, which resulted from well-intentioned policies and practices that bring systematic harm to a person's life and dignity. It was disingenuous to show up at someone's home to provide help and support, but also to monitor and document their behavior and their choices. This duplicity of child welfare seemed equivalent to a person who pats you on the back with one hand and then uses the other to pick your pocket.

Erica's case was a formative and jarring experience for me. It motivated my estrangement from the profession. None of this is surprising looking back at my life in the world of CPS. Still, my friendship with Erica was a casualty that I did not expect. I was stuck between showing loyalty to my professional mentor, caring for a child who was harmed during an act of discipline, and loving and supporting the closest friend I had. But it wasn't just Erica who experienced CPS's benevolent harm due to my indifference. I still had a caseload filled with families who were in the same boat, and no one benefited from me standing still.

Madisen had grown in the past seven months since I'd last seen her. She was much taller and a bit leaner. Even though she was five years old now and had visibly sprouted, seeing Erica pick her up made her look small. Focusing on her smallness made me think, for a moment, that maybe foster care didn't leave any scars. Maybe this short blip did not steal any part of her childhood that mattered.[3] Maybe all of our days at the park, feeding the geese, and our potluck dinners overshadowed the night I left her screaming on the floor of a strange home. I told myself that I was just doing my job, but I was also someone she loved and trusted who was leaving her again.

Erica had to take Madisen back to Ms. Lisbon's house after we left the park. She asked me to take some pictures of them. I turned it into a mini photoshoot: Erica and Madisen walking hand in hand, Madisen in motion throwing bread to the geese (actual footage of her defying park rules), and a beautiful shot of Erica hoisting Madisen up around her waist, both looking at each other with big smiles. Seeing Madisen hold on to Erica was a warm but somber reminder of when I first met her as a toddler. Two-year-old Madisen clung tightly to Erica's waist as if Erica could vanish. In a way, she had seen Erica vanish these last few months due to CPS. Her tight grip now made sense.

• • •

Before I left Tallahassee, I met with a former professor to discuss my doctoral journey. This professor supported my application with a letter of reference. When I let him know that I was accepted into Howard University, he congratulated me and shared his new apprehension about encouraging any of his students to go into child protective services. He spent years teaching about child welfare and, in many ways, he had encouraged students to go into the child protective services field. But lately, with the evidence of poor outcomes for the workforce and disparate outcomes with families, he said he no longer felt comfortable advocating entering the field of child protective services.

"It feels like I'm sending them into genuine peril. I honestly think that they would be much more fulfilled going in a different direction."

This was disheartening to me. I knew he was right. The feelings that I had developed while working in CPS were not healthy. The system was harmful and deliberately disruptive to families. CPS exploited parents' and families' most vulnerable and painful moments. These moments needed careful consideration and understanding, but our system made clumsy interventions with unchecked power, regulation, and coercive authority.[4] When I considered my role in the work and my current career path, I felt torn. I knew how hard my colleagues worked, but I also knew that the hard work was not producing the desired outcomes for families.

At Howard University, our professors drilled into us that this educational experience would be anchored in truth and service. I relished and welcomed these sentiments on the heels of my time in CPS. As an investigator, I searched for the truth in abuse allegations, but the more cases I carried, the more complex and elusive the truth became.

I threw myself into my courses. My first and still one of my favorites was the History of Social Welfare. This course opened my eyes to the foundations of racism in the welfare state. I devoured any course that focused on Family Theory. I wanted to understand family dynamics and the inherent strength of family connections. I took every Policy course that was offered so I could understand the process of policy making, but also the impact of the policies. Child welfare works with a variety of social service systems, so I also devoted my time to taking courses on Systems Theory to learn how to dissect the intricacies of bureaucratic partnerships.

During my second year, I spent much of my time in Statistics courses. They were challenging but enlightening. The textbook, written by our professor, showed us how to understand and use data in our work.[5] It was exciting to know that there were several pictures of child welfare, and one was painted in numbers. My research and coursework revealed that the disproportionality data, which has been persistent over the years within the child protective field, was one of the most searing indictments of its failings.

What I appreciated about my time at Howard was how my professors challenged us to become advocates for the most marginalized people, even if that meant uncovering our own moral culpability. Exploring the inequity and the systemic harm brought on families and the working conditions for the professionals within the system was an intellectual goal of the Howard program. It was encouraged by the faculty, and students felt empowered to uplift justice-oriented research priorities.

I was introduced to intersectionality while at Howard. I had witnessed how for many Black women, one interaction with CPS could do irrevocable damage to their family life. And I also saw through intersectionality how their multiple identities created vulnerabilities to the system. Black women are often erased by and in American institutions. Their intersecting identities became monolithic and were discarded. I would argue that many mandated reporters, the frontline agents who investigate families in CPS, and those caseworkers who surveil them through court orders are also anonymous and discarded by larger systemic actors. It is said that the client often vanishes behind their case, the caseworker vanishes behind their function . . . both muzzled by the impersonal bureaucracy.[6] The uniqueness of each parent and their respective challenges should not be lumped into generic assessments. The anonymity and monolithic perception of Black women by CPS—which mirrors society—has created deleterious consequences for Black families. When I was a caseworker, our training prepared us to *investigate* an "abuser," hold that "abuser" *responsible*, and *save* their children, without much attention to culture, context, or the weight of injustice.

I kept in touch with Katrina over the years, and she bore the brunt of my musings and my increasing levels of awareness about child welfare. She was still working in child protective services. She had rapidly ascended the career ladder and was well on her way to becoming a regional director. She had moved on from Tallahassee and was now working in Sarasota, Florida. Although she was working in a different part of the state, she felt that very little had changed. In Sarasota, the child welfare system was infamous due to the reputation of the attending child abuse pediatrician, Dr. Sally Smith. She was well-known, but not exactly for what you would expect. A *USA Today* investigation into Dr. Smith carried the headline "Bad Medicine: Critics Say Powerful Pediatrician Too Quick to Diagnose Child Abuse, Traumatizing Families." In response to this and other reports, Dr. Smith has denied any wrongdoing.

For Katrina, this media storm was a nightmare. But other disturbing realities were emerging around the state. A recent documentary called *Innocents Lost* was growing in popularity. The documentary tracked the deaths of children who had a history with child protective services, highlighting statewide cuts in funding, persistent workforce issues, and the many ways the deaths could have been prevented. The documentary's timeline traced these deaths back to 2008, the year I did my internship at CPS. It was harrowing and validating at the same time. I couldn't be happy about a disturbing picture of the field in which I once worked, but it did create a shift in my priorities. The need for reform was not new, but at that moment it was viral and visceral.

"Do you remember Mr. Dima? The Polish man who basically threw us out of the house?" Katrina asked me. Despite all the chaotic exchanges I had in that job, I could never forget that family.

"His wife had a car accident while under the influence. The person in the other car was seriously hurt. Mrs. Dima's been arrested." As Katrina explained what happened, the image of the little boy standing in his doorway years ago appeared at the forefront of my mind. And I thought of Mrs. Dima and her bizarre behavior that night.

"Wow." My stomach shifted at what she'd just told me. But there was more.

Katrina shared with me that the family had additional CPS reports, but nothing ever came of them. We talked a bit about how CPS often overreaches with families, but sometimes they may not do enough.

Katrina texted me a link to the news story. I scanned the article, and even though I knew there was nothing more that I could have done with my previous CPS case, there was something about that family that always concerned me. I felt conflicted because although she was wrong for driving under the influence, I felt sad about what her arrest would mean for her son. He must be at least ten or eleven by now. I wondered what the last few years had been like for that family. There was so much going on from the moment I met them, but CPS allowed it to be swept under the rug. The system did not seem able to effectively determine which families needed remediation and intervention, and which families did not. Implicit bias often traps families, but it also allows some families to remain untethered and unhelped. I didn't want to sink under the feeling that CPS should have removed the child that night when I was at their home, but it is clear that the family, in particular the mother, needed some sort of help. But CPS does not force its services onto every family, only some.

CHAPTER 17

TORN APART

2015–2020

THEY HAVE FINALLY TERMINATED DIDI'S PARENTAL RIGHTS!" ER-
ica announced over the phone. We talked on occasion after I left Tallahassee. Her involvement with CPS had continued over the years. I
didn't know how to feel about this news, but I wasn't overwhelmed
with happiness. Erica went on to explain that once the termination of
parental rights process was over, she was going to adopt Madisen. After
observing the plethora of systemic issues within child welfare, this sort
of news always made me feel conflicted. I knew that Madisen could
not be adopted until she was eligible, which would require her biological parents to either sign over their rights (which Jeffrey did willingly)
or have them terminated by the state. Most would support a decision
like this one, because Madisen would finally have a permanent home.
But I couldn't help but consider Didi . . . and the hand that she was
dealt. I couldn't help but think about how ill-equipped CPS was to
understand Didi and partner and work with her toward a future where
she could be well and parent her children and meet their needs.

CPS has never been equipped to understand or address the decades-
long housing crisis in this country or the impact of homelessness
and mental illness on parents like Didi. Which begs the question of
whether CPS should even be involved with these sorts of cases. The

intersections of inequity and the overlapping systems that fail families are astounding. Erica sounded thrilled to be able to finally embody what she'd always tried to be for Madisen: a mother. But what world—what systems—would we have needed in which Didi could have done the same?

Over the past five years, Madisen's behavior had been up and down, but Erica rode every wave. Madisen had virtually no contact with her biological mother, who, according to Erica, had gone dark during the CPS termination and adoption process. Madisen had intermittent contact with Jeffrey but very little time with her siblings, who all remained in New York.

"How do you feel about everything?" I asked Erica.

"I'm really happy. Once I adopt Madisen, I will be done with CPS. If I never see them again, it will be too soon." Erica's voice rang with anticipatory hope for freedom. "Madisen is so excited! She's ready to change her last name to Gaines."

"It's a big deal!" Erica went on with exuberance. "They are doing a write-up in the newspaper, and we are meeting with the governor. They are having a big adoption event, and all *forever families* are invited." Forever families is a term used by adoption agencies when they find a child a permanent home, thereby providing them a forever family. Erica went on explaining what the next few weeks would hold for them. It had been several years since CPS ostracized Erica during her case. I recalled how she shuffled her feet slowly into the Leon County Jail, and now she was preparing for a celebration *with them*. It sounded like Erica was expecting me to join in her happiness, but I was awestruck by the irony. I mostly kept silent on my end.

"Well, I hope everything works out. And tell Madisen I said hello." I ended our call before she could invite me to the ceremony. In the child welfare field, there are a host of adoption ceremonies and events, and I had attended my fair share of them when I worked in CPS. But I could not stand them anymore. I remember attending a conference around that same time, and a former adoptions caseworker was speaking to the audience. She explained the moment she knew that she could not be a caseworker anymore. It was when her job began giving bonuses whenever they finalized an adoption. Where were the financial incentives when we reunified families? she asked. There were none.

• • •

With everything that Katrina had told me and all the things that I saw in the media, I was not surprised when Florida began making sweeping legislative changes to establish a research-based center to influence better decisions and more accountability in child welfare. The FSU College of Social Work rose to the challenge, advocating for a Policy Institute that would curate best practices and advise the child welfare system and policy makers on efficiency and effectiveness. There was a national search for a leader to carry out the mission. They were looking for a leader who had been academically trained, had experience in child protective services, and possessed various competencies, including teaching, research, and an understanding of the intractable issues within the workforce. They were looking for me. I started working there in 2017—turns out, there was a market for what I wanted to do after all.

Nationally, child protective services' workforce turnover rates are generally between 30 and 40 percent. Child welfare has four million calls per year, approximately ten thousand cases reported daily to abuse hotlines across the country. Those calls included seven million children and resulted in six hundred thousand verified cases of abuse. This accounts for less than 10 percent of all reported calls.[1] Our massive mandate to report child abuse needed parameters. Given the sheer volume of calls and cases, it is no wonder the workforce is crumbling.

Families continue to be reported to CPS no matter how many investigators and caseworkers are available. Without a society-wide shift in law, perception, and awareness, mandated reporters will remain the antiheroes who are driving millions of families into the system. The CPS workforce is not sustainable and has always been dangerous for the well-being of children and families, in more ways than one. The danger derives from the harm caused by unnecessary and life-altering intrusions into family homes. Combine this with the small percentage of cases that actually require this kind of intervention, and the scope of the problem comes into clear view. An overworked staff makes the likelihood of providing unbiased advocate-based services to families much less likely. Children and families deserve an effective, keen caseworker, not one who is hanging on by a thread. Much of our caseworkers' capacity to critically think and meaningfully engage with families relies on how much awareness, time, and bandwidth they have in the moment. Child welfare professionals are tasked with making life-altering decisions about families, and they are often doing so while running on fumes.

In June 2018, I gave a TED Talk about a particular community and its efforts in mitigating the impact of implicit racial bias on decisions to separate families.[2] The community created blind removal meetings, which were internal meetings in which family separation decisions were made without knowledge of race, ethnicity, income, language barriers, or even immigration status.[3] That same year, the Trump administration made a policy decision that awakened something across the United States. The decision created a crisis at the US-Mexico border. Migrant families were separated when they attempted to enter this country. Watching children be pulled out of their parents' arms and placed in cages was something that people were unable to unsee. For many there was no rational explanation for this kind of inhumane treatment of children and parents. The visibility of these acts showed that xenophobia and racism were embedded in the structure of America.

Although the forced separation of families seeking asylum had been occurring, covertly, for a while, the exposure became pervasive in

June. There were images on the news of screaming mothers and wailing babies being torn apart. Videos emerged of hundreds of children sitting on top of each other in confinement. Watching this unfold on the news was horrific on many levels. Sometimes in America, *What you don't know won't hurt you*, but watching this occur repeatedly in videos was painful and shameful. No one could deny what they now knew. So many domestic family separations happen that are preventable. I imagined that the people who advocate for transforming child protective services gave a collective sigh, because the family separations at the hands of CPS have lost shock value.

As my TED Talk made its rounds, I started to receive half a dozen emails per day asking me to contribute to or weigh in on the national discussion about systemic racism and family separation. One request came from a media outlet that requested I write a piece on the long-lasting trauma of family separation in response to Trump's new policies. I agreed, as long as I could draw a parallel to other instances of inhuman separations. Soon, I published a piece titled "The Long History of Separating Families in the US and How the Trauma Lingers."[4] This article gave me space to weigh in on the policies that were ripping families apart at the border. I included how this was not exactly new behavior for the United States. Systemic exclusion and traumatic separations had affected poor African Americans, Native Americans, and Japanese Americans for generations.

In another written piece, I shared a question that plagued me: *What will it take for child welfare to embrace real change and become an anti-racist system?*[5] Unfortunately, video footage of what CPS does in its day-to-day work will not be captured by a cell phone and broadcast on national television. No one will see us strapping babies into the car seats that CPS investigators drive around with each day. No one will see caseworkers driving away from an angry crying mother, law enforcement leading the way. But it's still happening every day. The truth is, if America is drawing a hard line against family separation—these same individuals can bring their pencil over to the child welfare system. Advocacy is needed even if you don't see it. Sometimes what you don't see should still hurt you.

• • •

Through the next couple of years, I continued to advocate for systemic change. I did so through training, research, and policy work. Additionally, I was invited to speak at conferences about my research, and it was an opportunity to impart knowledge and inspire a new way to work. I regularly spoke about the power dynamics within our field and how our system often exacerbates the powerlessness that families already feel. I also talked to audiences about how important it is to consider how much our mindsets impacted our decisions on our cases. One day, after I finished the keynote address at a conference, an attorney raised her hand and stated that she had never truly thought about how much power the courts have and how that power disproportionately impacts Black women. She shared with us that she was working on a CPS case, and they were developing a court-mandated case plan for this Black woman to complete in order to get her children back. At the top of the case plan required by the court system was: *Acquire your GED.* The attorney shared that although she always knew the requirement wasn't appropriate, she did not realize the extent to which mindset fueled it.

I was shocked by this but ultimately not surprised. This was quite indicative of the assimilationist mindset (see p. 241) where there is a standard that the child welfare system regularly wants Black mothers to reach, even though the standards are often steeped in whiteness.[6] At that same conference, I remember fielding a question from a participant who saw no issue with requiring a mother to achieve an educational attainment like a GED. "What's wrong with that? They should get GEDs! It's a great way to improve themselves!" It sounded so much like Jolly K and Parents Anonymous.

I wasn't exactly prepared for that and what I said next was not a part of my prepared keynote. But it dawned on me at that moment that my father, an immigrant from Jamaica, never finished high school and never acquired a GED. And I told the audience this. I told them that I had never thought about the situation of my own father until that moment—and this is why it should not be *required* to parent. Loving and caring for a child isn't actually taught in GED courses. I explained to the audience that if a mother on your caseload shares with you a personal desire to get her GED, that is an opportunity for you to partner with her and facilitate a goal that is driven by her. But making it a mandate, in order to parent her children, is wielding power in the most dangerous way.

I continued to meet countless women who wanted and needed to be heard and supported through their CPS cases. And I realized that I was further from the field, but closer than ever before. I have read that it's important to "keep close" to the people who were marginalized and suffering.[7] A person could do good work from a distance, may even make some important changes, but they would never truly understand the people they are fighting for unless they had proximity. Staying close and having proximity would help them recognize the humanity in the person and thus create more awareness, by advocating for and initiating overdue change.

Interestingly enough, when I was a CPS investigator, with proximity to the families on my caseload, I felt distant. When it came to closeness, I was in their homes, opening their cabinets, requesting medical records, and conferring with their neighbors. I had a front-row seat to their vulnerabilities and their challenges. Yet, working closely with families as an investigator made me feel the furthest away from the issues they were facing. The issues that plagued them were inconsequential compared to the CPS directives and procedures that lay ahead. I was much too close.

I was looking at the families who I worked with but not *seeing* them. When I encountered a family, I could hear myself recite procedures and instructions as if I were an onlooker watching a robot. I watched parents shift from confused about my presence to fully irate—and I knew they were justified. I became comfortable intruding in people's private homes and asking questions that aren't easy on a good day, let alone a day when you are facing the loss of your children. The angst and stress marred me while I worked and while I slept. My best friend fought the system for months, and she was condemned. So many stones were thrown at her, and some of those stones came from me. I used my delegation as a mandated reporter as a weapon against my own sister, hiding behind the responsible and civic duty of reporting.

When I left my CPS job, I wanted distance. I wanted to be far away from any child protective caseload. And that is when I became proximate to the issue. I sat in the ivory tower of my university and dissected policies, dove into history, and examined nationwide data on child welfare. It was the clearest picture I had ever seen. The child welfare system had been uniquely positioned to target poor and minority families, and it would continue its assault for many years to come unless something revolutionary occurred. Not everyone needs distance to fully see, but I did. A little bit of distance made the difference for me. Though, now I've been thrust back into closeness with Black women who are constantly bracing for CPS impact. My road to *seeing* began while I was in the field, but I capitulated from a distant place. All of that to say, being close and connected to those who are experiencing harm is ideal—but do not be fooled that closeness means awareness and advocacy. In CPS, closeness could simply mean having direct access to render harm to vulnerable families.

CHAPTER 18

WHITE FRAGILITY

2020

IT WAS 2020 WHEN I JOINED JATOIA'S CASE AS AN EXPERT WIT-ness. The CPS system had formally filed paperwork to terminate her parental rights (TPR). Building a family and becoming a mother was Jatoia's dream, and the thought of having that taken away from her seemed unfathomable. Unlawful, even. She continued to attend community meetings with Restorative Justice Durham and Southerners on New Ground, two organizations that had been hugely supportive of Jatoia. It seemed like every time Jatoia was reaching her breaking point, someone at those community events would give her encouragement or ask her questions that made her think of new strategies or ideas. These community forums would become even more supportive after Jatoia learned the truth behind Kenny's injuries.

During the summer of 2020, Lawrence wrote an email to their caseworker disclosing his role in Kenny's injuries. He wrote that one evening he was under the influence of drugs and alcohol, and he was carrying Kenny outside and accidently dropped him. He picked him up right away and tried to soothe his crying. Once he got him settled and swaddled that evening, he remained panicked and never told Jatoia or anyone else.

This news created a clear path to her exoneration, and her criminal case was quickly dropped. But Jatoia felt deeply confused and hurt. Her thoughts went back to the moment when she knew that she was going into early labor. Then she thought of when they all came home from the PICU with Kenny, getting everything set up for their new baby. It was a stressful time but she was so happy to finally have both of her boys at home. She recalled the emergency room visit, the issues with her mother and stepfather, the removal, and then the arrest and her months spent in jail. Everything flooded back to her. All of the nights she couldn't sleep, reflecting every day, and analyzing every moment. She constantly questioned herself, wondering what she had missed. She thought of the anxiety and rage she felt as each day passed while she sat in jail without understanding how she got there. And after all this time, Lawrence was now admitting to hurting Kenny.

"Some days, it doesn't feel real, and I ask myself, 'Is this real?' Like one day, I am in denial but then another day I am very emotional about everything and I have to give myself pep talks," Jatoia said to her therapist during one of their sessions.

Elizabeth was just as shocked with this new information, but it re-energized her persistence about maintaining Jatoia's parental rights. She advised Jatoia again to get a restraining order against Lawrence. She predicted that CPS would still question Jatoia's allegiances. The idea of getting a restraining order had come up before, but for some reason, Jatoia did not go through with it. This time, she did. She filed a Domestic Violence Order of Protection. She had mixed feelings but she got it done and he was served.

Even with Lawrence's confession and Jatoia's swift action in getting an order of protection against him, nevertheless, CPS persisted. They moved forward in their pursuit of terminating her parental rights. The CPS legal team had to clearly outline the grounds on which they wanted to terminate Jatoia's and Lawrence's rights. In light of Lawrence's recent confession, CPS had a strong case against him, but their rationale for Jatoia's parental termination mystified most people. She not only cooperated fully with the process, but she maintained her innocence from the outset and never changed her story or waivered in her position. She did not hurt Kenny and she did not know how he was hurt. Until now.

The TPR petition read:

- Jatoia Potts has abused or neglected her children, and there is a reasonable likelihood that they will be neglected if they are returned to the mother.

- Jatoia has willfully left the children in foster care for more than twelve months without satisfactorily showing that there was progress towards correcting the conditions that led to the removal.

- Jatoia Potts has willfully failed to pay child support for the cost of care although she is physically and financially able to do so.

- Jatoia Potts has committed felony assault or aided and abetted the voluntary assault on a child residing in the home.

• • •

Jatoia was gearing up for the fight of her life. The CPS system had a mountain of support for their TPR petition, including their attorneys, law enforcement, and the guardian ad litem (court-appointed volunteers who advocate for the child's best interest). The first part of the termination of parental rights process is an adjudication hearing in which the state (petitioner) has the burden of proof to show with clear, cogent, and convincing evidence that the grounds for TPR exist. Then, there is a dispositional hearing that has the purpose of determining if the decision of the court is in the best interest of the children. This is the hearing in which Jatoia would have the opportunity to bring forth witnesses and expert testimony.

After several delays, the hearing occurred and the interactions that Elizabeth had with CPS were consistently contentious. They were emphatic in their pursuit to terminate Jatoia's rights, standing behind the declarative position that "the child(ren) were left in foster care for over 15 months and the parent(s) have not made reasonable progress to correct the conditions which led to the removal." However, Elizabeth immediately noted how they had disregarded the impact of pretrial detention and that astronomical bail amounts limit some parents' ability to get out of jail and tend to their children.[1] Parents who are incarcerated experience challenges in their ability to render effort toward their child's well-being. Elizabeth articulated these realities throughout the termination hearing.

The state also submitted as evidence the fact that Jatoia requested that visitation be suspended while she was incarcerated. "The state was willing to organize visitation for the minor child so that he could stay connected to his mother," they argued. But Jatoia's reasoning for that decision was because she cared very deeply for him. Jatoia recalls the social worker's clarification: "You want to suspend your visitation?" Jatoia could not have known that her decision would eventually become a self-inflicted and terminal wound.

When children visit their incarcerated parents, their experience can be stressful. This could be due to the correctional environment or because of the lack of preparation and lack of follow-up support after the visit. The child welfare system regularly disregards this potential dynamic when they require that incarcerated parents visit their children in order to maintain their parental rights.

The CPS petitioner also shared that the mother refused to pay child support. Elizabeth pointed out that, in reality, Jatoia did make some payments, but due to financial hardship, she was not able to pay them all. Not only did Elizabeth counter this with information about the impact of the pretrial detention on Jatoia's employment, but she also included the research on how unaffordable bail affects families. The real issue remains that the child welfare system is funded at over twelve billion annually,[2] and CPS decided to punish Jatoia for not paying child support to a system that took her children.

Any piece of evidence that points to Jatoia and her ability to care for her children or improve the conditions that warranted the removal must acknowledge that incarceration (in this case wrongful incarceration based on Lawrence's confession) should be seen as inhibiting parental capacity. Elizabeth continued to highlight how the petitioners rarely discussed incarceration or its impact on Jatoia's ability to parent. Despite her efforts, their evidence was accepted as convincing, and the TPR was granted. But there was still the dispositional hearing left to go.

Elizabeth asked that I present my testimony at the deposition; I began my preparation. In addition to my testimony, she requested testimony from Jatoia's family and her therapist. Elizabeth sent me the documentation needed to complete a written affidavit and present live testimony at the trial. During each of our meetings, she explained to me that the CPS legal team was adversarial. She encouraged me to stay as calm as possible. After the second or third time she mentioned this, I started to wonder if Elizabeth believed I tended to become angry and irrational. It turns out that she had been dealing with the CPS legal team for over a year at that point and had experience with their hostility and outright disrespect.

An expert witness is a person with extensive education, experience, and skills in a specific field or discipline beyond that expected from a layperson. The expert witness's duty is to apply their expertise to a professional opinion given to a court as a decision nears. In doing so, the expert witness seeks to explain and clarify complex matters that the average person would not typically understand. Elizabeth's goal was for my testimony to provide insight on racial disparity and disproportionality within the child welfare system, with emphasis on the data that corroborates the poor outcomes for Black parents and their children. Specifically, the fact that one in one hundred children will be legally and permanently separated from their parents through termination of parental rights, and risks are higher for Black children.[3] She also wanted the court to hear about the long-term impact of family separation on children. She asked that I be prepared to talk about the presence of intimate partner violence (IPV) within child welfare cases and the necessity to handle those cases with specialized skills. I was certainly ready for that one. Lastly, she wanted the court to understand what the data show about termination of parental rights and the increased likelihood of termination for Black parents.

Preparation continued on my end, but Jatoia's world came to a halt when her mother, Margaret, passed away in October 2020. It was remarkable that her mother was able to fight for so long. Jatoia remembered the long nights, the hacking coughs, the wheezing, the end of lung cancer. Her mother was tired. She lived well past her initial prognosis, but it stung that she wasn't able to see the boys before she died. Jatoia had asked the CPS caseworker about the possibility of her mother seeing the boys, maybe even talking to them on the phone— but the answer was no. With an active petition for termination of parental rights, there would be no visitation for any family members. Living or dying.

Ever since the upheaval, when her boys were initially placed at her stepfather's home, things were never the same between Jatoia and her stepfather. The next few weeks brought challenges relating to decisions, arrangements, and burial. It was the height of the pandemic, so there was no in-person funeral for her mother. This was another wound for Jatoia. She reflected on the good times that she had with her mother, and she found joy in knowing that her mother loved LJ and Kenny so much. Her mother stepped up to care for them even when her health was at its lowest. As many people do, Jatoia drew strength from knowing that her mother would want her to fight like hell for her kids.

• • •

After several delays, the dispositional hearing occurred in May 2021. It was virtual due to the ongoing risk of the coronavirus, so I awaited Elizabeth's text alerting me of my turn to testify. She let me know that I could join the trial link. By the time Elizabeth had brought me on to this case, I had been an expert witness in three other trials. They each had presented their own unique challenges, but disrespect and rudeness from the CPS team were not among them. It was a battle that, despite Elizabeth's warnings, still took me by surprise.

In addition to my own research and literature reviews on racial disparity, IPV, and termination of parental rights, I had gone through hundreds of pages of court documents, assessments, transcripts, case notes, and medical reports. I wasn't terribly nervous, but I was anxious because I internalized the weight of the outcome of this trial. I knew that the decision was not mine, and all I could do was my very best at explaining the rampant disparity in child welfare decisions, especially for low-income Black mothers. I hoped that my testimony would contribute to a deeper awareness that subjective decisions had affected Jatoia's case and that there was still time to change the trajectory of this TPR petition.[4]

When I logged on, in my line of sight I saw Elizabeth, then the judge—a formidable Black woman—then two white women who were on the CPS legal team. There were a few other small boxes on the screen with only names and cameras off. I was taken aback to see that a Black woman was at the helm of this case. Later I found out that although Jatoia had a revolving door of social workers leaving and coming, this judge had been with them from day one. Therefore, her decisions were not rendered with fragmented information. She had the entire picture.

When a person is called in as an expert witness in litigation, they become part of a process known as voir dire, which ensures that the judges and attorneys know the witness is properly qualified as an expert. The qualification process starts with both attorneys asking the expert witness a series of questions about their professional experience and qualifications. I was asked about my education and experience, and the CPS attorneys also asked me about my familiarity with North Carolina's child welfare system. I answered that I was not an expert in the specifics of North Carolina's system but explained that I would discuss the decades-long disproportionality and disparity challenges that were also present in North Carolina. States differ in how they operate their child welfare systems, but the one thing they have in common is overrepresentation of Black and Indigenous families throughout their systems of care.

"I just don't understand this," one of the CPS lawyers said, mostly under her breath. She muted and started to toss papers around on her desk. Her frustration was very obvious. She unmuted and asked, "Why are you here as an expert on systemic racism and disparity? None of that was present in this case. You can't prove that anyone from CPS was racist toward Ms. Potts, so again, I don't understand how this is relevant to this case."

I was stoic as I explained that I was not there to prove a direct and explicit act of racism toward Jatoia Potts, but that systemic racism is prevalent in and throughout child welfare case decisions. Without consideration of the potential harm of systemic racism and implicit bias, they would be discounting very real and documented inequities throughout the history of CPS. I also noted that classism was at play.

The CPS attorneys continued to dramatically adjust themselves in their seats and drop their heads into their palms. Their exasperation checkered every word they said. In some ways, it was comical to watch their thinly veiled white fragility. If I had not been in a professional setting, I might have giggled.

Their questions continued to come out like venom. Feminist writer Sara Ahmed argues that "whiteness often establishes institutionalized habits of entitlement and stratification of who is deserving and who is not." The CPS attorneys had clearly established their feelings when it came to Jatoia. Elizabeth and I didn't return their troublesome energy, but they rallied with their bullying. And ultimately, it worked. Although the court documented that I was indeed an expert in child welfare policy and practice, Judge Yevette Harrell agreed with the CPS legal team about relevance. Therefore, she would not hear my testimony. After an abrupt "thank you," she removed me from the hearing. I later read that the court tendered me "an expert" and found me "well educated" but did not feel that my knowledge about institutional racial bias was relevant to North Carolina's child welfare system, and thus was irrelevant to Jatoia's case.

The rest of that trial spanned five days while Elizabeth presented nine additional witnesses on Jatoia's behalf. Some were family, friends, even a social worker Jatoia had worked with while she was incarcerated. Elizabeth had never heard of TPR hearings going on that long. And neither had I. Even Jatoia was able to address the court and render testimony, which she saw as her one last chance to defend her right to mother her children. While Jatoia answered questions, a brief recess became necessary because her nose began to bleed. These nosebleeds came on due to stress, Jatoia knew, and that trial's stress was unbearable. Tears joined the bleeding as she worked to clean herself up. She was in a knot of worry, reeling from the high stakes.

A simple text from Elizabeth alerted me about the results of all of their efforts: "We lost." I didn't press or ask the millions of questions I had because I knew that this was a blow for Elizabeth and the rest of her team. Jatoia's case took the wind out of me. It made me feel like quitting. If the conversation of clear disparity and disparate outcomes within child welfare was seen as irrelevant to a court proceeding where an exonerated Black woman was on the cusp of losing her parental rights, then where do I go from here? A realization hit me with nauseating force: the system had more power than I ever knew. And, safety and family well-being were not part of their standard operating procedure.

Not long after Jatoia's rights were terminated, I received a call from a woman I had recently met at a conference.

"I just met someone whose son was taken by CPS after she took him to the hospital for help." The tone of this conversation was immediately triggering. This felt like a bad record playing again. "Dr. Pryce, she wants to talk to you. Her name is Syesha Mercado."

CHAPTER 19

THE FIRE NEXT TIME

2021

THE YEAR I BEGAN MY CPS INTERNSHIP WAS THE SAME YEAR SYE-sha Mercado rose to fame on the show *American Idol*. But long before *American Idol*, she had lived in Florida, on the Gulf Coast in the city of Sarasota. She studied performing arts and theater in high school and throughout college; she excelled in several stage productions, including *Seussical the Musical*. Syesha has shared her musical gift in venues nationally and around the world, bringing connection and warmth to her fans. She is also a decorated actress, starring in musicals and plays that have brought her critical acclaim. But in 2021, she was in the limelight for something entirely different. Child protective services took custody of both of her children.

The CPS onslaught began for Syesha when she and her partner, Tyron, "Ty," took their infant son to the emergency room in Sarasota, Florida. Both parents were trying to transition their son, Malik, from breastfeeding to formula, but it was a challenge. Syesha and Ty became concerned that Malik wasn't consuming enough, so they went to Johns Hopkins All Children's Hospital. Immediately, she felt the judgmental glances and accusatory questions. The physicians who examined Malik told Syesha and Ty that his B12 levels were extremely low, and that he needed an infusion. Syesha and Ty asked questions about the diagnosis and treatment plan. They were adamant about understanding everything that was given to their child, from birth until that moment. But it became clear to Syesha and Ty from the stance and demeanor of the doctors at Johns Hopkins that they did not want to be questioned. Syesha and Ty were not the sort of parents who made decisions based on something a "powerful" person recommended.

As was customary due to his age and the allegations of medical neglect, Malik needed to be examined by the hospital's pediatric child abuse physician. Dr. Sally Smith was still at her post. Shortly after her examination of Malik, Dr. Smith spoke with Syesha and Ty, sharing that the baby was very ill. He needed immediate intervention, in the form of B12 intramuscular infusions. While Dr. Smith continued speaking, Ty was already on his phone looking up information and trying to understand more about what was going on with Malik.

Dr. Smith interpreted their apprehension as noncompliance. Intuitively, and very much like Jatoia, Syesha began recording their exchanges on her phone. She was firm in her position and used her phone to document what was happening: "I am not saying no to any medical treatment for my son. I am asking for more information." Syesha and Ty were eventually told that Malik was being admitted to the hospital because he was "extremely malnourished." Without B12 intramuscular shots, "he would surely die." A medical diagnosis of this magnitude garners swift and unabashed intervention from CPS. A court petition was already underway, and so was the complete condemnation of Syesha and Ty. They were not permitted to be alone with their son and eventually were escorted off the hospital property and barred from returning.

Despite viable kinship placements, namely Ty's mother, who attended the emergency court hearing, Malik was placed in the legal custody of total strangers on March 11, 2021. I met Syesha soon after that.

• • •

Many of my past CPS cases required a physician's opinion about the origin of the alleged abuse. When I had cases with children who needed to be examined by Dr. Tess, the previous CPS physician in Tallahassee, there was very little opposition from me regarding her medical conclusion. In fact, there are rarely viewpoints from within CPS that override a physician's opinion or diagnosis. For a caseworker, a medical conclusion seems clear and definitive. It didn't make sense to question it. Most caseworkers throughout the country approach assessments this way. But my wariness about this process started way back with Erica. After Jatoia, I simply couldn't trust physicians in the process in the same way I had as a caseworker. With Syesha I realized how arbitrary these physician interventions could be and how much power we turned over to doctors in child welfare situations. The notion that physicians are infallible continues to be one of the most harmful parts of child protective services.

The shock of having Malik taken rippled through Syesha's body. The shock felt untethered, drifting from her head with sharp pains, then down to her stomach, with nausea and cramps, then up to her chest, with tightness and pressure. She felt physically ill. She processed all that occurred in a delayed fashion, reliving the moment over and over again. She kept wondering, "How did this happen?" Her focus eventually turned to Dr. Smith.

Syesha would have no way of knowing how much controversy Dr. Smith had generated until she and Ty started their own research into the child welfare system in Sarasota. They read case after case in the media, all of which depicted a physician who seemed to rarely listen but regularly made claims and accusations. They found a 2016 case about a child named Maya Kowalski,[1] who came into the hospital complaining of persistent stomach pain. Dr. Smith examined Maya and ultimately accused Maya's mother of inflicting harm on her daughter. Dr. Smith believed that Maya's mother had Munchausen by proxy syndrome, which is a very rare condition where a parent willfully harms a child or creates fake symptoms all in an effort to get attention. Due to this, child protective services petitioned the court to remove Maya from the custody of her mother, and the petition was successful. Not all parents are able to endure the long suffering required to deal with CPS. Maya's mother fell into a deep depression, and after months of being alienated from her daughter, she eventually took her own life. Their family subsequently filed lawsuits against several defendants, believing wholeheartedly that Maya's mother was driven to this act by CPS. Dr. Smith and her employer reportedly settled the lawsuit for 2.5 million dollars.[2]

Surprisingly, there were some rare occasions when judges, not caseworkers, challenged Dr. Smith for her inaccurate conclusions. She once examined a young boy's head injury and determined that it was inflicted by his father. The boy was removed from his father's custody, but Florida's Second District Court of Appeal overturned the removal, sending the boy back home. The court found that Dr. Smith's conclusion was based "primarily on her assessment of the father's credibility, not on the available medical reports." Smith wasn't completely immune from criticism, but she remained an influential decision-maker controlling the fates of families.

Syesha was known for using her voice to sing and recite lines as an actress, but she had never used her platform to speak out about social issues. Every new injustice she experienced at the hands of CPS moved her to speak out about the system. She was reckoning with the way CPS is portrayed in the media. She realized that the system wanted you to believe that children were being rescued from bad parents, but Syesha knew from experience that the system could take a child from just about anyone. It was powerful. More powerful than she ever knew.

Syesha and Ty began an online campaign, raising money to help with legal fees and speaking to news outlets about what had happened to their family. With each new article that was written, with each new social media post, Syesha received dozens of messages from Black mothers who were lost in their own CPS cases and unsure of who to trust or even how to begin to put their families back together. Hearing story after story, relaying the same miscarriages of justice, fueled Syesha's sense of responsibility to advocate for change. She heard the women's voices cracking with fear and shame. Even through her own pain, she spoke words of encouragement to them. "You are not a bad parent, you are not an abusive parent, do not let CPS trick you into believing that narrative about yourself. You and your family deserve better."

Syesha's story gained national momentum. It dovetailed with other community activists who were on the same mission to stop CPS from pulling Black families apart. Syesha, in partnership with a few other grassroots organizations, planned a virtual town hall—wherein they would share their stories and create a space for community organizers to establish an action plan. They scheduled the virtual town hall for May 9, 2021, which was declared Syesha Mercado Day in the city of Sarasota. It was also Mother's Day. The irony wasn't lost on the participants as they logged on to the virtual event. Many sent sympathetic "Happy Mother's Day" messages in the virtual chat box.

The moderator kicked off the event. "One day, we hope that protocol will not continue to supersede humanity." There were hundreds of people who joined, many of them in their own fights for their families. It was upsetting and sad and exhilarating all at the same time. People were turning their pain into purpose. They were coming together to learn, share, and mobilize.

Syesha and Ty addressed the group, sharing the emotional narrative about what had happened to them at Johns Hopkins. Syesha cried throughout her message, stopping at times to gather her emotions. Her pain was palpable. For the next two hours there were more speakers, questions, and facilitated discussions. Near the close of the virtual event, the moderator shared a powerful quote to encourage Syesha and Ty. It was from James Baldwin's *The Fire Next Time*: "And now, [Syesha], you must survive this because we love you, and for the sake of your children and your children's children."

• • •

On my calls with Syesha and Ty, they asked questions about the CPS process, vented their concerns, and sought advice on how to find their way through the complexities that awaited them. As someone who had done that job, I was able to alert them to what was next and how far this could go. They knew that their words were being twisted by CPS into a narrative painting them as negligent parents who refused to help their child. They knew that they could not trust CPS to have the best interests of their family at the center of the case. They also knew that the more time that passed, the more time they missed bonding with their young child. The deliberate and systemic delays of the CPS process made them anxious and fearful.

"How long can this process last?" they asked me.

With Jatoia as my most recent frame of reference, I answered honestly, "It really just depends. I just finished working on a case that had been going on for over four years." This information silenced them enough for me to offer a bookend of encouragement. "But, you all have so much support. You've engaged a great attorney, and you're cooperating with everything that CPS is asking of you. This may move faster." It hit me at that moment that Jatoia also had public support, had a great attorney, and had cooperated fully with CPS. When I am serving as a sounding board for mothers going through CPS, I try to be honest. But I never want to add to their fear and angst. I was still reeling from Jatoia. I never said this to Syesha, but in my mind, Malik was as good as adopted. It was hard to believe that the most implausible outcome would not happen when you had just watched it play out.

Ty also asked about the case planning process. He felt that the court-ordered case plan tasks were just a generic tactic to delay reunification. He did not want their compliance to denote some sort of placid culpability. His attorney advised them to complete all the tasks, no matter how irrelevant they were. The attorney's role was to do all he could to see to it that their legal journey was a fair one, but also to clear the path to reunification for this family. The path was burdened by the case plan. A stipulation of the court-mandated case plan was that both Syesha and Ty receive a psychological evaluation. This was required during my very first case as an intern, then again with Erica, Didi, Jatoia, and now Syesha. For over a decade, this blanket assumption that something psychological was at play with parents was still an active (and assumptive) practice. The CPS team advised them on a few options for the psych evaluation in the community of practitioners and partners with whom they work. Ty was uninterested in working with anyone who partnered with CPS.

"If we have to do this, can you recommend a psychologist who is not connected to this system? I do not trust them. I want someone who has some sort of cultural sensitivity and who is objective."

I appreciated his forethought; I set out to contact folks in my network who could help. This advocacy from Ty was right on time. With the country still reckoning with the horrific murder of George Floyd, many organizations were pivoting toward diversity, equity, and inclusion. That year, the American Psychological Association had rendered a public apology for their part in perpetuating systemic racism in psychology. They wrote: "we have failed in our role in leading the discipline of psychology, and have been complicit in contributing to systemic inequities, and hurt many through racism, racial discrimination, and denigration of communities of color."[3] Ty was not overreaching with his desire to engage in a psychological evaluation with someone who brought a deep awareness of the missteps in psychological services as well as cultural sensitivity and objectivity.

Soon Syesha shared with me that she was pregnant with her second child. She struggled with fears about it. She was not concerned with the viability or health of the pregnancy. She was scared of CPS. "We have to take that baby too," one of the CPS investigators told Syesha. It haunted her days. Although I was indoctrinated with this procedural lunacy, I knew it was not supported by the law and is not equally applied. There is no automatic removal of a child when their sibling is in foster care. There may be a trigger for a new investigation or new allegations, but telling a pregnant mother that their newborn needs to come with CPS is a display of explicit bias and faulty interpretation, not official policy.

Ty had children from a previous relationship and had sole custody, so he did his best to shield them from this entire situation. But it seemed that his other children weren't of concern to CPS, and Ty started to realize why. They were not Syesha's biological children. This case was built on pathologizing Syesha as an "abusive mother." They did not trust that she could have a baby and raise her child without inflicting harm. And to Ty, that was the real travesty—CPS's tainted and filtered view of Black motherhood.

"It was excruciating to see how Syesha was treated as a mother," he explained. "This process has been awful for me, but the way they have treated Syesha is downright criminal. They have no understanding or respect for her as a mother."

• • •

The courts ordered that visitation with Malik be supervised. At the beginning they could only see him virtually. Then they saw him once per week for one hour. At the supervision that week, Syesha, Ty, and Malik were at a park in Sarasota; they met the caseworker there. Ty took a video of Syesha as she sat on a patch of grass holding tightly to Malik. She rested her cheek on top of his head. She sang an original lullaby to him, something from her heart to his. She missed him and longed to hold and love him every single day, not just once a week. During visitation, it's always heartwarming to see how much children relax into their mother and father. They hold on to their parents, rest in their arms, study their face, grip their fingers. They soak up every part of this temporal moment. I watched Malik on the video radiate with contentment. Being held by his mother should not be a timed and transient experience for him. It should not be something that his subconscious longs for while his conscious world is surrounded by strangers. As Syesha continued to sing softly to him, Malik fell asleep, safe in the arms of his mother.

"I sing to Malik on every visit and even when I'm not with him," Syesha said. "And I believe that something beyond me is getting the melody to him. I want my voice to be in his heart."

In the midst of handling the case and visiting her son as much as possible, Syesha quietly delivered her new baby. She chose to be away from the traditional and often stressful hospital environment and had an intimate home birth experience with a midwife. She gave birth to a baby girl, Anastasia. During the most painful time of Syesha's life, Anastasia brought joy and hope and a renewed spirit to fight for her family. Syesha was instructed by CPS to file paperwork notifying them of her daughter's birth. Instead, Syesha called her attorney to let him know that Anastasia was here and healthy and to seek his advice on what to do next. Even though her CPS investigator had threatened to take the new baby before she was born, the next few days still came at Syesha fast. CPS was keeping track of traditional pregnancy time frames and began frequenting the home more than usual. They arrived unannounced, and law enforcement started to make their rounds.

"We know you had your baby, and we need to have the baby examined by our physician," the CPS investigator told Syesha. That statement created a panic that tore through Syesha. *Who would examine her? Would it be Dr. Smith again?!* Even the thought of this made Syesha desperate. She had to somehow figure out how to protect her baby from child protective services. She knew that she would likely never find something more ironic than that.

CHAPTER 20

THE FIRE THIS TIME

2021

IN THE EARLY EVENING OF AUGUST 10, 2021, I RECEIVED A FACE-Time call from Ty. CPS was back at his house to take their new baby. He held the phone up in front of him so I could see and hear the entire exchange. Syesha was not home, and he was alone with his children, and he wanted a witness. I watched over FaceTime as Ty's children stood around the living room, trying to distract themselves with toys. I had shouldered my share of shame over the years when I reflected on my role and time in CPS, but I had never felt more shame than in this moment. I thought of myself in a similar scenario, ten years ago, when CPS was at my sister's home, and I witnessed her CPS situation via the phone. As a new CPS investigator, I was tacitly chiding my sister for that domestic situation, and I was hoping CPS would be the impetus for change. What a difference a decade can make, because this time I was furious. I wanted to physically remove those people from Ty's home.

There were five white women, one of them a sheriff's deputy in uniform, one hand resting on her holster. Just as terrifying as the cop's gun was the lead investigator's weapon, a court order to pick up Anastasia. I noticed a younger looking woman who stood awkwardly off to the side, waiting in the wings for direction. She did not say a word. She moved timidly through the home, and I realized she must be an intern. Maybe it was her first day.

They all began walking through Ty's home, opening doors and peering into closets, searching for Syesha and Anastasia. I was holding my breath as I watched, knowing that I could never unsee this. The imagery was painful. These white authority figures stood in the home of a Black family, holding papers that said they could apprehend their newborn. I watched these agents of the state search each room of Ty's home.

This scene was a painful reminder that we haven't moved on from historical forms of oppression. In the antebellum South, when slaves tried to escape, sometimes they were hidden away and protected by other people. And when the slave patrol came by, doing their rounds, they would walk through homes searching for runaways. That was the imagery that came to mind as I witnessed what was happening in Ty's home. How could anyone deny that there was a subset of Americans who were still being unfairly and disproportionately patrolled?

"Where is the baby?" the first white woman demanded.

"She's not here right now. What's the problem, officer?" Ty was even-tempered. This was his disposition in most situations. He was steady, but I could tell he was fearful. Fear for his new baby, fear for Syesha, and even fear for himself—law enforcement was armed and in his home. He addressed the law enforcement representative as "officer" and addressed each CPS worker by name—often stopping mid-sentence to address them respectfully.

"I just need to understand why and how—wait, what's your name, ma'am?" He paused and she answered. "Debra. Okay, Debra, why are you here to take my daughter?"

"Where is the baby? We need you to produce the baby . . . now," she stated without answering his question.

Produce the baby. I'd never heard anyone say that. Not Lydia, not

LeAnn, none of my previous colleagues. But it had been a while since I was in the field. Apparently now investigators demand that human beings . . . be produced.

"Syesha isn't here. The baby isn't here," Ty said. "Can I see the paper-work?"

I watched the investigator brandish a set of papers that she had rolled into a tube shape. She walked a few steps over to the small dining table and laid the papers down, trying to smooth them. Ty, still holding his phone, started to review each report, page by page.

"The father says the mother and the baby are not home." I heard the investigator relaying an update to someone on her phone. Likely her supervisor.

"When will the mother and baby be back here?" Another question posed to Ty.

"I'm really not sure where they are, but we can follow up with you as soon as we talk to our lawyer." His voice was calm. I am not sure how many people could have remained levelheaded with CPS and police violating their home this way.

"Look. We need you to produce the baby right now," the investi-gator repeated. She was growing more impatient. After all, this was not her first time coming to that house to take a baby away. They had sent law enforcement on multiple occasions to stop by and patrol the area, hoping to finish the job of completely tearing this family apart. I wondered if they realized what they were doing. Did they feel this morally at all?

"Where is Syesha?!" Her voice was elevating now. But Ty repeated his answer, that she was not home and they would follow up as soon as possible. It was true that Syesha and the baby were not home at the time, but it was clear that CPS would not stop.

• • •

Despite the fact that she was healthy, having been examined by a physician and given a clean bill of health, the next day Anastasia was taken into CPS custody. She was only days old and breastfeeding. The removal was streamed live on Instagram. Most folks do not get the chance to see the forced separation of families by CPS. On the video, you see Syesha in the back seat cradling her newborn, whom she had just breastfed. Ty is driving and has to pull over to the side of the road, where they are surrounded by law enforcement and CPS. There were so many police that you would have assumed they were a threat to national security. Syesha is heard asking, "What have I done? Did someone report that I hurt my baby?" Syesha appears defeated and forlorn as she hands them her daughter.

The events that led up to that moment were horrific. It was an awful sight. And now that it was recorded, now that millions had seen it, maybe people would realize the problems in this system. This was torturous and inhumane. There was nothing CPS could say, explain, or justify about this situation. I had never seen anything so harmful and disturbing. And this time, it was captured on tape.

The video made me physically sick. I felt helpless. We rallied with Syesha, hosted events, had Zoom calls, had conference calls, made phone calls, raised money, but the state still took her baby right out of her arms. This was senseless. All parties involved, from the intern to the judge, shared responsibility. A Black woman, not convicted of any crime, had to hand over her healthy baby to a sea of state agents, without knowing where the baby was going or who would be her caregiver. I thought of my nightmare from ten years ago, when I was scarred and disfigured. Those people who took Syesha's baby out of her arms had clear and unblemished faces, but they too were scarred and disfigured in many ways. They also had scarred that family. That is the moment I knew that families were not the only ones lost in this system. So were we. The investigators. The case managers. The social workers. Law en-

forcement. The mandated reporters. Those child welfare professionals taking away Syesha's newborn baby had clearly lost some part of
themselves. They callously carried out court-ordered protocols, with
no human compassion. They did not see what was right in front of
them. A mother breastfeeding her baby and crying out to understand
why she had to lose her. They only saw the next step in a painful and
systemically harmful process.

• • •

Having their newborn taken broke something inside Syesha and Ty,
but it also built something. They became laser focused on community
activism and prepared to host another event—this time it would be
in person in Sarasota. It would be an event with invited guests who
would fly in from around the country, with the goal of raising awareness, education, and support for mothers who were experiencing similar situations. Most of all, Syesha and Ty wanted this event to be a call
to action—for everyone to feel encouraged, motivated, and equipped
to speak up for those who are being treated unfairly by CPS.

When Syesha asked me if I would be a speaker at the event, I said yes
right away. But I was unsure how my involvement would be perceived.
At the time, I was the director of a research center that was focused
on enhancing child welfare through research, policy, and training. Although racial justice became my life's work, this was not the focus of my
day job. When fliers began to circulate with my face on them, next to
hashtags like #EndCPS or #StopCPS or #CPSLegalKidnapping, I was
bracing for the backlash. But then I thought of Erica. And I thought
of my sister. And I thought of my very first case during my internship,
Naomi. Then I thought of Jatoia, and every parent who is tormented by
the premature indictment of abuse. How could I face them if I cowered
so easily? The stakes were high for Syesha and Ty. The state had their

children, but that did not stop them. I wasn't going to let anything stop me either.

Out of all the invitations to speak that I have ever received, this was the most inspiring to me. I wouldn't be talking to academics, or social workers, or policy makers, or child welfare leaders. I was going to speak directly to parents who were reeling from the system or currently lost in it. I would be speaking to community members who wanted to learn how they could find a place in the movement. I would be speaking to community activists who have the brightest minds and the biggest hearts, and I would offer them encouragement to fight on.

The event was hosted at Payne Park in Sarasota. There were microphones set up at the top of the amphitheater where speakers would address the crowd. A small café was up near the stage area, where people could buy pastries, coffee, or tea. Families arrived and spread out blankets and sat in lawn chairs. Reporters were set up, near the front, with cameras and microphones to interview speakers and attendees. Music blared from the speakers of a DJ's console to the left side of the area. Many of the people in attendance carried signs. I noticed a few of the signs as I made my way over. One large sign said: "Dr. Sally Smith Must Be Stopped." Another one said: "Stop CPS." And another one: "Some Cops Are Called Caseworkers."

Syesha and Ty would address the crowd, the first time they had spoken publicly since they had their second child taken out of their custody for reasons that were still lost on them. After they finished, there would be a series of activists who would speak, and then parents who would share their stories. People were overcome with emotion. Some folks held others as they cried, and some people sat by themselves shaking with tears. It was impossible to take in this display of humanity without resolving to do all that is within your power to change this system. When it was my turn to speak, I took a deep breath and joined the movement:

BLACK MOTHERHOOD IS ON THE LINE

Over ten years ago, I started my career in child protective services; I wanted to help children and keep them safe. As I continued in my work as an investigator, it became clear that the measures that we used were alienating, isolating, punitive, and misguided. These were not safety measures. The CPS approach lacked many things: context, compassion, and cultural humility. The mandates and requirements created a scenario in which identifying family strengths was like finding a needle in a haystack. Of all the things we had to do, it was the smallest priority of them all.

Black women sit at the intersections of multiple injustices connected to race, gender, and class. And we are tired of redistributing funding streams that all link back to foster care and family separation. We are tired of the platitudes. The fabric of our society has been afflicted with systemic disadvantages for Black mothers and their families. Until our society and our communities embrace equity and liberation for families, our current, narrow view of abuse will continue to oppress the most vulnerable. Our system continues to judge parents harshly, and it is unable to assess familial situations that have been exacerbated by broader structural failings.

I believe we have reached an inflection point in the child protective services system. We are tired of Black women having to see their babies for one hour per week and be watched by a nearby social worker. We are tired of Black women having to prove themselves worthy enough to raise their families. We are tired of Black women having to prove their mental fitness in a world where mental health is a joke. We are tired of Black women having to grieve their living children and watch them be raised by another woman, sometimes just a few blocks away. And we are tired of the child welfare system mythologizing a painful past while perpetuating patterns of harm.

As I look out at each of you, this is a beautiful image of what a community should be. A community should not be composed of patrollers, reporters, and bystanders. A community takes an active role in learning, advocating, and providing support for families. A community should want to see Black women have what they need to love and care for a soul they brought into the world. We want a community that fights for the right to seek assistance with housing without fear of being reported. And, the right to request medical assistance and not receive predatory questioning and examination.

When I think about the restorative justice framework that is used in some criminal proceedings, it is inspiring to see how they conceptualize the community. In restorative justice, the emphasis is not on perpetrator and victim, because those dichotomies limit the complexities and nuances of this world. In child protective services, that dichotomy is the central premise and the foundation of their ongoing work. There are perpetrators and there are victims, but we know that this is shortsighted.

When Syesha and Ty asked me to speak at this event, I accepted the invitation but harbored reservations. I wondered, *What would it look like for me to be there? How might that be perceived?* But when you are clear about the hill on which you will die, then decisions start to become easier. This is my hill. Black women. Black motherhood. Black families. I watched CPS and the police enter Syesha and Ty's home, five of them, walking through searching for Syesha and her newborn. I watched that happen in real time and I still can't shake the violence inherent in that level of stalking and surveillance. It was disturbing and it added to the depth of exhaustion for all of us fighting against the policies and procedures of CPS.

Maya Angelou writes that "history, despite its wrenching pain, cannot be unlived, but if faced with courage, need not be lived again." Maya's words ring true because it has become strikingly clear to me that history is repeating itself in a different form, a form that is masquerading as child protective services. Black women have raised generations of people, but too many have had their babies taken away by the state. Black women are compassionate, generous, loving, and poised—even through their pain—but they continue to have their lives shaped and overdetermined by the most pathological stereotypes constructed to contain them.

Black women are just as human as anyone else, and they can grow, and they deserve a community in which to grow where they are not ostracized or isolated. bell hooks said that "rarely, if ever, are any of us healed in isolation. Healing is an act of communion with others." Yet the CPS process regularly alienates many parents by using destructive labels. I know that each of you are different and do not deserve to be lumped together, because your individual experiences matter. But I see two very clear commonalities with every Black mother here. First, you all are carrying one of the most painful and historically reverberating burdens there ever was, the loss of your children. And second, you also carry the irrepressible fervor to create a world where Black women can love their children fully and without disruption. And that is, quite literally, our ancestors' wildest dreams.[1]

WHAT WE CARRY

2023

AFTER ERICA ADOPTED MADISEN, SHE RAISED HER WITH LOVE and adoration. The bond between them grew each year, and their love anchored them. Madisen struggled with her identity for years. This happens regularly for adoptees, even those who don't have as traumatic a childhood as Madisen did. She has carried some grief for the relationships that she never had with her siblings. She has also carried a deep wound from the absence of Didi, a mother she learned had left her and never returned.

Didi's younger sisters lamented the loss of their niece from their family. They acknowledged Didi's challenges, but they were also Madisen's family and wished that they had been considered in the ordeal. When you pull a child away from her entire family and they are adopted, it is not necessarily the end of the world. But it is the end of a world. A world where that child could have cultivated lasting and trusting relationships with siblings, grandparents, aunts, and uncles. Most know that the child welfare system is reactionary. It never slows down enough to consider the lasting impact of the decisions the systems make and the impact on the children, parents, and extended family. Madisen is a young adult now. She thrives in many areas of her life—and plans to reconnect with her siblings and biological family in more meaningful ways going forward.

With all that Madisen carried as an adoptee, Erica provided her with love and the space to hold gratitude and grief. Erica remained vocal about the destructive nature of CPS. She encountered many opportunities that were thwarted due to her involvement with CPS, mainly employment opportunities. The reality and long-standing negative effects that CPS has on a person's life are hard to track or enumerate. Ultimately, Erica was never convicted, and her record was expunged. But her arrest still had potential for future impact.

The system villainized Erica, facilitated her arrest, painted a picture of her that begets terror and fear, and then put her on a pedestal during the adoption process. She considers CPS to be a manipulative system that builds its case decisions on single snapshots of a person's life. The experiences that she had with the CPS system were life-altering; throughout the years between reunification and adoption, she had a constant CPS presence in her life. They were relentless. In some ways, she never really felt settled again. Liberty and autonomy truly feel precarious after an experience with CPS.

• • •

A few months after the Sarasota Town Hall, Syesha was reunited with her children. She and I had a conversation about a year later. We had been playing phone tag and trying to connect. I was looking forward to talking to her and hearing how she was doing now that her family was back together. We weren't exactly friends, but we did have an understanding of the CPS experience. What she went through over the past year was horrific, and I was desperate to understand the resilience that it takes to stand upright after that.

I've seen Syesha sing on national television, address a crowd by giving a speech, become hysterical with tears and riddled with fear of CPS, and cry softly through pain. I've also seen her so exhausted that she was immune to any feelings at all. And when I imagine her now, with her two children, Malik and Anastasia, I smile. But I also stand in wonder—how precious each moment with her family must be.

"How are you holding up?" I asked her.

I could hear her little girl playfully cooing in the background, Syesha likely multitasking. I, too, was making dinner and trying to be mindful of my clattering pots.

"You know, Dr. Pryce... I'm good. We're good. When I think about everything that happened—" She stopped for a moment. I'm not sure if she was thinking or if she was busy with her children. She picked the conversation back up, "You know when you have a really bad dream?"

Boy, did I.

"Yes," I responded. "Does your CPS experience feel like that?"

"Sometimes it does. When you have a bad dream, you remember it, but it feels sort of far away, half remembered. Still stings when you think about it, but it feels a bit removed from reality. That CPS situation feels like it was a part of another dimension of consciousness. But then some days, the terror of it all comes back to me."

"We are just really focused on being present with our children. We have started a nonprofit organization called Sing 2 the Children, where we create resources for parents who might find themselves in a similar situation. Would you be open to being a part of what we are working on?" she asked me.

"I absolutely would. Please keep me posted on how I can help. I think it's amazing that you are doing this."

"What happened to my family might feel like a bad dream, but we know it wasn't. It was real. And yes, I have my children back, but what about the agonizing months away from them? And what about the parents who never get to bring their children home?"

I realized that some mothers who found their way back to their children would never turn that experience into service to others. And I do not fault them. But then there was Syesha, and Jatoia, who were doing what I'm not sure I could do. Committing to ensuring that no one else goes through the same thing, and if they do, they don't go through it alone.

"Dr. Pryce, I want to thank you. CPS is such a powerful system and I know you often felt like there was nothing you could do."

She was right. I'm not a lawyer and I'm no longer employed by CPS, so I often feel like I can't affect their case outcomes. I was likely a broken record when I lamented, "I wish I could do more."

"But you did more than you know. You listened to me and Ty. And even better, you heard us. It takes effort to not believe the lies that are fed to us as parents. Not even for a moment did you make us feel like what we went through was warranted, and we appreciate you so much."

Before I ended the call with Syesha, I shared with her how much I appreciate them. She and Ty changed the way I do and see my work. They inspired my activism; they showed a level of bravery that I had never had.

• • •

When Jatoia's legal rights were terminated, it felt like an assault on her entire family and community. There was collective outrage. Her story was shared across social media, and news stations highlighted her story across the state of North Carolina. Elizabeth, still recovering from the disappointment of losing the TPR case, prepared an appeal for the Supreme Court of North Carolina. She recruited several organizations as amici to render their endorsements of support, including the American Civil Liberties Union (ACLU), the National Association for the Advancement of Colored People (NAACP), and the North Carolina Coalition against Domestic Violence (NCCADV). The issues that were being presented in the appeal were (1) did the court make an error in their decision to terminate the parental rights of Jatoia Potts, and (2) did the court make an error in excluding my testimony in the trial.

Since its inception, the ACLU has been at the forefront of efforts to protect constitutional and civil rights, particularly for folks who have been historically marginalized. The ACLU had a strong interest in supporting the appellate petition on behalf of Jatoia. With decades of case law as precedent, the ACLU submitted their argument, citing (1) the sanctity of the parent-child relationship, which is protected under the Fourteenth Amendment, and (2) the trial court's failure to consider Jatoia's exhaustive efforts to remedy every situation that was presented as a barrier to reunification.

The North Carolina chapter of the NAACP is the oldest and largest civil rights organization in the state, with a special focus on activism, social justice, and litigating the civil rights of Black Americans. The focus of the NAACP's report was the failure to hear and consider the role of racial bias in the child welfare system. The NC-NAACP felt that the sensitive yet salient issue of race was unfairly handled in Jatoia's proceedings. They cited numerous scholars who have documented the disturbing patterns of families who are lost in the child protective system, many of whom are struggling with persistent challenges, including poverty, domestic violence, and mental health. The NAACP stated plainly that the trial court abused its discretion in failing to consider expert testimony, particularly in a case with a nonoffending Black woman. They respectfully urged the Supreme Court to reverse the lower court's opinion on the consideration of my testimony as evidence.

The NCCADV submitted a report in support of Jatoia's appeal; it focused on the importance of trial courts to consider the safety needs of survivors of domestic violence. It is imperative that courts do not signal to survivors of domestic violence that their fitness as parents is being scrutinized in relation to how they are managing their victimhood and trauma. The NCCADV urges more awareness of how trial courts treat victims of domestic violence. The report sought to demonstrate how more attention to the survivors will better equip courts to protect children and promote safe parent-child interactions.

When decisions such as these go to the High Court for appeal, generally the decision and the final ruling is five pages or less. Elizabeth was astonished when she received the Supreme Court's decision. Not only was it nearly one hundred pages, but it also upheld the CPS decision to terminate Jatoia's parental rights.

That ruling made it all final and irreversible. The race for Jatoia had ended. LJ and Kenny were officially eligible for adoption. When I finished reading through the Supreme Court decision, all I could think of was Mrs. Sims, the foster mother, calling her best friend, excitedly announcing, "They have finally terminated Jatoia's parental rights!" Again, I was at a moment where I saw the rare occurrence when someone's lowest point in life becomes the highest for someone else.

• • •

On January 4, 2024, Jatoia's eldest son, LJ, turned eight years old. She has not seen him since their last day of visitation in September 2019, when he was three years old. When this day comes each year, as well as Kenny's birthday, she is painfully reminded that she will not get the chance to see her boys grow up. She has not seen a picture or heard their voices in years. The following was our final interview:

JESSICA PRYCE: I'm glad we have the chance to connect and catch up. How have you been?

JATOIA POTTS: I'm doing okay, just taking things one day at a time.

PRYCE: I can understand that. I see you're still in Durham. Does it feel like home?

POTTS: Not really. And I don't understand them, the foster parents. Maybe they thought that I would just go back to Georgia? But, I'm a real mom and my kids live here. I'm not leaving. It will just never make sense to me. I'm sure they are telling their friends that they saved these two boys, but that's just not true. Did Elizabeth tell you that we have a big interview coming out tonight?

PRYCE: Yes, and I'm so glad that you're still able to get this story out there.

POTTS: So again, I just don't understand these foster parents. The story is going out statewide so I'm sure that someone from their community or church will see it. I really think they thought I would just give up. I still just keep thinking about how my kids are going to want an explanation from their foster parents. When they grow up, they will want to know why they were kept from their mother.

PRYCE: I agree.

POTTS: I completely see now that no matter how much love you have for your children, the system stacks everything against you until you have no choice but to give up. Literally no choice.

PRYCE: Absolutely. I talk about this very thing quite a bit in relation to the power that CPS has at their disposal. You mentioned during one of our discussions that at the beginning you were in regular communication with the foster parents, is that right?

POTTS: Yes, we talked and I remember at the first visitation, the foster mother made a comment that she had no idea that my sons had an "active mom." I think these people assume that all kids who come into the system have parents who don't care. But, yeah, we would text and call and they would send me pictures of my kids. I was never mean to them, always respectful. Because I knew they had the power.

PRYCE: When did that change?

POTTS: It started to change after I was arrested. They did not want LJ to have visitation with me anymore because of his behavior. But I remember hearing things about this behavior and him choking dolls and lashing out. He never did that with me. I always raised my son to be kind and gentle.

PRYCE: No pictures or anything after visitation ended?

POTTS: Nothing. They were done with me. I would love to see them now, even a picture would be nice.

PRYCE: That seems like a reasonable request. I also remember you mentioning that you asked your caseworker to share photos. Did that ever happen?

POTTS: I think so but I can't be sure. I'm not sure how much the foster parents could dictate to the caseworker. One of my caseworkers really felt sorry for me so she might have.

PRYCE: And I recall you said that you had four different caseworkers throughout your case and how that level of turnover really impacted the timeline.

POTTS: Definitely. It's like white people are controlling everything but they have Black people doing the work. Every caseworker I had was Black. My paw-paw says that it literally reminds him of the slave patrols from back in the day. When I tell people that I had four Black women as caseworkers, a Black woman judge, and a Black couple is trying to adopt my kids. People are like, what?

PRYCE: I remember you told me that in the trial, the judge cried before she made her decision.

POTTS: Yes, she was crying so hard, she literally needed a moment to gather herself before she told us her decision. I wanted to say . . . you know I carried them, right? You know they were in this body. [Jatoia pointed to herself.] Our lives are forever linked so no termination of my rights can change that. No matter what this court says.

PRYCE: That's so true, Jatoia. I know the Supreme Court made their ruling. But can anything else be done?

POTTS: As far as my parental rights, that part seems like it's done. But I now work with Elizabeth at Emancipate NC. I handle all of their community organizing and activism work. My focus is on CPS reform and creating alternatives to policing. I spend my days connecting with people and connecting with organizations. I'm still fighting but in a different way.

PRYCE: Wow, that is great that you have found such a passion and purpose for this work. I know it can't be easy to do with all you've gone through.

POTTS: It is hard, but you know what, I look at it like leaving clues for my kids. I know one day they will find me. I know they will find me because I'm not going to stop doing what I'm doing in the community and speaking out about this.

PRYCE: And Elizabeth told me that Lawrence's father is petitioning for adoption?

POTTS: Yes, now that the appeal is over, adoption is next. We wanted to at least try to get the boys adopted into my family. But the foster parents put in their petition as well.

PRYCE: Jatoia, what do you think life is like for your boys?

POTTS: Well, there are so many eyes on the foster parents [the Simses] because of all the community work that we do, so I'm sure my boys are being well taken care of. I'd like to think that LJ thinks about me. . . . I'm sure he must remember me, some parts of me, I hope. But I know even the best memories fade over time. The boys are being loved, I'm sure of it. It's not hard to love them. They have beautiful souls.

PRYCE: Jatoia, do you know how Lawrence is doing?

POTTS: Not good at all. His father told me that he was homeless and was recently arrested. It's all pretty sad. I'm just like, that could have been me. This CPS process will make you lose your mind if you do not take care of yourself, and I'm pretty sure that's what has happened to him. It could have easily been me.

PRYCE: How have you been able to cope and take care of yourself?

POTTS: Losing my kids is something that I have to deal with every single day, and some days I just have to tell my friends and family that—I don't want to do anything today. Some days it's too hard to do anything at all.

PRYCE: I'm so glad you have a community of support who you can be honest with on those days.

POTTS: Honestly, some days I don't know how or why I'm still doing this work but then I keep going. And I think about how when I had my kids, they were always with me. So I still consider them with me and I will always carry them with me.

PRYCE: Jatoia, I know within your advocacy work you are aware of the limited availability of good attorneys for parents who are going through a CPS case. What has it meant having Elizabeth in your corner?

POTTS: Everything. She is so smart and passionate about social and racial justice. I don't just feel like she's working on my behalf, it's clear that this actually matters to her. And I think that's rare.

PRYCE: I can confirm that it is rare, so many people need attorneys like that. Win or lose, parents need someone in their corner.

POTTS: I agree.

PRYCE: Jatoia, I know holidays were so difficult during this case. How was this past holiday?

POTTS: Well, I put up a Christmas tree and it's February and it's still up! [laughs] I haven't put up a tree since before this all happened, so it's a big deal that I wanted to get into the Christmas spirit this year.

PRYCE: Oh, that's nice to know. Sounds like some parts of the things you once enjoyed are back, perhaps some healing is happening. And actually, I wanted to ask you about healing. What does healing look like for you? What does healing mean for you at this stage?

POTTS: The first time I lost my kids, when they came and took them and put them in foster care, that was the lowest I've ever felt in my life and I somewhat feel like I never bounced back. I've just been completely numb since that moment. And I'm still haunted by my last visitation with LJ. I hugged him and kissed him and tried to soothe him. I said, "I'll see you next week. I'll be back, baby, don't cry." But then they stopped my visitation and he never saw me again. I think about that all the time. So, I think full healing for me is when my kids find me, and they realize that I never gave up. They will see that I've spent my life waiting for them.

IT ENDS WITH US

THERE ARE SOME CHILDREN WHO NEED IMMEDIATE PROTEC-
tion, some families who need state intervention, and some parents
who need judicial accountability. Those types of cases are in the minority nationwide, and they constitute none of the Black mothers in
this book. The families in this book, even my own, presented complex
circumstances that were exacerbated by the state child welfare system.
Each of the children mentioned in this book spent a combined ten
years under court supervision or in state custody separated from their
homes and families, and some will never come home. Some parents
will grieve their living children for the rest of their lives. Their present-
ing issues were related to poverty, domestic violence, accidental harm,
or alleged medical neglect. I did not want to write a book about egre-
gious child deaths or nefarious parents, because the data are clear that
those are not the majority of what our system sees. Ultimately, I wrote
a book that shows the internal and conflicting struggles of carrying
child abuse cases, how those cases are experienced by Black women,
and the emotional and moral toll that it takes on everyone involved.

This book was written to illuminate the challenges that Black parents and their extended families face every day, and how their unique
positions in society make them even more vulnerable to CPS intervention.

This book was also written to describe the experiences of child welfare professionals who juggle daily decisions alongside ethics and procedural requirements. Over the years, I have maintained a level of compassion for people on both sides of the clipboard. When I was in the field, we carried clipboard binders, which held papers inside them, but also allowed for documents to be clipped to the top. That clipboard held full reconnaissance on the family. The family's vulnerability and objectivity were visceral. I've held the clipboard, but I've also seen and felt the impact on the other side, through my friends and family. Families are exposed in a way that they do not even realize when they are undergoing a CPS investigation. While we currently have this inept system of child protective services, I believe that in order to engage with families meaningfully and ethically, we need to understand the professionals and start the transformation process from within.

It is hard to imagine that a CPS investigator could become transformative in the life of a family, but I saw it play out recently when I watched a documentary commissioned by the New Jersey Department of Children and Families. There was a scene in the documentary when a Black mother walked up and hugged her CPS investigator; I had to push rewind. As a previous investigator, I can tell you that none of the people on my caseloads handed out hugs! The woman talked about how the investigator approached her at the onset of her case by sharing how much of a team they needed to be. The investigator told this mother that removing her children was the last thing she ever wanted to do. The mother reflected that it was through her interactions with that investigator that she realized that CPS could serve in a different function from simply pulling families apart. The Black woman added, "having this investigator show up as a human has helped me through another stage of my healing."

I do not believe that the investigator in that documentary is the norm. In my professional experiences, child protective services investigations have been Orwellian. It is a process that reflects the kind of dystopian government overreach so often talked about in our political discourse. But it is also Orwellian in the sense that the system's name—child protective services—too often belies what actually happens when CPS intervenes. The truth is, children in the system are not always protected. They are removed [protected] from their parents but are often open to a host of other social and relational troubles while in foster care.[1]

The CPS system generally manages the structural failings within society by highlighting individual flaws within parents. These systems punish parents for being low-income without interrogating the generational, racial, and/or systemic disadvantages that vulnerable families experience. We know that poverty is a powerful factor in the outcomes associated with the work of child protective services. But there are others. Gender and race are also overdetermining factors. If you are a Black woman, you are more likely to be subjected to well-meaning professionals who are guided by a racist, classist, and sexist system of services. When multiple pillars intersect in your individual identity, you and your children all at once become more susceptible to child welfare involvement. This book shows this phenomenon through an intersectional lens while illuminating the consequences that are compounded for Black women.[2]

Black feminist legal scholar Kimberlé Crenshaw coined the term *intersectionality* in 1989, and subsequent scholars have expounded on that seminal work. Crenshaw's work is an incisive approach to capturing the dynamics of race, gender, class, and other individual characteristics of identity as they interface with society and discriminatory practices attached to (and attacking) those identities. One of her more devastating conclusions is that Black women are "theoretically erased." The uniqueness of each woman is ignored by the system. Being an economically poor parent puts you at greater risk of CPS involvement in your family life. Being a Black mother increases that risk. Experiencing low income, racial injustice, and gender inequity introduces a devastating set of stressors. Unfortunately, the intersection of these challenges for Black mothers is not taken into careful consideration by our child welfare system. In this sense, CPS seemingly holds a different (and discriminatory) set of rules for impoverished Black mothers. Any mother facing the reality of losing their child/children might feel humiliated and terrified by the thought of separation. But for Black mothers with this intersecting threat of discrimination, the stakes for any interaction with CPS are unusually high. Child welfare will continue to have a deleterious effect on Black women unless there is a deliberate effort to change the foundation of the system.

I often teach about how child welfare has evolved as a system. But evolution is not revolution. Evolutionary change (changes that make the system better) and revolutionary change (changes that make the system profoundly different) are often at odds with each other, but I believe they should work in tandem. Engaging in evolutionary change is sensible as long as there is a priority of effort, working concurrently, to shift the foundational fabric of the system. Considering the framework for my development, I realized that *agents* tend to favor the maintenance of their current system, *advocates* repeatedly seek evolutionary changes, and *activists* display unwavering commitment to revolutionizing how this system fundamentally operates.

An important distinction between evolutionary and revolutionary work is the reality that the former centers on *survival*. When you are simply evolving as a system, you will do whatever it takes to keep the system going in the same direction—even if evidence informs a different course of action. Although the child welfare system has survived all these years, it hasn't thrived, and neither have the families it serves. Revolutionary change is not consumed with resembling the checkered past of child welfare policies and procedures. It is actively pursuing a different set of foundational premises. Whenever I speak publicly, I take audiences through examples of social policy dating back one hundred years, and I describe how each policy has passively evolved. Evolutionary change is normal and at times natural, but it is also neutral. It is expected and embraced. In some ways, evolutionary change has made child welfare better, year after year. I've seen with my own eyes that the system has experienced slight improvements over time. For example, there was a time when children were taken away from their parents and placed in foster care, and they would not see a therapist or a physician for months. As it was, CPS removed children from their homes and then did not provide the care they needed while in state custody. Then policies evolved. Now, in many states, there are mandates that require a foster child see a therapist or a doctor within the first few weeks of their time in care. Although this may not always happen, there are policies in place to guide the procedures. This is an instance where evolutionary change made positive improvements for system-involved children. But that change did not make the system operate differently, only slightly better. A revolutionary change means that a child would not have to be separated from their parents in order to access critical medical and mental health treatment. A revolutionary shift means that parents and children get what they need from a system that will make exhaustive efforts to keep them together.

Revolutionary change is not neutral. It is never expected and rarely embraced—at first. Revolutionary change would radically alter the operations within child welfare. It would never settle for incremental improvements; it is committed to challenging the foundation of child welfare and creating a humane experience for families. Evolutionary change maintains the status quo. It claims to "protect" children and "help" families, which is noble but shortsighted. Revolutionary change must reach beyond noble ideas and platitudes. Revolutionary change would be a CPS system that approaches the relational connections between a child and their family as sacrosanct. The commitment to strengthening families should be CPS's ultimate, if not singular, goal.

My journey with child welfare started over fifteen years ago. As an intern, I was simply trying to learn the system and be helpful. I needed to understand how everything worked in order to be successful at what I believed was a profession committed to protecting children and serving families. As an observer of the inner workings of the system, I began to experience the abundant fault lines. CPS did not hold the relationships between children and parents as a sacred connection. Moreover, CPS was rarely equitable. The system simply did not account for the structural disparities that some families face.

Watching people in your life—people who are close to you—struggle through the CPS process is a form of torture, especially when you consider how many families you have put through the same process. I started to understand the ways in which my colleagues and I had been deployed as a tool of the state to investigate families while simultaneously mandated to consider their well-being. It's a tall order to prioritize the well-being of a family that you can very easily pull apart.

The impossibility of the job was one of the reasons that I decided to return to school. I knew that knowledge—subject matter expertise—was an important path forward for me. If I understood my role in the CPS system as an agent, then I needed to learn much more about the history of the system and its structures to find my place in transforming it. Taking a deep dive into the system's history helped me see the patterns of change that had been occurring in the system. The steady evolution was clear, and the way in which the system fell short, time after time, was glaring.

I taught my first graduate school course, as an adjunct, at the University of Maryland in 2013. When I taught about evolutionary and revolutionary change within systems, I often discussed one of my favorite games: Jenga. There are various versions of Jenga. Some games are life-size and as tall as I am. When you play Jenga, the point is to take a block and place it back on the top of the Jenga system without making it fall down. If you have ever played this game, you know it is fun, but it can also be stressful. All of the players are committed to keeping the Jenga system standing tall. The various blocks are gently manipulated, but the foundational block that built the Jenga tower is never touched. It can't be! Strategic players avoid the foundation at all costs. This is a reminder that the folks who are thwarting the true revolution of child welfare are usually well-intentioned, intelligent, and highly strategic thinkers. These folks have skillfully maintained a massive and growing child welfare system for decades and have yet to prove that it is both efficacious and safe.

In America's child welfare systems, we constantly move blocks (policies and programs), and we sometimes make the system better. We evaluate policies, and we maybe even add funding to new programs. We conduct trainings and develop staff according to the new, evolved programs and policies. But for the most part, we put the same blocks back into the same system. We rarely remove a block and throw it away, even though some parts of the system should be discarded completely. We just keep restacking, and we remain ever so careful to keep the system upright. I will never discourage or discount systems that work to do and be better, but at this point, refusing to ever alter the foundations of child welfare is negligent and will result in continued workforce dysfunction and community harm.

Families in our communities need the child welfare system to look and feel different. We need to show up in people's lives in a way that communicates compassion and a humane understanding of the structures that underpin their family's challenges. It is time to dig into the foundational assumptions, mindsets, and biases that guide every policy and operational procedure within the system. And yes, that digging will pull apart a system that we have always known—and it will take courage to create something new.

• • •

A few years ago, a quick Google search about rebuilding the Jenga tower produced some astonishing results. There are people who have successfully stacked one thousand blocks on a single block. The new Jenga tower now flowers outward rather than straight up. This new system revolutionizes the initial version by building the structure on one single block. One single value, assumption, or foundational belief. It's inspiring, but to be honest, the new Jenga gaming system makes me nervous. The new version feels precarious and unrealistic to me. It feels a bit scary. My uncertainty about this foundational shift makes me leery of rebuilding anything at all. It seems like it will be too hard.

This is how most people feel about revolutionary change. This is how people feel about becoming a child welfare activist. It reflects the exact kind of feedback I receive when I do workshops or give talks about ways to advance antiracist policies and procedures in the child welfare system. People get nervous. They feel uncertain and scared that this is an unrealistic and possibly unnecessary change. Why can't we keep the other Jenga system? It was fine!

Seeing another way to build Jenga changed my world. That a new system—same game—could be built on top of one single block still amazes me. It is an apt metaphor for my professional goals associated with the child welfare system. It represents the possibility of building from a new foundational block to guide our revolutionary work going forward. I encourage leaders to choose a new and braver foundation on which to build a new system. Sometimes the new foundation may not seem sturdy enough to bear the weight of such profound change, but we owe families the agility to take measured risks toward transformation. As a leader who wants to equip, empower, and compel other leaders to change our child welfare system, I also hold myself accountable to not being content with simply moving the pieces around in the system.

I encourage all child welfare professionals to join me in considering what they are currently working toward in their respective agencies. I sincerely believe that many of us enter the CPS profession as service-oriented optimists who believe that we are changing children's lives for the better. I also know and believe that after spending time as a CPS agent, inflicting unintentional harm, the cases you carry begin to assume a weight on your soul that is almost impossible to lift. This heaviness can be exchanged for the hope that revolution is possible, even probable.

Imagine what the system should be and begin to think about all of the ways that you—as a child welfare professional—might engage a family in a way that centers compassion, that appreciates the humanity of the people you are trying to help, and that realizes the limitations of the CPS playbook as it is currently written. For me, the revolution started internally through every phase of my professional and personal development, and I believe that many in our workforce are feeling the internal shift but are unsure how to maneuver when their system is lagging behind. Many professionals share with me that they feel overwhelmed by the fractured system and are not sure if they can alter such dysfunction. When I hear those sentiments, I'm reminded of a quote: "Profound change is more honest than grandiose."[3] This compels me to tell child welfare professionals that the revolution is honest, not loud. The revolution will begin with honest introspection and then intentional steps *toward* families in partnership, not away from them.

There are several schools of thought on how to bring about this sort of change, and each one has its own merit. For me, I desire to create a different foundation that leads to a shift in how we care for our workforce, how we center families, and how we partner with parents. I intend to lead from the middle. Child welfare professionals are in the middle, with federal and state oversight on one side and the families they serve on another. Their input, knowledge, and buy-in is critical if we want to shift how this system operates. Along with the workforce, parents and families should be at the table as co-architects of the new system. Their insight and experience are crucial, and that is a key reason that the voices of Black women ring loudly throughout this book.

My journey from agent to advocate to activist was facilitated by personal and professional moments of clarity. Although my phases were somewhat distinct, that may not be the case for all professionals. Professional development is dynamic, and it doesn't always chart a linear path. Wherever you are in the child welfare sphere—front line, agency leaders, court officials, educators, medical personnel, volunteers, foster parents, therapists, or even law enforcement—I invite you to consider what phase of development you are in and consider how the attributes associated with that phase influence how you engage families.

After spending time with the women featured in this book, I am compelled and inspired to bring the current child welfare system to a historic ending. When I finish speaking to audiences, I always invite the audience to *let it be us*. Let it be us who finally end the torrent of harm from the child welfare system. Let it be us who will work concurrently with policy makers but who will not wait for them to catch up. Let it be this generation of child welfare professionals who begin a revolution with the next family they encounter. The current method of protecting children has to end at some point, and I implore the child welfare workforce to let it end with us.

ACKNOWLEDGMENTS

I WANT TO THANK EACH AND EVERY BLACK WOMAN WHO GAVE their time and their heart to this book. I also want to thank my former colleagues for your time and transparency. Your commitment to this work was inspiring. Thank you for responding to every email and every text message and for trusting that your story could create more change than we can imagine. The process of writing this book was grueling, sacrificial, and edifying. Mostly, it was an honor. Thank you.

I'm grateful to my editorial team: Gabriella Page-Fort, Daphney Guillaume, Jennifer Baker, Jessica Berry, Ayana Byrd, Lori Tharps, and the team at Scriptocentric, LLC. Thank you for your partnership, patience, and honesty. I also want to thank Tracy Sherrod, who is an icon in publishing and saw the vision for this book before I did. And to my agents at McKinnon Literary, thank you for your representation and encouragement. I also want to thank the host of people who read my entire manuscript and offered feedback, insight, and enhancements: Virginia Deberry, Abigail Williams-Butler, Caroline Mendez, and Savannah Bowen.

Over the years, I have benefited greatly from amazing professional and personal mentors who have helped cultivate my work and voice. To name a few: Reverend George L. Williams, Joan Zlotnik, Katharine Briar-Lawson, Mary McCarthy, Margaret Ashmore, Fran Gomory, Anthony James, Belinda Williams, Shanna Batten Aguirre, Phyllis Miller, Mary Dunson, and Gwen Waxkirsh.

I want to thank my family and friends as they have provided ongoing love and support throughout the past six years of researching, developing, writing, rewriting, revising, and finalizing this book. Special acknowledgment to my parents, Viola Pryce and the late Ramsay Pryce. Thank you to my siblings and nieces and nephews. Also, a big thank-you to my Florida network (especially KD, JN, and AC), gratitude to my comrades from Howard University (HU!!), my beloved BBBS crew (I don't need to spell out that acronym), and my soul-sisters from Pan 19 (I have an idea for our next book club: you're holding it).

I'd be remiss not to thank my hometown, Fruitland Park. I call it the "city that built me," and I truly mean that. A special thank-you to my hometown shero, Mrs. Henrietta B. Mcgriff, who was my person and my best friend for over twenty-five years. I will never forget you. Also, sincere gratitude to Mrs. Yvonne Thornton, who told me when I was a preteen, "You're going to be a writer one day," to which I replied, "Me?!"

The most important acknowledgment that I could give is to God, who authored and finished everything at Calvary.

DEVELOPMENTAL FRAMEWORK FOR CHILD WELFARE PROFESSIONALS AND COMMUNITY PARTNERS

	PHASE 1: AGENT →	PHASE 2: ADVOCATE →	PHASE 3: ACTIVIST
MINDSET	SEGREGATIONIST	ASSIMILATIONIST	ANTI-RACIST
GUIDING SENTIMENT	Pity	Empathy	Compassion
POWER DYNAMIC	Hierarchical and Imbalanced	Negotiated and Reciprocal	Shared and Balanced
BELIEF SYSTEM	"These people are permanently inferior, and they cannot be helped. We must save them from themselves."	"These people are only temporarily inferior, and they can be helped. We can rehabilitate them. We can help them become better parents."	"These people are people, and they were never inferior. They have strength, value, and inherent worth."
OPERATING SYSTEM	Punishing	Saving	Liberating

Our **mindset** about families (how we view them) impacts our **feelings** about them, which informs how much **power** we give to them. All of which influence our **beliefs** about their potential, which overdetermines what we will do (how we **operate**).

PHASE 1: AGENT

- Do I ask the hard questions about systemic harm, or do I keep them to myself?

- Am I vocalizing my concerns and using my voice effectively?

- Am I hiding behind bureaucratic pressure and solely following policies and procedures without considering their harm?

- Do I prioritize finding a guilty and offending parent over considering nuances and individuality?

PHASE 2: ADVOCATE

- Am I asking myself the hard questions and seeking answers?

- Do I actively educate others and promote awareness for systemic shifts and policy changes?

- Am I reconnecting with social work values of social justice, dignity, integrity, and the importance of human relationships?

- Am I aware of the barriers marginalized families face?

- Am I mindful of the impact my actions and decisions have on families and their well-being?

PHASE 3: ACTIVIST

- Have I cultivated the courage to challenge others with the hard and pressing questions about systemic harm?

- Am I willing to speak up and embrace discomfort to drive true change?

- Do I prioritize equity, liberation, and the value of humanity in my work?

- Am I standing up for what is right, even if it means taking risks?

- Am I actively working toward an anti-racist and family-centered child protective system?

CASE-BASED DISCUSSION QUESTIONS AND CONVERSATION PROMPTS

Naomi Harden

In chapter 1, the reader is introduced to a mother, Naomi Harden, whose home has been reported for environmental hazards, and her parenting behaviors have been seen as neglectful.

- What phase of the developmental framework (Agent, Advocate, Activist) led the investigation? How did it affect the interaction?

- When the CPS investigators made contact with Naomi, were any of their procedures and behaviors especially punitive and dehumanizing? If so, which ones?

- In what specific ways could the CPS investigators have prioritized Naomi's autonomy and dignity within their interaction?

- Why do you think that Naomi asked the intern, "Do you have any children?" What was the subtext of her question? What was she *really* asking?

- At the school, it was clear that Naomi's children were overburdened at home and needed some sort of help. How do you think the CPS system can balance the urge to "save" children with the commitment to strengthen their family unit?

INTROSPECTION

As a child welfare professional, what procedures do you carry out with families despite the pain and stress they are facing? What are you feeling when you are operating in that manner? What part of your development has been illuminated?

What evolutionary and revolutionary ideas do you have regarding how to keep something like this case outcome from happening again?

Diedre "Didi" Lawson

In chapter 2, the reader is introduced to a mother, Diedre "Didi" Lawson, who is experiencing several challenges, such as homelessness and displacement, poverty, and sexual abuse as a child.

- What phase of the developmental framework (Agent, Advocate, Activist) led each CPS interaction with Didi? In her childhood and her adulthood? How did it impact the interaction?

- How did Didi's childhood trauma affect her adulthood choices and behaviors?

- In many ways, Didi was an absent parent and difficult to reach as it related to her responsibilities with Madisen. How has the system historically dealt with parents who behave in this way? What community partners should be at the table when making decisions about an absent parent?

- Essentially, Didi never finished her court-ordered case plan. Take some time to ponder her evasiveness and refusal. And, do you think it *was* evasiveness and refusal?

INTROSPECTION

As a child welfare professional, what did you feel when reading Didi's story? Did you experience empathy toward her or frustration with her choices or both?

What were your thoughts about her rights being terminated?

What evolutionary and revolutionary ideas do you have regarding how to keep something like this case outcome from happening again?

Erica Gaines

In chapter 2, the reader is introduced to Erica Gaines, who was devoted and committed to her goddaughter, Madisen.

- What phase of the developmental framework (Agent, Advocate, Activist) led Erica's physical abuse investigation? How did it affect the interaction?

- Due to Didi's transition, Erica tried to step in as caregiver; what barriers did she face in requesting public assistance for Madisen?

- In what specific ways could the CPS investigator have prioritized Erica's autonomy and dignity within their first interaction?

- Could there have been a better plan for Madisen's placement rather than traditional foster care? If so, what could that plan have been?

- Did you feel any empathy toward the lead investigator, Lydia? If so, discuss how there is often a dehumanization of professionals and families.

INTROSPECTION

Corporal punishment is a controversial topic and brings up different emotions for people. As a child welfare professional, what were you feeling during the description of the spanking? In your professional opinion, was Madisen in danger in Erica's custody?

What evolutionary and revolutionary ideas do you have regarding how to keep something like this case outcome from happening again?

Jatoia and Lawrence

In chapter 4, the reader is introduced to a mother, Jatoia Potts, who was reported to CPS for medical neglect and physical abuse.

- What phase of the developmental framework (Agent, Advocate, Activist) led the investigation of Jatoia? How did it affect the interaction?

- When the CPS investigators made contact with Jatoia, were any of their procedures and behaviors especially punitive and dehumanizing? If so, which ones?

- In what specific ways could the CPS investigators have considered Jatoia's unique experience of being a young mother with a medically needy child?

- In what ways did agents with a segregationist mindset and advocates with an assimilationist mindset affect this case?

INTROSPECTION

As a child welfare professional who has likely seen similar cases, what feelings came up for you with this case? As you read, at what point in the case did you see the impact of racial and/or economic inequity?

What evolutionary and revolutionary ideas do you have regarding how to keep something like this case outcome from happening again?

Natasha and Matthew

In chapter 6, the reader is introduced to a mother and father, Natasha and Matthew, whose son suffered an accident while he was watching a movie at home with his father.

- What phase of the developmental framework (Agent, Advocate, Activist) led the investigation that commenced at the hospital? How did it affect the interaction?

- When the CPS investigator made contact with the family at the hospital, were any of their procedures and behaviors especially punitive and dehumanizing? If so, which ones?

- How did this case mirror the hospital interaction with Jatoia Potts? What other procedures persist across families, across systems, and across states?

- In what specific ways could the CPS investigator have prioritized this family's well-being in such a moment of crisis?

- Do you think that most families would have faced arrest with a similar incident? Why or why not?

INTROSPECTION

As a child welfare professional, have you ever had to interview someone at a hospital or in a similar crisis? How did you prepare? Did you adapt any of your approach methods based on the situation?

What evolutionary and revolutionary ideas do you have regarding how to keep something like this case outcome from happening again?

Rachel

In chapter 8, the reader is introduced to Rachel, who was reported to CPS for a domestic violence incident.

- What phase of the developmental framework (Agent, Advocate, Activist) led the investigation? How did it affect the interaction?

- When the CPS investigators made contact with Rachel, were any of their procedures and behaviors especially punitive and dehumanizing? If so, which ones?

- When voluntary services are offered in situations like this, are they truly voluntary?

- In what ways can the victims' advocate community and the child welfare community better understand each other and work in tandem?

- Some professionals are encouraging a paradigm shift from "mandated reporting" to "mandated supporting"; what do you think about that shift and how do you think it could affect child welfare?

INTROSPECTION

As a mandated reporter, have you ever filed a CPS report on a family? What were your feelings when you did? What ideas do you have about how to train and educate mandated reporters on issues of equity and justice?

What evolutionary and revolutionary ideas do you have regarding how to keep something like this case outcome from happening again?

The Dima Family

In chapter 8, the reader is also introduced to Andrew Dima, who has been reported for the possible physical abuse of his son and has a history of domestic disturbances in the home.

- What phase of the developmental framework (Agent, Advocate, Activist) led the investigation? How did it affect the interaction?

- When the CPS investigators made contact with Mr. Dima, he did not give them access to his home or his family. How is it possible that he is not mandated to allow them in his home when so many other parents assume they are required to?

- When it comes to potentially combative situations with clients, how should CPS investigators respond to this sort of behavior and tension?

INTROSPECTION

As a child welfare professional, have you ever felt intuitively that a family needed intervention but you were not permitted to assess? What moments in your work brought the realization of equity and bias playing out in cases?

What evolutionary and revolutionary ideas do you have regarding how to keep something like this case outcome from happening again?

Justine Atkins

In chapter 12, the reader is introduced to a mother, Justine Atkins, who has been reported to CPS because her five-year-old autistic daughter wandered out in the middle of the night.

- What phase of the developmental framework (Agent, Advocate, Activist) led the investigation? How did it affect the interaction?

- When the narrator made contact with Justine, were any of the CPS procedures and behaviors especially punitive and dehumanizing? If so, which ones?

- In what specific ways could the CPS investigator have prioritized Justine's autonomy and dignity within their interaction?

- It seems that the narrator experienced particular shifts in how she saw this case and how she saw herself leading it. In what ways did she begin to shift?

INTROSPECTION

As a child welfare professional, have you ever had a case where you clearly saw a person's humanity and a genuine mistake, yet you had to carry out procedures? How did that affect you on a deeper level? What moral considerations came up for you?

What evolutionary and revolutionary ideas do you have regarding how to keep something like this case outcome from happening again?

Syesha Mercado

In chapter 19, the reader is introduced to a mother, Syesha Mercado, who was reported to CPS for medical neglect.

- What phase of the developmental framework (Agent, Advocate, Activist) led the investigation? How did it affect the interaction? How did it affect what happened after Syesha had her second baby?

- When the CPS investigators made contact with Syesha, were any of their procedures and behaviors especially punitive and dehumanizing? If so, which ones?

- In what specific ways could the CPS investigators have prioritized Syesha's autonomy and dignity within their interaction?

- What protective measures could have been in place in that particular hospital, with that particular physician, since there was a history of highly controversial medical determinations?

INTROSPECTION

As a child welfare professional, what did you feel as you read through Syesha's story? In particular, how did you feel during the scene where they were searching for her and her new baby?

What evolutionary and revolutionary ideas do you have regarding how to keep something like this case outcome from happening again?

TOOLS FOR MANDATED REPORTERS

The Child Abuse Prevention and Treatment Act mandates certain individuals to report known or suspected child abuse or neglect. The law also requires that the reporter's identity be kept confidential. At least forty-seven states designate individuals who typically have frequent contact with children as mandatory reporters, such as social workers, educators, medical professionals, mental health counselors, childcare providers, and law enforcement.[1] In many states, there is a recognition that mandated reporting contributes to the racial disparities that are plaguing the system. For years, mandated reporters have been conditioned to overreport, and equipping them with training on context and community factors is essential to correcting this. To assist mandated reporters in assessing their rationale for calling child protective services, the following resources are recommended.

RESOURCES:

- STRENGTH-BASED REPORTING: Emphasizes the importance of identifying the strengths of families when making a report to child protective services.[2]

- MANDATED SUPPORTING FRAMEWORK: Emphasizes the importance of changing the narrative, which has been that reporting families to child protective services is the best way to ensure child safety.[3]

- INSIDE MANDATED REPORTING: Presents one county's innovation around mandated reporting and their efforts in understanding who is making the most reports and why.[4]

- FROM FAMILY SURVEILLANCE TO ASSISTANCE: Emphasizes the importance of shifting from surveillance of families to intentional support.[5]

There are several states developing tools that provide more options for mandated reporters to assist families rather than report them. Many champions for this overdue work are shifting language from mandated *reporting* to mandated *supporting*. You are invited to join this important work by exploring resources in your community and how they might help families in need.

CONSIDERATIONS BEFORE REPORTING TO CPS

Are you a teacher, librarian, nurse, or neighbor worried about a child's safety? In some roles, individuals are "mandated reporters," with a legal obligation to report certain child safety concerns, while in others they are entirely at their own discretion in deciding when and how to intervene on behalf of an at-risk child. As we work to transform how mandated reporting works and to drive better outcomes for families, here are some questions to consider before choosing to report a family to child protective services:

- How long have I known this family and have I had the time to build a trusting relationship with them?

- Do I know of any circumstances that have emerged in this family's life within the last six months that have impacted their stability and/or safety?

- Have I considered what community or social supports could help this family? For example, social/emotional support, nurturing and attachment, parent and child development, social connections, and faith-based alliances.

- Is there a trusted colleague or community advocate who I can connect with to brainstorm ideas to assist this family?

- Are my own values impacting my view of this situation at all? If so, how might I extricate my own personal worldview from this family's current situation?

- Do I have a sense of what will happen next when child protective services enter into the lives of families?

- Answer the following: If this family had resources such as _____, my concern for them would be resolved.

- Do I understand the harms associated with family separation and also understand that my report could result in this family being separated from one another?

INTRODUCTION: IT STARTS WITH US

1. R. M. Whitman, "Remembering and Forgetting Dreams in Psychoanalysis," *Journal of the American Psychoanalytic Association* 11, no. 4 (1963): 752–74, https://doi.org/10.1177/000306516301100404.

2. Kimberly Bundy-Fazioli, Katharine Briar-Lawson, and Eric R. Hardiman, "A Qualitative Examination of Power between Child Welfare Workers and Parents," *British Journal of Social Work* 39, no. 8 (2009): 1447–64, https://doi.org/10.1093/bjsw/bcn038.

3. Dorothy E. Roberts, "Prison, Foster Care, and the Systemic Punishment of Black Mothers," *Faculty Scholarship at Penn Carey Law* 432 (2012), https://scholarship.law.upenn.edu/faculty_scholarship/432?utm_source =scholarship.law.upenn.edu%2Ffaculty_scholarship%2F432&utm _medium=PDF&utm_campaign=PDFCoverPages.

4. Josephine G. Pryce, Kimberly K. Shackelford, and David H. Pryce, *Secondary Traumatic Stress and the Child Welfare Professional* (New York: Oxford Univ. Press, 2007).

5. Pryce, Shackelford, and Pryce, *Secondary Traumatic Stress.*

6. Kasia O'Neill Murray and Sarah Gesiriech, "A Brief Legislative History of the Child Welfare System," Pew Commission on Children in Foster Care, published November 1, 2004, https://www.pewtrusts.org/-/media /legacy/uploadedfiles/wwwpewtrustsorg/reports/foster_care_reform /legislativehistory2004pdf.pdf.

7. Ibram X. Kendi, *How to Be an Antiracist* (New York: One World, 2019).

8. Zlatana Knezevic, "Social Change in Developmental Times? On 'Changeability' and the Uneven Timings of Child Welfare

Interventions," *Time and Society* 29, no. 4 (2020): 1040–60, https://doi .org/10.1177/0961463X20938590.

9. Tricia N. Stephens, "Distinguishing Racism, Not Race, as a Risk Factor for Child Welfare Involvement: Reclaiming the Familial and Cultural Strengths in the Lived Experiences of Child Welfare-Affected Parents of Color," *Genealogy* 5, no. 1 (2021): 11, https://doi.org/10.3390 /Genealogy5010011; Darcey H. Merritt, "Lived Experiences of Racism among Child Welfare-Involved Parents," *Race and Social Problems* 13, no. 1 (February 2021): 63–72, https://doi.org/10.1007/s12552-021 -09316-5.

10. "Read the Code of Ethics," National Association of Social Workers, accessed September 6, 2023, www.socialworkers.org/About/Ethics /Code-of-Ethics/Code-of-Ethics-English; Frederic G. Reamer, *Ethical Standards in Social Work : A Review of the NASW Code of Ethics,* 2nd ed. (Washington, DC: NASW Press, 2006).

11. Kendi, *How to Be an Antiracist.*

12. Jordan Flaherty, *No More Heroes: Grassroots Challenges to the Savior Mentality* (Chico, CA: AK Press, 2016).

13. Zuleka R. Henderson, Tricia N. Stephens, Anna Ortega-Williams, and Quenette L. Walton, "Conceptualizing Healing through the African American Experience of Historical Trauma," *American Journal of Orthopsychiatry* 91, no. 6 (August 2021): 763.

14. In order for child welfare to make strides toward a different way of work, we believe that reconciliation with communities who have been harmed is a necessary step. This article discusses the pathway to truth, reconciliation, and reparation of systemic harm. Amelia Franck Meyer and Jessica Pryce, "Truth, Reconciliation, and Reparation in Child Welfare," *The Imprint*, March 8, 2021, https://imprintnews.org/child-welfare-2/truth -reconciliation-reparation-child-welfare/52475.

PROLOGUE: WHAT I KNOW FOR SURE

1. Social work education programs collaborate with child welfare agencies in efforts to promote the recruitment and retention of competent and professional child welfare workers. Title IV-E training funds have been a major source of support for these efforts by facilitating the social work education of students, child welfare workers, and currently employed workers who return to school. This study describes the status of Title IV-E funds in bachelor of social work and master of social

work programs. There were sixty-five respondents representing thirty-one states and ninety-four social work education programs. These programs are geared toward stimulating preparation and longevity in the field. The author matriculated through a Title IV-E program prior to entering her position with CPS. Joan Levy Zlotnik and Jessica Pryce, "Status of the Use of Title IV-E Funding in BSW and MSW Programs," *Journal of Public Child Welfare* 7, no. 4 (2013): 430–46, https://doi.org/10.1080/15548732.2013.806278.

CHAPTER 1: DO BETTER

1. Readers are encouraged to read up on mandated reporting and its impact on racial disparity and disproportionality. Many child welfare leaders are exploring their mandated reporting data to uncover who is making the most reports. For example, in Los Angeles County in 2022, educators called in 23 percent of the child abuse reports yet only 6 percent were verified for abuse. Just as in the case with Naomi, educators and school officials are responsible for a large percentage of families being reported to CPS, and it is important to note the prevalence and the outcomes of those cases, thereby ascertaining if the call was warranted. "Mandatory Reporters of Child Abuse and Neglect," Child Welfare Information Gateway, published 2019, https://www.childwelfare.gov/topics/systemwide/laws-policies/statutes/manda/.

2. US Department of Health and Human Services, Administration for Children and Families, Administration on Children, Youth, and Families, Children's Bureau, *Child Maltreatment Report* (Washington, DC: US Department of Health, 2008), chapter 2, available from https://www.acf.hhs.gov/sites/default/files/documents/cm08_0.pdf.

3. Allegation narratives were reconstructed based on interviews with former co-workers and my firsthand account of the case that is being described. Readers are encouraged to review resources from the Child Welfare Information Gateway on community and environmental factors that impact impoverished families, as well as the confounding impact of mental illness. "Community and Environmental Factors That Contribute to Child Abuse and Neglect," Child Welfare Information Gateway, accessed September 6, 2023, https://www.childwelfare.gov/topics/can/factors/environmental/.

4. US Census Bureau, "Tallahassee Demographic Mapping," Calendar Year 2008.

5. "Tallahassee, Florida Demographics Data," Towncharts.com, accessed December 15, 2016, https://www.towncharts.com/Florida /Demographics/Tallahassee-city-FL-Demographics-data.html.

6. US Census Bureau, "Tallahassee Demographic Mapping," Calendar Year 2008.

CHAPTER 2: EVICTED

1. US Department of Housing and Urban Development, Office of Community Planning and Development, *The 2008 Annual Homeless Assessment Report to Congress*, https://www.huduser.gov/portal /publications/pdf/4thHomelessAssessmentReport.pdf; Julia Haines, "The 25 U.S. Cities with Largest Homeless Populations," *US News*, March 22, 2023, https://www.usnews.com/news/best-states/slideshows /cities-with-the-largest-homeless-populations-in-the-u-s.

2. HUD, *The 2008 Annual Homeless Assessment Report*.

3. The housing crisis undeniably intersects with the child welfare crisis. There is so much for child welfare to learn about the long-term impact of evictions on the stability of families. Research has found that renters whose previous move was involuntary were almost 25 percent more likely to experience long-term housing challenges. Matthew Desmond, *Evicted: Poverty and Profit in the American City* (New York: Broadway Books, 2016), 351; SAMHSA, HRC Facts Sheet, "Current Statistics on the Prevalence and Characteristics of People Experiencing Homelessness in the United States," published July 2011, samhsa.gov.

4. This article explores how poverty and housing instability further strain families—primarily single mothers—who struggle to raise children in unstable or unaffordable conditions. This phenomenon represents a uniquely distressing experience, particularly among families with children who experience school changes and disruption of social networks while adjusting to new environments. Readers are encouraged to read this article as a companion and explanatory resource for much of Didi and her family's experience. Katherine E. Marcal, "The Impact of Housing Instability on Child Maltreatment: A Causal Investigation," *Journal of Family Social Work* 21, no. 4–5 (2018): 331–47, doi:10.1080/10522158 .2018.1469563.

CHAPTER 4: ATLAS OF THE HEART

1. The author employed the use of in-depth interviews as a method for delving deeply into participants' perspectives and experiences. Jatoia's story, in particular her backstory, was captured through a series of interviews designed to extricate personal details about her upbringing, her goals and aspirations, and her road to motherhood. If details were altered, that was done to protect privacy.

CHAPTER 5: ALL ABOUT LOVE

1. "The Gap: A Shortage of Available Homes," National Low Income Housing Coalition (NLIHC), accessed September 6, 2023, https:// nlihc.org/gap.

2. Armando Lara-Millán and Nicole Gonzalez Van Cleve, "Interorganizational Utility of Welfare Stigma in the Criminal Justice System," *Criminology* 55, no. 1 (February 2017): 59–84, https://doi.org /10.1111/1745–9125.12128.

3. The context of the housing crisis and its impact on families like Didi's cannot be overstated. The child protective services system is encouraged to consider the social strain of unstable housing and to partner with housing organizations on innovative ways to support families with the goal of keeping them together. US Department of Housing and Urban Development, Office of Community Planning and Development, The 2009 Annual Homeless Assessment Report, Submitted to Congress, available from https://www.huduser.gov/portal/publications/pdf /5thHomelessAssessmentReport.pdf.

4. Josh Leopold and Amanda Gold, *The Costs and Potential Savings of Supportive Housing for Child Welfare-Involved Families* (Washington, DC: Urban Institute, 2019), https://www.urban.org/.

5. During the time frame when Didi was being asked to leave her "crowded" home, there was a study being conducted in Milwaukee that focused on "doubling up" in rental units during 2009–2011. Although typically seen by housing advocates, policy makers, and many CPS workers as problematic, that was not revealed to be a concern for tenants. This study was purely focused on renters/tenants and did not inquire about child maltreatment or well-being, though it's worth noting that impressions of "overcrowding" vary. Christine Flanagan and Mary Schwarts, "Rental Housing Market Condition Measures: A Comparison of U.S.

Metropolitan Areas from 2009 to 2011," published April 2013, https://www2.census.gov/library/publications/2013/acs/acsbr11-07.pdf; Matthew Desmond, *Evicted: Poverty and Profit in the American City* (New York: Broadway Books, 2016), 359.

CHAPTER 6: THE NEW JIM CROW

1. Dina J. Wilke, Sarah Rakes, and Karen A. Randolph, "Predictors of Early Departure Among Recently Hired Child Welfare Workers," *Social Work* 64, no. 3 (2019): 188–97, https://doi.org/10.1186/s12960-023-00829-1.

CHAPTER 7: NO WAY TO TREAT A CHILD

1. In recent decades, states have increasingly adopted differential response methods alongside or in place of traditional child maltreatment investigations due to concerns about the limitations of adversarial approaches. Traditional methods often place excessive blame on parents. To address these concerns, safety plans were introduced as an investigative tool, combining elements from both differential response and traditional methods. These plans aim to collaboratively address immediate risks identified during initial assessments while allowing traditional investigations to continue, ideally reducing the need for emergency child removals. However, if misused, safety plans can infringe upon parental rights without proper due process and add more complications to a fraught situation. This article by Ryan Shellady examines the construct of safety plans and their utility and impact on cases. Ryan C. F. Shellady, "Martinis, Manhattans, and Maltreatment Investigations: When Safety Plans Are a False Choice and What Procedural Protections Parents Are Due," *Iowa Law Review* 104 (March 2019): 1613.

CHAPTER 8: MY SISTER'S KEEPER

1. N. J. Sokoloff and I. Dupont, "Domestic Violence at the Intersections of Race, Class, and Gender: Challenges and Contributions to Understanding Violence against Marginalized Women in Diverse Communities," *Violence against Women* 11, no. 1 (2005): 38–64, https://doi.org/10.1177/1077801204271476.

2. Asha DuMonthier, Chandra Childers, and Jessica Milli, "The Status of Black Women in the United States," Institute for Women's Policy Research, 2017, https://iwpr.org/wp-content/uploads/2020/08/The-Status-of-Black-Women-6.26.17.pdf.

3. Carolyn C. Hartley, "Severe Domestic Violence and Child Maltreatment: Considering Child Physical Abuse, Neglect, and Failure to Protect," *Children and Youth Services Review* 26, no. 4 (2004): 373–92, https://doi.org/10.1016/j.childyouth.2004.01.005.

4. Wanda Wiegers, "The Intersection of Child Protection and Family Law Systems in Cases of Domestic Violence," *Canadian Journal of Family Law* 35, no. 1 (2023): 183–239.

CHAPTER 9: THE COLOR PURPLE

1. Emma Johnson, "Single Mother Statistics for 2023: Surprising Facts about Single Moms," Wealthy Single Mommy, updated May 24, 2023, www.wealthysinglemommy.com/single-mom-statistics/.

2. Dr. Gil, a social scientist, testified before Congress and discussed the reality that since spanking is a lawful form of discipline, it is not uncommon for accidents to happen during this experience, which could result in bruises or marks, unintended by the parent. He commented about the tendency of child welfare to interpret social problems through an individual lens rather than sociocultural. Ultimately, he offered: "The decision to take a child out of their home, even temporarily, is a grave decision that must be made in a culturally competent way that values context over prescriptions and expediency." Testimony of Dr. David G. Gil, Brandeis University, at Hearings of U.S. Senate Subcommittee on Children and Youth on the "Child Abuse Prevention Act," S.1191 (93rd Congress, 1st Session), March 26, 1973, https://eric.ed.gov/?id=ED080196.

3. Erin Digitale, "Child Abuse Reports by Medical Staff Linked to Children's Race, Stanford Medicine Study Finds," Stanford Medicine News Center, published February 6, 2023, https://med.stanford.edu/.

4. "Child Abuse and Neglect Statistics," Child Welfare Information Gateway, accessed September 6, 2023, https://www.childwelfare.gov/topics/systemwide/statistics/can/.

5. Testimony of Dr. David G. Gil, Hearing on the "Child Abuse Prevention Act."

CHAPTER 10: THE THREE MOTHERS

1. Kinship care placements should be prioritized for several reasons. They preserve family bonds, allowing children to remain within their extended family or community, which promotes stability and continuity. Studies have shown that it reduces the trauma associated with separation from their parents. Additionally, kinship caregivers often have a deeper understanding of the child's needs, leading to more personalized care. Kinship care can also support family reunification efforts, when appropriate, and ease the strain on the foster care system. "Placement of Children with Relatives," Child Welfare Information Gateway, published 2023, https://www.childwelfare. gov/topics/systemwide/laws-policies/statutes/placement/.

CHAPTER 11: THE AUDACITY OF HOPE

1. Child Welfare Information Gateway, *Case Planning for Families Involved with Child Welfare Agencies: State Statutes Current through April 2018*, April 2018, https://www.childwelfare.gov/pubPDFs/caseplanning.pdf.

CHAPTER 12: TWICE AS HARD

1. Ignacio Navarro, "Family Engagement in 'Voluntary' Child Welfare Services: Theory and Empirical Evidence from Families under Differential Response Referrals in California," *Child Welfare* 93, no. 3 (2014): 23–46, https://www.jstor.org/stable/48623436.

2. Amy S. He, Jon D. Phillips, Erica L. Lizano, Shauna Rienks, and Robin Leake, "Examining Internal and External Job Resources in Child Welfare: Protecting against Caseworker Burnout," *Child Abuse & Neglect* 81 (July 2018): 48–59, https://doi.org/10.1016/j.chiabu.2018.04.01.

3. Emma Ketteringham, "Live in a Poor Neighborhood? Better Be a Perfect Parent," *New York Times*, August 22, 2017, https://www.nytimes.com/2017/08/22/opinion/poor-neighborhoods-black-parents-child-services.html.

CHAPTER 13: THE GREAT ALONE

1. Mical Raz, *Abusive Policies: How the American Child Welfare System Lost Its Way* (Chapel Hill: Univ. of North Carolina Press, 2020), 117–24.

2. Caroline T. Trost, "Chilling Child Abuse Reporting: Rethinking the CAPTA Amendments," *Vanderbilt Law Review* 51, no. 1 (1998): 183, https://scholarship.law.vanderbilt.edu/vlr/vol51/iss1/4/; Alan J. Dettlaff and Reiko Boyd, "Racial Disproportionality and Disparities in the Child Welfare System: Why Do They Exist, and What Can Be Done to Address Them?" *The ANNALS of the American Academy of Political and Social Science* 692, no. 1 (2020): 253–74, https://doi.org/10.1177/0002716220980329.

CHAPTER 14: THE WILL TO CHANGE

1. Sam Smink, "Falsifying DCF Records: Former Investigator Says 'It's Common Knowledge,'" WPTV, published July 28, 2017, https://www.wptv.com/news/local-news/investigations/falsifying-dcf-records-former-investigator-says-its-common-knowledge; Daralene Jones, "9 Investigates DCF Investigators Accused of Falsifying Records," WFTV 9, published March 1, 2017, https://www.wftv.com/news/9-investigates/9-investigates-dcf-caseworkers-accused-of-falsifying-records/498567274/.

2. Rudolph Alexander Jr. and Cora L. Alexander, "Criminal Prosecution of Child Protection Workers," *Social Work* 40, no. 6 (November 1995): 809–14, https://doi.org/10.1093/sw/40.6.809; Andrea Ball and Eric Dexheimer, "Dozens of CPS Caseworkers Caught Lying, Falsifying Documents," *Austin American-Statesman*, January 13, 2015, https://projects.statesman.com/news/cps-missed-signs/wrongdoing.html.

CHAPTER 15: A LITTLE LIFE

1. Michael R. Menefee, "The Role of Bail and Pretrial Detention in the Reproduction of Racial Inequalities," *Sociology Compass* 12, no. 5 (2018): e12576, https://doi.org/10.1111/soc4.12576.

2. Child welfare agencies reject approximately 40 percent of all Interstate Compact on the Placement of Children (ICPC) placement requests, often

denying home studies for seemingly arbitrary reasons. In most states, there are no distinct standards for evaluating the suitability of parents' or relatives' homes compared to other foster placements. This is despite the constitutional right of parents and children to live together. Some common reasons cited for denying parent home studies include insufficient living space, unstable housing situations, the necessity for a parent to sleep on a couch to accommodate children, disqualification due to shared housing arrangements, and financial instability. These factors contribute to the challenges parents and families face when attempting to maintain or regain custody of their children within the child welfare system. Vivek S. Sankaran, "Foster Kids in Limbo: The Effects of the Interstate Compact on Children in Foster Care," *ABA Child Law Practice* 33 (2014): 140, https://repository.law.umich.edu/articles/1921/.

CHAPTER 16: THE IMPOSSIBLE IMPERATIVE

1. Jill Duerr Berrick and Erika Altobelli, *The Impossible Imperative: Navigating the Competing Principles of Child Protection* (New York: Oxford University Press, 2018).

2. Amy S. He, Erica L. Lizano, and Mary Jo Stahlschmidt, "When Doing the Right Thing Feels Wrong: Moral Distress among Child Welfare Caseworkers," *Children and Youth Services Review* 122 (March 2021): 105914, https://doi.org/10.1016/j.childyouth.2020.105914.

3. Some would say that Madisen's stint in care was relatively short, and although I hoped that it did not have a traumatic impact, there is hidden trauma in short stays in foster care. Although some assume the most damage is done when children languish in care for years, it is important to note how short stays impact youth. Thousands of youth are taken away from their families and returned within ten days, which can feel like "kidnapping." Eli Hager, "The Hidden Trauma of 'Short Stays' in Foster Care," The Marshall Project, February 11, 2020, https://www.themarshallproject.org/2020/02/11/the-hidden-trauma-of-short-stays-in-foster-care?utm_medium=email&utm_source=govdelivery.

4. Kelley Fong, "Getting Eyes in the Home: Child Protective Services Investigations and State Surveillance of Family Life," *American Sociological Review* 85, no. 4 (August 2020): 610–38, https://doi.org/10.1177/0003122420938460; Kelly Fong, *Investigating Families: Motherhood in the Shadow of Child Protective Services* (Princeton, NJ: Princeton Univ. Press, 2023).

5. Soleman H. Abu-Bader, *Advanced and Multivariate Statistical Methods for Social Science Research* (New York: Oxford Univ. Press, 2010).

6. George Konrad argued that "the client often vanishes behind their case, the caseworker vanishes behind their function . . . both muzzled by the impersonal bureaucracy." George Konrad, *The Case Worker* (New York: Harcourt Brace Jovanovich: 1974): 75.

CHAPTER 17: TORN APART

1. "Child Maltreatment 2019: Summary of Key Findings," Child Welfare Information Gateway, published April 2021, https://www .childwelfare.gov/pubpdfs/canstats.pdf.

2. Jessica Pryce, "To Transform Child Welfare, Take Race Out of the Equation," TED Residency, May 2018, video, www.ted.com/talks/jessica _pryce_to_transform_child_welfare_take_race_out_of_the_equation.

3. Blind removal meetings were a county-led strategy aimed at nullifying the impact of implicit bias. Although this strategy has been piloted in this county as well as other areas of the United States, more data is needed on its long-term impact. The viability of this method should be considered within the context of each jurisdiction and, if implemented, should run concurrently with additional system-wide changes. J. Pryce, W. Lee, E. Crowe, D. Park, M. McCarthy, and G. Owens, "A Case Study in Public Child Welfare: County-Level Practices That Address Racial Disparity in Foster Care Placement," *Journal of Public Child Welfare* 13, no. 1 (2019): 35–59, https://doi.org/10.1080/15548732.2018.1467354.

4. The legacy of family separation in the United States lingers and also perpetuates itself within the foster care system. Any discussion of the trauma of separating families must include the impact of unnecessary separations within a child welfare context. Jessica Pryce, "The Long History of Separating Families in the US and How the Trauma Lingers," The Conversation, published June 26, 2018, https://theconversation.com /the-long-history-of-separating-families-in-the-us-and-how-the-trauma -lingers-98616.

5. If we desire for the child welfare system to move from neutrality into real and sustained change toward equity, the policies and organizational practices within it must be antiracist, anti-oppressive, and anticolonial. Being an antiracist organization requires a visceral interrogation of privilege and power, and a collective commitment to do this work differently. Jessica Pryce, "What Will It Take for the Child Welfare

System to Become Anti-Racist?" *The Imprint*, June 25, 2020, https://imprintnews.org/child-welfare-2/what-will-take-for-child-welfare-system-become-anti-racist/44702.

6. Ibram X. Kendi, *How to Be an Antiracist* (New York: One World, 2019).

7. Bryan Stevenson is an attorney who works on behalf of the wrongly accused but also those who lack adequate legal counsel in their criminal cases. His work reminds me of Elizabeth Simpson from Durham, North Carolina. They understand more than most about the rights of citizens, and they rarely shy away from identifying the violation of human rights. Like the child welfare system, Black and Indigenous folks disproportionately experience inequity within the criminal justice system. Bryan Stevenson worked closely with his clients and also walked alongside their family members through trial after trial, keeping close proximity, never losing sight of their humanity. Bryan Stevenson, *Just Mercy: A Story of Justice and Redemption* (New York: Spiegel and Grau, 2014).

CHAPTER 18: WHITE FRAGILITY

1. Will Dobbie, Jacob Goldin, and Crystal S. Yang, "The Effects of Pre-Trial Detention on Conviction, Future Crime, and Employment: Evidence from Randomly Assigned Judges," *American Economic Review* 108, no. 2 (February 2018): 201–40, https://doi.org/10.1257/aer.20161503.

2. "Child Welfare: Purposes, Federal Programs, and Funding," Congressional Research Service, updated May 26, 2023, https://sgp.fas.org/crs/misc/IF10590.pdf.

3. Christopher Wildeman, Frank R. Edwards, and Sara Wakefield, "The Cumulative Prevalence of Termination of Parental Rights for US Children, 2000–2016," *Child Maltreatment* 25, no. 1 (2020): 32–42, https://doi.org/10.1177/10775595198484.

4. Erin Digitale, "Child Abuse Reports by Medical Staff Linked to Children's Race, Stanford Medicine Study Finds," Stanford Medicine News Center, February 6, 2023, https://med.stanford.edu/news.

CHAPTER 19: THE FIRE NEXT TIME

1. Dyan Neary, "What Happened to Maya," The Cut, June 13, 2023, https://www.thecut.com/article/child-abuse-munchausen-syndrome-by-proxy.html.

2. Olivia Evans, "Dr. Sally Smith Settled with the Kowalski Family for $2.5 Million," Yahoo!, published June 21, 2023, www.yahoo.com /lifestyle/dr-sally-smith-settled-kowalski-180000730.html?fr=yhssrp _catchall.

3. "Apology to People of Color for APA's Role in Promoting, Perpetuating, and Failing to Challenge Racism, Racial Discrimination, and Human Hierarchy in U.S.," Resolution adopted by the APA Council of Representatives on October 29, 2021, www.apa.org/about/policy/racism -apology.

CHAPTER 20: THE FIRE THIS TIME

1. *The Fire This Time: A New Generation Speaks about Race*, edited by Jesmyn Ward (New York: Simon and Schuster, 2016), illuminates the darkest aspects of our historical legacy, which I included in my closing speech at the rally. This book also grapples with our present challenges, envisioning something revolutionary. As James Baldwin's prophetic "fire next time" becomes our own urgent concern, *The Fire This Time* aims to contextualize the current moment within a historical framework and, above all, to propel us toward a brighter future, one where the health and wellness of Black families become more than an outcome, but a collective mantra.

CONCLUSION: IT ENDS WITH US

1. Erin Sugrue, "Evidence Base for Avoiding Family Separation in Child Welfare Practice," Alia, July 2019, www.ncsc.org/__data/assets/pdf _file/0031/18985/alia-research-brief.pdf; Roxanna Asgarian, *We Were Once a Family: A Story of Love, Death, and Child Removal in America* (New Yok: Farrar, Straus & Giroux, 2023).

2. Abigail Williams-Butler, "Intersectionality and Structural Gendered Racism: Theoretical Considerations for Black Women, Children, and Families Impacted by Child Protective Services in the United States," *Critical Social Policy* 43, no. 3 (2023): 514–35, https://doi.org /10.1177/026101832211253.

3. Ronald A. Heifetz and Marty Linsky, *Leadership on the Line* (Boston: Harvard Business Review Press, 2017).

RESOURCES: TOOLS FOR MANDATED REPORTERS

1. "Mandatory Reporters of Child Abuse and Neglect," Child Welfare Information Gateway, published 2019, https://www.childwelfare.gov /topics/systemwide/laws-policies/statutes/manda/.

2. Jocelyn D. Wormley, "Strength-Based Reporting: A Trauma-Informed Practice for Mandated Reporters, to Address Behavioral Health Concerns in Children at Risk of Child Welfare Involvement" (thesis, University of Southern California), Proquest (28317912).

3. "Mandated Supporting," JMACforFamilies, accessed September 6, 2023, https://jmacforfamilies.org/mandated-supporting.

4. Jeremy Loudenback, "Inside Mandated Reporting Reform in Los Angeles County," *The Imprint*, July 20, 2023, https://imprintnews.org/top-stories /a-look-at-mandated-reporting-reform-in-los-angeles-county/243115#0.

5. Margaret Sturtevant, "Shifting Mandated Reporting Laws from Family Surveillance to Assistance," *The Regulatory Review,* December 14, 2021, https://www.theregreview.org/2021/12/14/sturtevant-shifting-reporting -surveillance-to-assistance/.

ABOUT THE AUTHOR

JESSICA PRYCE is on faculty at Florida State University's College of Social Work. For the past fifteen years, she has worked in child welfare from multiple angles, including direct casework, research, teaching, training, and policy development. She has provided training for more than two hundred child welfare organizations, empowering professionals to reimagine their role and their work. She currently lives in Florida where she partners with child welfare leaders who are working on system-wide culture shifts and organizational change. Pryce holds a master of social work degree from Florida State University and a PhD from Howard University.